THE APPLE SOURCE BOOK

Also by Sue Clifford & Angela King

England In Particular,
A Celebration of the Commonplace,
the Local, the Vernacular
and the Distinctive

THE
APPLE
SOURCE BOOK

Particular uses for diverse apples

SUE CLIFFORD & ANGELA KING
WITH PHILIPPA DAVENPORT
COMMON GROUND

This collection and parts of text © Sue Clifford, Angela King and Common Ground
An Apple for all Seasons © Joan Morgan
Ten Green Apples © Carol Trewin
The English and Their Apples © Philippa Davenport
Recipes © the contributors 2007
Illustrations © the illustrators 2007

The Apple Source Book was first published by Common Ground in 1991
and reprinted 1991, 1994.

This new and extended edition first published in 2007 by Hodder & Stoughton
A Hachette Livre company

Common Ground is a charity (no: 326335) and has been grateful for grant support from
the Cobb Charity, John Ellerman Foundation, The Garfield Weston Foundation,
The Headley Trust, The Tedworth Trust, the Defra Environmental Action Fund
and many others over the years.

The right of Sue Clifford and Angela King to be identified as the Author of the Work has
been asserted by them in accordance with the Copyright, Designs and Patents Act 1988.

A Hodder & Stoughton book

1

A CIP catalogue record for this title is available from the British Library

ISBN 978 0 340 95189 7

Designed & Typeset by willwebb.co.uk
Typeset in Adobe Garamond & Trade Gothic

Printed and bound by L.E.G.O. SpA, Vicenza, Italy

The paper used to manufacture this book have been sourced from a Forest Stewardship
Council accredited paper mill in Sweden.

Hodder & Stoughton Ltd
A division of Hodder Headline
338 Euston Road
London NW1 3BH

Our warmest thanks to all the cooks, chefs, food-writers, gardeners and illustrators who have contributed to this book, and to all those who care and work for the future of orchards.

We also love almonds, apricots, bullaces, cherries, damsons, elder, figs, hazelnuts, medlars, mulberries, peaches, pears, plums, quinces, sloes and walnuts.

Traditional Orchards: Well Worth Preserving

CONTENTS

'The fruit of Apples do differ in greatness,
forme, colour and taste; some covered with
a red skin, others yellowe or greene, varying
indefinitely according to soyle and climate;
some very great, some little, and many of
a middle sort; some are sweet or tastie,
or something sower; most be of a middle
taste betweene sweete and sower, to
which to distinguish I thinke impossible;
notwithstanding I heare of one that
intendeth to write a peculiar volume
of Apples, and the use of them …'

John Gerarde 1597

INTRODUCTION

Over the years we have bred or chanced upon hundreds of varieties of apples that suit the vagaries of the British weather, the mysteries of locality and our taste. In half a lifetime we have squandered this cultural inheritance. Monoculture has taken over our countryside and monotony our shops. Because superstores and most other food outlets concentrate on selling the apples, pears, cherries and plums that travel well, have long shelf-lives and are easiest to grow, we are deprived of the enormous choice of varieties we could be enjoying. Worse, the tragic loss of traditional orchards continues: since 1950 nearly two thirds (57 per cent) of England's orchard area has disappeared.

Yet we should be as proud of our orchards – as protective of them, the hills, valleys and people who support them, and as imaginative about the food, drinks,

songs and stories they generate – as the French are of their vineyards and wines, the Italians of their olive groves and oils.

Traditional orchards are cultural landmarks and give us distinctive landscapes. They are the source of genetic variety, local recipes and customs. They are beautiful to be in and are havens for wild life. What is Kent without its apples, its sixty-foot high cherry trees and intimate cobnut plats, Gloucestershire without its magnificent perry pears, the Vale of Evesham without its plums, Shropshire without its hedgerow damsons, Devon or Somerset without its cider orchards?

The price of apples and apple concentrate on the world market erodes the viability of the old orchard down the lane; the price of land sees off the remnant orchard in the suburb. Every apple you buy grown in far-away places adds to the carbon burden in the atmosphere. In the price we fail to count in what orchards mean to us culturally, aesthetically and ecologically.

It is not so hard to start a counter-momentum. Eat English apples in their season – from July to March; ask your greengrocer/farmers' market/local shop for particular varieties as they ripen; write letters to the press about the lack of choice; support growers who sell a decent range; ask local chefs to be more inventive and to use varieties in their season; organise a local Apple Day on October 21st (start with supper at home); get together and create a Community Orchard; learn to prune and graft, press your own juice, make cider, go wassailing, enjoy our own cultural landscapes and culinary heritage. Become a connoisseur of the different flavours of apples and other fruit and find new uses and recipes for them.

This book aspires to encourage the cultivation of local varieties for local use in their season, to link the fruit with the tree, the variety with the recipe, the orchard with the land. That richness of local distinctiveness, the intimate relationship between nature and culture, needs constant tending. We all have some responsibility and the power to change things.

Common Ground offers the fate of the orchard as allegory for the variety and richness we are losing in our everyday surroundings and across the Earth, and the apple as a symbol of hope. To find the Blenheim Orange in Woodstock, the Galloway Pippin in the Borders presents more than a wider palette: it can etch a philosophy of living well with the world.

THE CASE FOR VARIETY

You could eat a different kind of apple every day for more than six years and still not come to the end of the varieties we can grow in the British Isles. An amazing 2,300 varieties of dessert and cooking apples have been grown here, as well as hundreds of cider apples, which are specific to the west. Apples do well across the country partly because we have loved them. In Victorian times gardeners and nurserymen worked hard to dabble and cross-pollinate, discover and graft, to bring on a wonderful inheritance of new varieties.

We may rejoice in our assertion that we grow the best apples in the world, but the truth is that they arrived here from the Tien Shan Mountains, which now find themselves on the border between China and Kazakhstan. They accompanied traders along the Silk Road to the Balkans, then came via the Romans and others to our shores. But it is we who have sifted and sorted the novel saplings and their fruits to find varieties that suit us and the places where they grow. Every apple pip offers a new shuffle of the genetic pack; varieties that flourish by the motorway and wildings from discarded apple cores may hold as much taste and goodness, or even economic promise, as a new variety from a horticultural research establishment.

Many apples are traceable to their orchards, woods, hedges and gardens of origin. Since a variety can be perpetuated only by grafting, or the tree being left to grow up again after it has fallen, our relationship with it keeps it alive. Unless we value it for its flavour, natural goodness, hardiness, heritage importance or beauty it will disappear. Currently the few varieties that add most to the national economy dominate, and hundreds of others are simply slipping away unnoticed.

Without the benefit of cold storage, the season for apples starts in July, with Emneth Early, Gladstone, Beauty of Bath, Laxton's Early Crimson and Discovery, and continues until spring, with May Queen. The early varieties have short shelf-lives, but the later ones, such as Blenheim Orange and Annie Elizabeth, can be stored in mouse-proof cool places into May. The Hambledon Deux Ans is reputed to last for two years. Chastise yourself, then, when you take from the superstore shelf Golden Delicious from France, Idared from the US or Granny Smith from Australia during our long season.

The Pitmaston Pine Apple from Worcestershire fits into the smallest hand; it is a delicate yellow, its juicy flesh paler lemon. Compare this elegant little dessert apple with Peasgood's Nonsuch, a giant from Lincolnshire, or Reverend W. Wilks from Middlesex, with its bright white flesh and greasy skin, which is creamy and pale with a few reddish stripes.

Laid out along a table for comparison on Apple Day, apples take the breath away with their variety, colour, aroma and presence. Tasting and identifying them requires the skill of the wine connoisseur. In north Devon, Orchards Live has compiled a list of nearly two hundred apples with a close Devon association, such as Devonshire Quarrenden, Fair Maid of Devon, Killerton Sharp and Whimple Queen. June Small, of Charlton Orchards in Somerset, has identified 156 Somerset apple varieties, many of which have links with particular villages, towns or parts of the county, such as Yarlington Mill and Bridgwater Pippin.

The trees have their preferences. D'Arcy Spice is suited to the dryness of Essex. Blenheim Orange is said to grow best on the stone brash and calcareous soil of Oxfordshire, within a few miles of Woodstock, where one Mr Kempster first grew it. Such was the word-of-mouth reputation of Kempster's Pippin (even before it was taken on by the big house and renamed) that coaches would stop to allow people to glimpse the tree, and graft wood was frequently stolen over the garden wall at night.

A tree that should carry Mary Ann Brailsford's name was planted by her as a pip in Southwell, Nottinghamshire, at the start of the nineteenth century. This is the mother of all Bramleys, named after the man who inherited her tree. Every pie made with Bramleys comes from a tree that originated as a graft, or a graft of a graft, from this single tree. Battered by nearly two hundred years of falling over and starting again, the original tree can still produce a ton of fruit and has recently given more grafts to reinvigorate the stock.

Isaac Newton's revelations are celebrated at his home, Woolsthorpe Manor in Lincolnshire. The orchard still contains the variety of the tree beneath which he sat when the apple dropped, now known as Isaac Newton's Tree or the Gravity Tree. Richard Cox, a retired brewer from Bermondsey, east London, whiled away his hours cross-pollinating trees in his garden at Colnbrook, Buckinghamshire (the place has found itself variously in Middlesex, Surrey and Berkshire). The Cox's Orange Pippin is just one of the varieties he created; he died in 1845 before it achieved popular recognition in the 1880s.

In the nineteenth century there was great activity and competition to introduce new varieties, spurred on by Royal Horticultural Society certificates and economic fortune. Thomas Laxton of Bedford, and his family after him, were among the most successful plant-breeders in the world, producing varieties such as Lord Lambourne, Laxton's Fortune, Laxton's Superb and Barnack Beauty/Orange.

Variety is apparent in other ways: a single Ribston Pippin (a Yorkshire fore-bear of the Cox) contains more vitamin C than a pound of Golden Delicious. In the Tamar Valley on the Devon/Cornwall border there are apple trees with aerial roots. Recipes for cider cake vary from village to village in the West Country, where there are cider gravies, peas cooked in cider, and Squab Pie pairs pigeon with apple. In Devon, apple cake is made with apple pureé, cinnamon and raisins, and in Dorset, with chopped cooking apple and currants; in Somerset, chopped apple is combined with cinnamon and mixed spice. In Cornwall the cake may resemble the French *Tarte Tatin*.

The hundreds of customs and games we have created around the apple echo the importance it has had in our lives. Almost every farm, from Northumberland to Cornwall, had its orchards; labourers were part-paid in cider. City folk travelled to pick fruit in Kent, the Garden of England, and the orchards of Herefordshire. Costermongers' (apple-sellers) cries rang out in street markets, and greengrocers put out tubs of water full of apples for games at Hallowe'en, which was known as Dookie Apple Night in Newcastle and Duck Apple Night in Liverpool. In Mobberley, Cheshire, and other places, Crabbing the Parson involved pelting the incumbent with crab apples on the local saint's day. Griggling, a-scraggling, souling, pothering and ponking, a-cattin, going a-gooding, clemening, worsting, howling and youling, and taking round the calennig are just a few of the local traditions.

It takes time for customs to differentiate themselves, just as an intricate landscape demonstrates the deep relationship that we and Nature have developed over hundreds of years. The rich repertoire of apple games and customs links season, produce and locality, yet we are in danger of forgetting what they mean because we have ceased to value our apples and orchards. They are the more vulnerable since some are peculiar to a single place.

Within a landscape, fruit trees flavour a locality. The individual geographies and histories of apples are not merely interesting, they are fragments of knowledge from which a future can be made. They may amount to the same thing, but gene banks, biodiversity and endemism do not have the same ring as Keswick Codlin, Teesdale Nonpareil, Cornish Gillyflower, Kentish Fillbasket, Lady Henniker, Roundway Magnum Bonum, Stoke Edith Pippin and Yorkshire Greening … neither do they carry the cultural resonance of Ten Commandments and Slack ma Girdle.

AN APPLE FOR ALL SEASONS

Joan Morgan

With Bramleys on sale all year round, we have nearly lost all notion of the seasons and successions of different cooking apples that were a traditional part of country life a hundred or even fifty years ago. Modern commercial storage has given us a sharp, fresh cooker, even until July, which is something our grandparents would have envied, but it has also left us with little choice. Few people now know of, let alone try, the dozens of varieties that used to grow all over Britain in gardens and orchards and provided a diversity of qualities, from the codlins picked at the beginning of August to the very last of the 'late keepers' out of the store after Easter.

It was in Victorian England that the notion of a culinary variety, one specifically grown for the kitchen and often especially valued for a particular dish, became firmly entrenched in our culture. Definite opinions were held as to which were the best varieties for apple sauce, apple dumplings, jelly or pies and, particularly, which were the best plainly baked. Summer codlins were ideal and provided the first baked apples of the new season. Keswick Codlin and Early

Victoria will quickly rise like a frothy soufflé, and need no embellishment except, perhaps, a little sugar and a dribble of cream, but are too juicy and insubstantial for pies and charlottes. For those, you had to wait for the autumn-ripening apples, such as Golden Noble, which is sharper, keeps a little of its form when cooked and fills a pie with soft, golden fruit. It has a distinct flavour that will stand on its own. Purists permitted no distraction from cloves or lemon peel in a pie of Golden Noble.

For apple sauce, Ecklinville Seedling was prized for its smooth, savoury quality, and the cider apple, Foxwelp, with a 'rough, piquant flavour', made a fine accompaniment to the Michaelmas goose or a roast leg of pork. In a more delicate style there were juicy Hawthornden and the Reverend W. Wilks. These were followed by the large, angular Warner's King, suitable for most uses – but not Apple Charlotte, which called for an apple that would make a stiff purée. Many cooks requested Blenheim Orange for this purpose: it is usually thought of as a dessert apple but, picked early, it cooks well and will make a firm sauce for the moulded Charlotte.

Then came the late-maturing apples, picked in October and kept until spring. The Victorian favourite was Dumelow's Seedling, which was sold in the markets as Wellington and is still to be found in old orchards. It has a translucent quality, is good for pies and makes a delicious creamy, brisk-baked apple or sauce; it is almost as sharp as a Bramley, but not quite as forceful. Dumelow's was overtaken at the beginning of the twentieth century by the larger, heavier-cropping Bramley's Seedling, which was favoured at first for dumplings but soon became recommended for every kind of dish. Alas, Bramleys are now picked as early as August, but these 'thinnings' are immature, sour and starchy, lacking the robust flavour of fruit left to develop properly on the tree. Not all late varieties are as strong: Annie Elizabeth, for example, is mild, needs no sugar and was claimed to be best of all for making stewed apples because 'the quarters never break'.

Culinary varieties are distinguished from dessert apples by higher levels of acidity, as well as their larger size. In the main, the intensity and proportions of acid and sugar provide the flavour, and the amount of acid determines the cooking properties. Generally, the more acidic an apple is, the more easily it will cook and form a purée. Less sharp apples tend not to break down so readily and slices will retain their shape during cooking, but if the apple contains too little acid it will cook poorly. The structure of the flesh is another factor. Summer codlins, which 'size up' quickly and have loosely textured flesh with a good deal of water, cook swiftly and often to a froth. Firm-fleshed, late-maturing varieties, such as Norfolk Beefing, are less juicy and hold their form. Indeed, the Beefing was recommended for drying and was also used in Norfolk Biffins, a popular Victorian sweetmeat, which was sold at the fruiterer's to be eaten with sugar and cream. Biffins were a speciality of Norwich bakers: after the bread had come out of the ovens, they put in the apples, covered with an iron plate to squeeze out the air as they cooked; since Norfolk Beefings are tough-skinned, they did not burst and, sealed in, the flesh became rich and sweet. You can achieve the same effect by baking your apples at the lowest possible oven setting; the Biffins will taste almost cinnamon-flavoured.

The quality of an apple is affected by the locality in which it is grown and the time of year at which it is picked. Many Scottish and northern varieties of high culinary repute often lack acidity in southern gardens and are rather bland. Lord Derby, for instance, which arose in Cheshire, remains green and sharp until Christmas in the north, but in Kent is at its best in September, soon losing its acidity and appeal. On the other hand, James Grieve is a valued eating apple in southern gardens; deprived of sun it is very sharp and is regarded in the north as a cooker.

The way in which an apple cooks depends to an extent on when it is used and how it is stored. Windfalls and early-picked fruit will be sharper and cook more easily than those harvested in their proper season. Even after picking, apples continue to develop, and if you have your own trees or buy fruit from a farm shop to store over the winter, you will find that their cooking properties change as the season progresses. Kept in a frost-proof garden shed or some other dark, cool equivalent of the old-fashioned fruit store, an apple's acidity will fall and its sugar level rise. Most will cook more firmly and taste sweeter, although many old culinary varieties become flat and insipid: lemon juice and spices came to the rescue supplying the lost acidity and flavour. Modern commercial storage maintains fruit in a state close to the condition in which it was picked. Before the invention of refrigerated and controlled-atmosphere storage, varieties that remained sharp through the winter without any trouble were highly valued.

Dumelow's Seedling was the most prized, lasting until forced rhubarb or even the early gooseberries appeared, and Bramleys, too, will keep sound in amateur conditions until the weather begins to warm up.

That apples matured and sweetened during the winter in the barn or store meant that many, like Annie Elizabeth, were dual purpose. Another was Forge from Sussex, still grown in its home territory of East Grinstead: a brisk cooking apple in September, it is sweet and quite perfumed by Christmas. By March even a Bramley becomes a sharp eating apple.

In its prime, a good English cooker possesses plenty of 'bite' and a savoury character that offsets the richness of pork or game. Cooking ameliorates sharpness and if apple is to contrast with buttery pastry, and zing through the sugar and cream, it needs plenty of flavour and piquancy. The greatest virtue of Bramley's Seedling must surely be that a pudding will emerge tasting strongly of apple, no matter how much sugar, cinnamon, lemon peel or cloves has gone into it. Delicate, mild-flavoured cooking apples are easily swamped and best used in simple ways. Similarly a dessert apple, such as a Cox, will be more interesting if cooked early and sharp.

An open tart calls for an apple that keeps its shape, yet is also richly flavoured, and here the familiar English cooker falls short. French cooks use Reine des Reinettes, which is another name for our King of the Pippins – a variety that became widely distributed across Europe and thereby gathered up numerous synonyms. Grown in the warmer French climate, it is larger and more colourful than it is in England, but it is still to be found in Herefordshire as Prince's Pippin and many old gardens contain a King of the Pippins tree. Reinette du Canada, a September–October eating apple, with an underlying astringency, is favoured in Europe for Tarte aux Pommes. It is similar to Blenheim Orange, but ripens later. Both are best used early in their season, since with keeping they develop characteristic dessert qualities and tend to be bland when cooked. They are not readily available, but many farm shops sell Newton Wonder, which is grown in hundreds of gardens. Not as acidic and aggressive as the Bramleys, it is good used raw in vegetable salads where its crisp, sharp taste is not overwhelmed by a vinaigrette dressing. A large Newton Wonder is perfect in baked red cabbage, will add flavour grated into stir-fried green cabbage, and much improves a bread-and-herb stuffing for the Christmas goose or turkey.

A fresh fruit salad, on the other hand, asks for the best dessert apples available, with an intensely aromatic, rich flavour – in autumn, a ripe Cox's Orange Pippin, Sunset, Holstein, Ribston Pippin or Orleans Reinette, any of which will add colour too. Later in the season, look out for Ashmead's Kernel, with its sweet, sharp taste reminiscent of fruit drops, the robust Suntan and Tydeman's Late Orange. In August and September Discovery, Miller's Seedling, the bright red Worcester Pearmain – when ripe it tastes of strawberries – and Ellison's Orange, with its lovely aniseed flavour, add depth and interest.

It is well worth exploring the diversity of flavours that apples offer and, if you can experimenting with them to discover how best to exploit the particular qualities of each variety.

· ·

Joan Morgan is a fruit historian and pomologist. She is the author with Alison Richards of The New Book of Apples, the Definitive Guide to Apples including over 2000 varieties. *In recognition of her work she has been made an Honorary Freeman of the Worshipful Company of Fruiterers and is one of the recipients of The Institute of Horticulture 'Award for Outstanding Service to Horticulture'. She is Chairman of the Royal Horticultural Society Fruit Trials Sub-Committee and Vice-Chair of the RHS Fruit and Vegetable Committee.*

TEN GREEN APPLES

Carol Trewin

A cider-maker recently told me that his customers were genuinely surprised to learn that cider-making is not a year-long activity. 'When visitors come down here they think we're picking apples all year round – they have no idea of blossom time or harvest,' he said. This is a small, traditional business for which the seasonal pattern of spring blossom, summer fruiting and autumn harvest are essential. For most artisan cider-makers this is an entirely natural way of life, unlike the pattern of the industrial processes found in the big companies that use imported apple concentrate – usually from dessert and culinary apples, rarely from cider apples – to keep their factories working all year round.

Perhaps in the age of mega-sized international businesses and global warming this lack of awareness of the seasons is not surprising. The onslaught of the superstores on our sense of seasonality (in the name of consumer choice) and our dislocation from the landscape that produces our food means that there is no reason for most consumers to be aware of blossom time in spring or that English apples can be available from August until the following March or April. How many of us care, when supermarkets give us a year-round supply of the same selection of around half a dozen eating apples (usually Cox, Gala, Braeburn, Golden Delicious and Granny Smith), most of them imported from the southern hemisphere? What this means is that even at the tail end of their season and the start of the English apple season, imports always seem to take precedence over home-grown produce.

One of the repercussions is that the decline of English apple production has continued. According to the Department for Environment, Food and Rural Affairs' own figures, between 2001 and 2004 a further 12,000 acres, or 21 per cent of the area that once grew the most popular cooking and eating varieties, went out of production (these figures from English Apples and Pears, the trade association for growers, register the main varieties, not the total grown). This is on top of the 57 per cent of our orchards that have been grubbed up and burned since the Second World War.

Why has this happened? And what has taken the place of our wonderful old varieties that measured the seasons?

The truth is that a combination of joining the EU, cheap fruit on world markets and the superstores' buying power has led to the destruction of many traditional English apple orchards. In the early 1960s and the 1970s the buying culture was steadily changing, driven by a post-war feeling of plenty and the idea that anything imported or foreign must be better than home-produced. So, imported fruit from Commonwealth countries, such as New Zealand and Australia, had a ready and easily accessible market. Then in the 1980s came 'Le Crunch', the highly subsidised and successful French campaign to promote Golden Delicious. English growers could not compete with this. At the same time the Common Agricultural Policy underwrote any surplus fruit produced in other EU member states, on this side of the Channel, though, the only payments to growers were for grubbing up orchards. Unable to compete on price, more English producers went out of business.

This left the superstore shelves wide open to imports from Chile, South

Africa, Italy, France, New Zealand and Brazil, ensuring a consistent, year-round supply of cosmetically perfect, unblemished apples. Most of the popular varieties, including 'new' ones such as Pink Lady (the first trademarked apple, it can only be grown under licence) and Fuji, have been developed for their keeping qualities, shelf life and appearance, with few concessions to taste, texture and flavour.

This has also influenced the varieties grown in most of Britain's large commercial orchards. According to English Apples and Pears, these are Discovery, Worcester, Cox, Bramley, Gala, Spartan, Jonagold and Egremont Russet. Their erstwhile competitors, Golden Delicious and Braeburn, have also been planted to satisfy perceived 'consumer demand', as the superstores claim.

As the superstores increased their dominance in the marketplace, responsible for 88 per cent of all food and drink retailing, the wholesale markets that could have sold English produce to smaller independent greengrocers simultaneously declined, giving most apple growers little choice other than to sell to the multiples.

In 2006 there were signs of a sea change. According to the retailers this has been in response to consumer demand, with each of the big four trying to out-compete each other in the level of their support for English apples and the number of varieties sold. Some of us have seen this before and the more cynical see it as more of a marketing ploy than a long-term commitment to supporting home-grown produce. However, regardless of the intention, any promotion that brings English apples to a wider audience has to be a good thing. The irony is that as more consumers find there are other, better options to buy interesting and, usually, fresher fruit, the superstores will find it increasingly difficult to satisfy their new-found interest in traditional apple varieties.

In a reaction against the corporate muscle power that dominates the UK's food and drink industry, growers have sought alternative outlets and developed new apple products. More farm shops are stocking locally grown apples or, in counties without a commercial apple-growing tradition, at the very least English apples. The growth of farmers' markets from a standing start in 1997 to more than 500 in 2007, has provided another valuable outlet for consumers hungry to allow their eating habits to follow the seasons. The movement to eat seasonally and to support local growers has been revved up by increasing concern about climate change and food miles. The last six years have seen a phenomenal growth of support for 'Buy Local' campaigns, particularly in the regional press. One of the few benefits of the 2001 foot-and-mouth outbreak was that it inspired the British public to support local farmers, which brought a better understanding of the links between the food we eat and the landscape. It reconnected us with the concept of local, seasonal produce.

A growing number of people are increasingly recognising the real cost of the greenhouse gases produced while apples are transported from the other side of the world. They are often picked underripe to prolong their shelf life so that they reach the consumer in a so-called state of ripeness, which, of course, is incomparable with a freshly picked apple that has travelled no more than a few yards from orchard to farm shop. What few consumers understand is that while ships are pumping out carbon dioxide on their transglobal journeys, apple growers are pumping carbon dioxide and other gases into cold stores to delay ripening and to preserve the fruit for months, guaranteeing that we can eat Coxes, Braeburn and Royal Gala all year round.

Some of the growers who have survived offer a fabulous range of apples from Beauty of Bath in summer to Court Pendu Plat, still eating well in early spring. Others have opted to turn their fruit into juice. Now we can choose from a range of blends and single-varietal juices, all with real depth of flavour, which bear no comparison with the cartonned, sugar-dense alternative found in most super-stores. While investment in machinery and labour is needed for juicing, the higher profits and improved cash-flow have been the salvation of many apple growers facing an uncertain future, and provided a use for otherwise unwanted fruit.

Charlton Orchards in Somerset decided not to supply superstores several years ago. Here, more than twenty-eight different eating and culinary apples are grown and sold either direct from the farm or at farmers' markets, with seven types of apple juice and other fruit, including plums, damsons and quinces. For those not lucky enough to live in Somerset, the company sends out boxes of apples by post. Elsewhere, farm shops have spotted that consumers are increasingly interested in the provenance and locality of their food, and are planting orchards specifically to guarantee their own supply of apples. In Yorkshire, not always thought of as an apple-growing county, Yorkshire Orchards claims to have more than a hundred varieties of dessert and culinary apples, all planted since 2002.

For growers with orchards stocked with local or unusual varieties it would seem there is a future, whereas commercial growers of acres of uniform, bland fruit for the superstores find themselves competing against world market prices and the multiples' rigorous demands on size, appearance and price. The biggest threat looming is from China, responsible for 40 per cent of the world's apples: there, 4.6 million acres of orchards produce around 20 million tonnes of apples a year, compared with England's 150,000 tonnes.

Apples have been grown here for more than two thousand years. It is the quintessentially English fruit, not only forming a rich part of our culinary and orcharding traditions but, at blossom time, showing how traditional orchards are a vital part of our landscape. They are a precious and beautiful sight, with deep historical and cultural resonance, that unites communities, provides habitats for wild life and food and drink for humans.

Carol Trewin is the food editor of the Western Morning News *and a fellow of the Royal Agricultural Society of England. She has written two books,* **Gourmet Cornwall** *and* **Cornish Fishing and Seafood,** *and has a long career in food and agricultural journalism.*

ORCHARDS

Apples, pears, damsons, cherries, plums, greengages, hazelnuts… An orchard may include several varieties of a single fruit, or a mixture of species. Single fruit trees in neighbouring gardens can offer the feeling of an orchard, for residents and bees.

Old orchards are the richest kind. Some have occupied the same land for centuries: the one at Bawdrip in Somerset can be traced back on maps to 1575 and perhaps earlier. Now, despite nearly a decade of local opposition, housing has taken its place. The wild life will leave, long-told stories will be forgotten and the community is left with a deep sense of loss.

Although orchards and fruit trees are to be found in every English county, the major commercial fruit-growing areas remain Cambridgeshire, Essex, Kent, Herefordshire, Worcestershire, Somerset and Devon. The eastern counties grow apples, plums and pears; Kent provides us with eating and cooking apples, cherries, pears, plums and cobnuts; the Vale of Evesham, apples, plums and pears; and the south-west, cider apples, perry pears and mazzards (cherries). Cherries were grown extensively in Hertfordshire and Berkshire, damsons in Cumberland and Westmorland, and apples in Middlesex.

Orchards, with their tall 'standard' trees, are important in the landscape. Traditionally standard cider apples were spaced out on a thirty-foot grid, and each majestic cherry tree on the north Kent coast grew more than forty feet from its neighbour. Perry pears were planted sixty feet apart, sometimes with grazing sheep, flowers or soft fruit beneath them. In today's commercial orchards, small trees stand in dense lines; some so intensive that they resemble vineyards.

Orchards are like wood pasture, full of micro-habitats, their biodiversity no less rich for having been maintained by many hands. They tell the seasons frankly, flaunting blossom, dropping fruit, enticing creatures large and small, enjoying winter wassailing. They display an intricacy of particularity to place. In

Westmorland, damson trees keep company with stone walls, and in Shropshire they march along hedgerows, as do cherries in some parts of Norfolk. Giant cherry trees, sixty feet high, mark the few remaining orchards near Faversham in Kent, while further south, in the Weald, squat cobnut plats pick out the ragstone of the Greensand ridge.

As demand for elderflower cordial grows newly planted elders are remaking the landscape in Leicestershire and Surrey. Since 1945 Gloucestershire has lost three-quarters of its orchards, but it still has many varieties of perry pear. These huge, long-lived trees, which can reach 60 feet and 350 years, are so particular about their conditions that some varieties will not grow more than five miles from where they arose; each parish produced its own single-variety or local-blend perry.

Every farm and substantial garden had its own orchard of fruit trees for domestic use. In Ryedale, Yorkshire, George Morris discovered that on marriage a woman would move to her husband's farm, taking with her graft wood to add to the orchard, which would become her domain. Typically, in apples alone, there would be Yorkshire Cockpit, Green Balsam, Yorkshire Greening (also called Yorkshire Goose Sauce), Backhouse Flowery Town (with its pink flesh), Yorkshire Beauty, Keswick Codlin, Warner's King, Lane's Prince Albert, Dog's Snout, Catshead, Burr Knot, Striped Beefing, Gravenstein, Lemon Pippin and Northern Greening. Now, the latter are often grubbed out because few realise that by Easter their hard and sour early persona is transformed. The whaling ships that left Whitby, in Yorkshire, for the southern ocean carried apples that took up to six months to mature and provided vitamin C against scurvy long before the arrival of oranges. The Vale of York's orchards declined steeply when Rowntree, the sweet manufacturers, began to use chemical pectin to set its fruit gums.

In sacrificing an orchard we risk losing varieties particular to a locality, wild life, songs, recipes, cider, festive gatherings, the appearance of the landscape and wisdom gathered over generations about pruning and grafting, aspect and slope, soil and season, variety and use. We sever our links with the land. Looked at from a different angle, if we lose real cider, we lose the need for cider barrels, flagons, wassail bowls, mugs, tools, troughs, presses ... people. We lose interest in artefacts and buildings often unique to their place, which are left to rot, mislaid or broken. With them fades the knowledge, the self-esteem and soon the varieties and the wild life. Everything is dependent on everything else: when finely tuned, culture and nature create a dynamic, intimately woven working world.

It would be wrong to assume that the city is bereft of orchards. Norwich, it was famously mused in Tudor times, 'was either a city in an orchard or an orchard in a city'. In north London, in 1989, the Hampstead Garden Suburb Horticultural Society organised an apple hunt to identify garden fruit trees planted by Dame Henrietta Barnett in 1899. More than forty varieties were rediscovered, scattered across front and back gardens, making an extensive orchard. Fruit trees can be trained to take up little space so it is feasible to grow them as espaliers against walls in the smallest of city gaps; several parks and allotments now await the first fruits of newly planted orchards.

Since fruit is so cheap on the world market many old orchards are being lost to other forms of agriculture and to building. Wiltshire has lost 95 per cent of its orchards since 1945, Devon 90 per cent since 1965. Many other counties have witnessed the demise of more than two thirds. However, renewed interest in orchards has stemmed from recognising the links between fruit variety and place. Community, city and school orchards are being created with varieties local to parish, town and county, reintroducing old knowledge and keeping it practiced in its locality.

CIDER AND CIDER ORCHARDS

Although cider is made in Sussex, Norfolk and Suffolk, in the 'eastern tradition' from eating or culinary apples, it is in the wetter south and west of England that cider-making flourishes. There are more than four hundred varieties of cider apple, many named after the place where they arose. In the heyday of cider-making, from around 1650 to 1750, much of Devon, Somerset, Shropshire, Gloucestershire, Herefordshire and Worcestershire were covered with orchards. Thirty- to forty-foot-tall cider-apple trees (and, in the latter three, perry-pear trees) were spaced thirty to forty feet apart so that grass could grow under them, allowing stock to graze. What a magnificent sight they must have been en masse.

Some of these traditional orchards survive in the main cider-making areas because they support other industries: sheep, cattle and pigs (in Gloucestershire, the Gloucester Old Spot is known as the 'orchard pig'), chickens, bees, mistletoe and overnight campers.

Modern bush orchards, widely planted from the 1970s, with the first branches reaching just two to three feet from the ground, can have a planting density of 160 to 360 trees per acre (rather than the forty to sixty in a traditional orchard) arranged in long lines of bare earth. They achieve a greater tonnage per acre but also suffer from and perpetuate the problems of monoculture.

Traditional orchards are shady wood pastures, grass always visible through the widely spaced rank and file, blousy in spring and filigree in winter. In the Somerset Levels spring floods demonstrate our forebears' knowledge of the land; old houses, churches and orchards stand dry on subtle island slopes.

Each cider-maker creates a unique blend of flavours, which will have developed over the years according to local preferences. As writes Liz Copas, in *A Somerset Pomona*, 'Bittersweets became the most popular in Somerset but pure sharps and sweets predominated in the southern part of the county near the Devon border. A different kind of sweet apple became the favoured taste in the eastern part from Wincanton to Shepton Mallet.' In *The New Book of Apples* Joan Morgan notes that 'Devonshire had become known for its sweet ciders as a result of the planting of pure "sweets", such as Sweet Alford, Sweet Blenheim, Northwood, Slack ma girdle and Sweet Coppin.'

In the hop-growing areas of Herefordshire, the trough mill, made of old red sandstone (granite in Devon), in which apples were first crushed using horsepower, was housed in the kell, or oast-house. In Somerset, the local limestone reacted with the acid in the apples and stone troughs were uncommon: instead wooden ones and grindstones were used, or the Ingenio apple mill that John Worlidge invented in the 1670s.

Elsewhere, cider-making might take place in the threshing barn, which had enough head room to accommodate the screw press. This squeezed the pulp through horsehair or straw 'cheeses' to produce juice, which fermented in oak barrels for about six months. The remaining pulp or pomace was spread along the hedgerows where pips germinated, sometimes resulting in promising new varieties (these seedlings are known as gribbles in Somerset). In Herefordshire it is enchanting to see occasional apple trees in hedges shining with winter red or yellow apples. Some of the best cider apples, including Redstreak, Foxwhelp and Yarlington Mill, are 'wildings' – discovered rather than bred.

Cider has a long and distinguished history: it was made in *pomaria* in monasteries as long ago as the thirteenth century. High-quality cider was once regarded as superior to the finest wines, and drunk from beautiful engraved crystal. It was popular in villages and cities when water was not to be trusted, and with sailors to protect against scurvy. Workers were part-paid in cider, a practice that extended to farm labourers in cider-making areas until the Truck Act of 1887 made it illegal.

There have been many attempts to improve the quality of cider and to develop new varieties. In Herefordshire during the 1640s, Lord Scudamore experimented with fermentation in bottles to discover he had made a sparkling apple 'champagne'. Impressed by the quality of Norman-French ciders, he advocated the planting of Redstreak. It became so popular that John Evelyn remarked: 'All Herefordshire has become, in a manner, but one entire orchard.'

Herefordshire has proved a crucible: a fruit breeder, Thomas Andrew Knight, wrote a *Treatise on Cider* in 1797 and the *Pomona Herefordiensis* in 1811. Dr Robert Hogg was commissioned by the Woolhope Naturalists' Field Club to survey the orchards, resulting in *The Herefordshire Pomona 1876–85*, and hundreds of Foxwhelp and Skyme's Kernel (and Taynton Squash pear) trees were distributed to fruit growers across the county. In 1912 the National Fruit and Cider Institute, founded in 1903, became the Long Ashton Research Station near Bristol. Before it closed in 1985, much work was instigated on varieties and orchard management, which favoured intensive bush orchards to enable mechanical harvesting.

From the late 1870s cider began to be made on a larger scale in small factories by firms such as Gaymers and Whiteways. Now four giants dominate, with Bulmers holding more than 60 per cent of the market share, with Magners hot on its heels. Real cider is the pure, fermented juice of apples, but cider made on an industrial scale and sold in kegs is carbonated and contains apple concentrate, water, sugar, yeast and other additives. But the use of apples alone does not guarantee superiority: scrumpy, the memorable rough, strong, home-made cider, has a bad reputation, which sophisticated artisan cider-makers are now routing.

The big manufacturers buy apple concentrate on the world market and locally may buy only from farms contracted to them. Hundreds of small

orchards become vulnerable. In the South Hams of Devon, Orchard Link has been set up to find markets for small apple-growers; it also has a mobile mill and press to enable people to produce their own juice and cider.

A new wave of single-variety and organic ciders has reinvigorated the retail scene, together with English distillations to rival Calvados. Apple brandy was first made in Hereford, as King Offa, in 1987. But it is Julian Temperley who has started a new industry with Somerset Royal Cider Brandy, made near Kingsbury Episcopi since 1992.

ATTRACTING WILD LIFE TO ORCHARDS

Gail Vines

Had our forebears set out to create havens for wild life, they could hardly have bettered traditional orchards. Nature revels in the sheer variety of these places.

Orchards defy tidy categorisation – neither woodland, grassland, hedgerow nor wood pasture, they have rarely featured in habitat surveys. Yet the wonder of these places is that they can be all of these habitats at once. At their best, orchards offer a patchwork attractive to creatures from beetles and bats to badgers and butterflies. On the scaly bark of old Bramley trees in No Man's, Kent's first Community Orchard, sharp-eyed botanists have spotted at least thirty-three species of lichen and moss – a world in miniature that testifies to the wholesome air enjoyed by walkers on the North Downs Way as they pass the orchard.

The orchard's history as a valued place is central to this natural bounty. Biodiversity thrives in places that are themselves diverse and have been so for a long time. Old orchards are a living sign of continuity in the landscape, and most species, like most people, appreciate places with a bit of history to them.

In some favoured spots, old orchards are an enduring feature of the landscape. Even though the trees may be relatively short-lived, an orchard may have occupied the same stretch of land for centuries. As fruit trees are periodically replaced and replanted, a diverse *mélange* gradually develops. Under the trees, a flower-rich grassland carpet evolves, reflecting years of grazing or hay-making. The combination proves irresistible to myriad pollinating insects, which in turn attract birds, bats and much more. The web of interconnections has yet to be fully charted.

Traditional orchards of tall trees offer the best opportunities. Full-sized 'standard' fruit trees harbour spiders, grubs and beetles for trunk-feeders such as nuthatches and tree-creepers, which find rich pickings under the bark flakes of apple and in the crevices between the chequerboard scales of pear. Orchard trees, with the exception of walnut and pear, rot relatively quickly, allowing colonisation by hole-dwelling birds including woodpeckers, which are among the most common orchard birds. Other species that make nest holes in the rotwood include starlings, tits and tree sparrows – now a rare species in Britain.

Orchard blossom is a magnet for wild life, and a vast range of creatures will help you harvest the fruit. Blue tits hunt over apple trees to pick off codling-moth caterpillars while wasps tackle aphids. Even the bud-eating bullfinch – killed until recently by commercial fruit-growers under licence from the Ministry of Agriculture, Fisheries and Food (MAFF) – has become welcome. This beautiful bird, with a voice like a squeaky gate, is now in serious decline, having lost some three-quarters of its population over the past thirty years.

Not a moment too soon, conservationists are taking a close look at old orchards, such as Tewin Orchard, near Welwyn Garden City in Hertfordshire, Britain's first orchard nature reserve. Leased from the RSPB, it is managed by the Herts and Middlesex Wildlife Trust. Among others, it has embraced a badger colony plus twenty species of moth, and butterflies such as the marbled white and the white-letter hairstreak. The orchard has not been sprayed since 1958, enabling a healthy grassland to develop. Wild flowers such as bird's foot trefoil, field scabious and various cranesbills flourish there.

Three types of uncommon bat feed in Tewin Orchard: the serotine, the noctule and the long-eared. The latter feasts on the insects that feed on overripe fruit, especially plums, just before it hibernates. A wide range of birds enjoy the orchard too, including tits, greenfinches, bullfinches, goldfinches, linnets, yellowhammers and blackbirds. In winter, flocks of fieldfare and redwing, sometimes seven hundred strong, feed on the fallen fruit. The abundance of songbirds provides sparrowhawks with a reliable food source. In summer, the overgrown cordons offer an attractive breeding habitat to a range of warblers, notably the garden warbler, the willow warbler, the lesser whitethroat, and the blackcap. Reed buntings have started to visit in summer as well as winter, bramblings turn up once in a while and hobby, goshawk and buzzard make a rare visit.

The Wildlife Trust manages Tewin Orchard to enhance the diversity of habitats available to wild life. Their most important rule is to avoid being too tidy, and they never cut down a tree until they have understood its role in the orchard. A gnarled old branch or trunk, pocked with rot-holes and covered with peeling bark may look insignificant, but it will provide dream homes and lavish catering for a host of creatures, such as the little owl, which likes nothing better than an old orchard as its home base.

James Marsden supports little owls and much else in his Herefordshire orchard. He is the policy planning principal specialist with Natural England, but also owns and manages about two hectares of traditional orchard at Gregg's Pit in Much Marcle for the benefit of local wild life and to produce his own cider and perry. In the *Common Ground Book of Orchards* as he describes: 'As a – very! – amateur entomologist, I have confined myself to recording butterflies and have been impressed by the numbers and variety of species attracted to my orchard. During September 1999 ripe plums inspired a feeding frenzy of butterflies, and on one sunny day I saw seven species in the orchard – comma, large white, painted lady, red admiral, small copper, small tortoiseshell and speckled wood. My records for purple hairstreak date from a month or two earlier in the year, when I saw these attractive butterflies feeding on oak in the orchard hedges, in perry-pear and cider-apple trees, and following the setting sun due west up the orchard on two warm evenings.'

Ideally, trees in an orchard should be of mixed ages. Young trees allow plenty of light to reach the ground plants while older ones provide food and shelter.

You can boost the diversity of life that makes use of an orchard by creating a patchwork of habitats, fitting to your locality, even if on a small scale. Encourage a flower-rich meadow, for instance, perhaps by directly planting wild-flower plugs or seeds sourced locally, then devising a sustainable grazing or cutting regime. Consider growing bee- and butterfly-friendly flowers, such as primroses, cowslips, knapweed, scabious, fleabane and wild basil. Your local Wildlife Trust should be able to advise on what will work best in your neighbourhood. Grazing by sheep, cattle, pigs or even hens can be beneficial to local flora and fauna, but only if carefully managed: hungry herbivores (including deer) can rapidly strip a

meadow, if their numbers are too high or the timing is wrong. Protect your trees with robust, stock-proof guards.

Plant a thick hedge with locally typical trees and shrubs, which may include native hawthorns, buckthorn, blackthorn, holly, yew, damson, bullace, crab apple and bramble, peppered with perennial wild flowers of the locality, and a surprising array of animals will notice the difference. The insects will be among the first to respond. Buckthorn attracts the brimstone butterfly, while the elm, still a distinctive hedgerow plant in eastern counties, is a favourite of the comma and white-letter hairstreak. In counties such as Hertfordshire and Norfolk, where plum and cherry prunings were often struck into hedges, the black hairstreak and the cherry-bark moth may flourish.

Rich grassland flora are to be found within traditional orchards on the limestone soils of the Cotswolds or the liassic limestone soils that underlie parts of Worcestershire, where bee orchids colonise old plum orchards. A 2006 study of three traditional mixed, but predominantly cherry, orchards on the edge of the Wyre Forest recorded 1,868 species of wild plants and animals in an area of 5.39 hectares – a remarkably high number which is encouraging Natural England to include traditional orchards in its national priority habitat list.

In recent years, a number of local biodiversity action plans have explicitly included orchards. Drawn up at county level throughout the British Isles, they set targets for practical nature-conservation schemes, especially in the West Midlands, where traditional orchards are still integral elements to the local economy and landscape. Here, birds associated with orchards include the spotted flycatcher, tree sparrow, fieldfare, redwing, song thrush and the greater and lesser spotted and green woodpeckers. In Devon, old orchards help to provide the kind of mixed grassland enjoyed by the cirl bunting, once so common that it was known as the 'village bunting'.

Commercial orchards are of less interest to bird life, although nest boxes can help. The spindle or bush trees are usually grubbed up at around fifteen years old, or earlier, so have no deadwood or rot-holes, and their short trunks hold no quarry for trunk-feeders, such as tree-creepers or beetles. What is more, the orchard floor is usually sprayed with herbicides to allow young trees to establish quickly without competition. Nectar-rich wild flowers are obliterated.

You can't help but notice the difference at James Marsden's Gregg's Pit. The land deeds show that there has been an orchard here since before 1785. Pests may never have been a problem because the orchard is rich in natural predators, as Marsden explains: 'Diversity offers intrinsic protection from pests. Old orchards like mine often contain a number of trees of considerable age – perry pears that are more than a hundred and fifty years old. Because of the replanting that has gone on over many years, a great mixture of trees of different varieties and ages are dotted throughout the orchard. The result is a highly valuable wild-life habitat very similar to the better-known lowland wood pasture.

'The mixture of fruit of early- and late-flowering species reduces the risk of damaging outbreaks of pests or disease. In Gregg's Pit Orchard, flowering starts in late March, with damsons, plums and perry-pears, and continues until early June with the last of the apples. And because few if any chemical sprays are used in many traditional orchards, natural predators of pests – ladybirds, hoverflies, earwigs, tits, finches and more – build up numbers high enough to combat any potential problem. In effect, ladybirds and bluetits act as nature's insecticides. Potential pests, such as codling moth, apple sawfly and aphids, may be present, but not in high numbers.'

It is well worth thinking about growing local cultivars resistant to diseases that are likely to be prevalent in your area. For instance, Cox's Orange Pippin has become a widespread apple variety, yet ironically it is one of the hardest to grow because it is vulnerable to a range of diseases. Commercial apple-growers may routinely spray a dozen or more applications of fungicide each growing season just to prevent scab – but good scab-resistant varieties are available and could be grown instead.

Fruit ripens in autumn and winter just when birds in particular need high-energy foods. Once eaten, the seeds usually pass undamaged through the digestive tract or else are regurgitated some distance from the mother tree so enabling the dispersal and regeneration of new trees. Some birds (and butterflies) become intoxicated after they have eaten fermenting apples. Reports of tipsy mammals are thin on the ground, but hedgehogs, hares, deer, foxes and badgers certainly visit orchards in autumn and winter to feed on the trees' largesse.

Gail Vines is a scientist and naturalist. She writes for New Scientist *and* Kew Magazine *and works as an editor for Plantlife International – a major organisation.*

COMMUNITY ORCHARDS

Community Orchards offer ways of reinforcing local distinctiveness, of saving vulnerable old apple, cherry, damson, pear and plum orchards, providing opportunities to plant new ones and thereby helping to counteract the massive loss of orchards since the 1950s. They are simultaneously places for quiet contemplation, open-air classrooms and centres for local festivities; acting as carbon sinks, reservoirs for local varieties of fruit, and refuges for wild life.

Community Orchards should be open and accessible at reasonable times. They may be owned or leased by a community group, voluntary organisation, parish council or some other tier of local authority. Local people can share the harvest or profit from its sale, and take responsibility for any work to be done.

Since 1992 when Common Ground put forward the idea of Community Orchards many have been established; they are various and variegated. In Birmingham a strip of allotments previously owned by British Rail, had been used as a dumping ground for green waste. Local people raised £7,000 to buy it for the Cotteridge Community Orchard and have planted thirty trees.

Since 1998 Gabriel's Community Orchard has been planted on sloping ground on the edge of Pilton in Somerset; the land was donated and the parish council acts as custodian trustee. After researching the fruit trees in the vicinity, eighty trees are being propagated in nursery beds and over 100 apples have already been sponsored and planted by the villagers. Enthusiasts gather to learn and practise pruning, grafting and other tasks, or to enjoy the open view to Glastonbury Tor and look forward to juice-making.

Friends of Reeth Orchard in Swaledale, north Yorkshire produce a colourful twice-yearly newsletter charting the progress of this once overgrown plot – now transformed after much hard work as a walled garden with mature and newly planted fruit trees, some espaliered. Seats and gates have been commissioned, and Reeth now has a beautiful space in the middle of the town for quiet contemplation, or for concerts and celebrations.

We need more such places where we can relax, play, work and learn. We need shared activities to enable people of different age groups and backgrounds to come together. In city, suburb or village, the Community Orchard is becoming the equivalent of local woodland a century or more ago – a communal asset for a parish. More than that, it can become the focal point – the moot, or open-air community hall. Orchards can work in housing and industrial estates, hospital and school grounds. They can improve our diet, offer healthy activity, enliven a curriculum and even speed the recovery of the sick.

At a time of unprecedented alienation from nature, and knowledge about where our food comes from, Community Orchards are reviving interest in fruit-growing. They provide a way to share knowledge and horticultural skills, and stimulate us into growing our food again. In the face of climate change the need to reduce food miles makes the provision of locally grown fruit the more urgent.

A Community Orchard could become part of a bigger picture, part of a chain that links the playing-field or recreation ground with the common, the park, the local nature reserve, a disused quarry, allotments and the churchyard. Natural England's goal is for people who live in towns and cities to have 'accessible natural green space less than 300m (in a straight line) from home': the Community Orchard can help to achieve it. As James Crowden wrote, in *Cider – The Forgotten Miracle*:

> *It is perhaps through trees, and orchards in particular, that we convey our sense of permanence in an otherwise largely impermanent world, and at the same time there is blossom, fruit, juice, beverage, even spirit, and firewood…*

APPLE DAY

Traditions have to begin somewhere and Apple Day, now regarded as a part of the festive calendar, was introduced on October 21st 1990. That day, Common Ground took over the Piazza at Covent Garden – originally the Convent Garden, which included an orchard – in London, to demonstrate the significance of the apple to British culture, landscape and wild life. It is now celebrated countrywide on or the nearest weekend to 21 October. Apple Day, and its herald, All Fruits Eve, was conceived as an annual celebration to link the fruit we eat with the people who grow it and the places they make in the process: our cultural landscape. The apple, with its powerful symbolism, rich in poetry and extraordinary variety, was chosen to stand for all fruits, but the event's success has led to more such celebrations: Damson Day in Westmorland, Plum Day in Pershore, Worcestershire, and Pear Day at Cannon Hall Museum, Yorkshire.

The apple is a wonderful emblem of diversity: the Carlisle Codlin, the Crawley Beauty, the Devonshire Quarrenden and the Worcester Pearmain's names tell us their place of origin; Ashmead's Kernel, Cox's Orange Pippin, Laxton's Superb, Peasgood's Nonsuch and Charles Ross commemorate the people who developed and raised them.

Celebration is a starting point for local action: it lifts spirits, builds alliances and opens eyes. We wanted to create a popular festival, a date in the calendar, to stimulate initiatives promoting the importance of our relationship with the land and the links between local production and ecological care, social customs and culture. By giving people reasons to value and conserve them we aimed to prevent further extinction of varieties and traditional orchards, and encourage people to celebrate and care for the cultural landscape.

On that first occasion we brought together forty stallholders from across the country who had different connections with the apple: organic growers; the Women's Institute, with chutneys, jellies and pies; a north London school whose orchard was used as classroom; nurserymen, who dispensed advice as well as trees; beekeepers and honey; juice-makers; cider-makers with presses; photographs of orchards of the West Country by James Ravilious; and a hundred varieties of apple to taste and talk about with apple 'doctors' and identifiers.

The intention was to encourage others to take the idea on and Apple Day has multiplied; at six hundred events in 1999, from small parties at home to gatherings that attract thousands, we gave up counting. It has been celebrated in village halls, the Houses of Parliament, school-meals services, museums, nurseries, allotments, bakers' shops, restaurants, doctors' surgeries, pubs, arts centres, agricultural and horticultural colleges, botanic gardens and Community Orchards, by farmers, fruit-growers, cider-makers, juice-producers, local authorities, English Heritage, the National Trust, the Women's Institute, the Wildlife Trust and the Soil Association. The success of Bath's first Apple Day encouraged the organisers to introduce, in 1997, two markets over the following weekends. It was the start of the countrywide reinvention of direct-selling farmers' markets.

WASSAILING

The Anglo-Saxon '*waes haeil*', means 'to be healthy'. Wassailing apple trees was thought to encourage a good crop. It usually takes place after dark on Old Twelfth Night, 17 January, but is sometimes held closer to Christmas and New Year. Now villagers go to their local orchard, sometimes lit by bonfires, and gather round the largest or most prolific tree – the Apple Tree Man. Fêted as the guardian of the orchard, cider or beer is poured over its roots and pieces of cider-soaked toast or cake are placed among the branches for the robins, guardian spirits of the trees. Often the tips of the lowest branches are drawn down and dipped into a bucket of cider. The wassailers fill cups with cider and toss it into the branches, then drink and sing a toast to the tree. In Carhampton, Somerset, it goes:

Old apple tree, we wassail thee, and hoping thou wilt bear,
For the Lord doth know where we shall be, till apples come another year,
To bear well and bloom well so merry let us be,
Let every man take off his hat and shout to the old apple tree.
(Chorus, shouted:)
Old apple tree, we wassail thee, and hoping thou wilt bear,
Hat-fulls, cap-fulls, three-bushel bagfulls
And a little heap under the stairs.
Hip! Hip! Hooray!

To drive away evil spirits and wake the sleeping trees, they blow cow horns, beat trays and buckets and fire shotguns into the upper branches.

The wassail bowl went from house to house in the evenings from the last weeks of Advent and throughout the Twelve Days of Christmas. In Gloucestershire, it contained a mixture of hot ale, spices, sugar and roasted apples, sometimes with eggs and thick cream floating on top, known as Lamb's Wool, it was also drunk on 25 November, St Catherine's Day. The bowl was made from turned ash or maple, often elaborately carved and kept for the purpose.

Wassailing the apple trees has continued in some places, such as Carhampton, for centuries, while in other areas it is undergoing a revival or reinvention.

At New Ash Green the Woodlands Group have spent three thousand hours in restoring an orchard at the heart of the village and had their first wassail on Twelfth Night, 6 January, 2007; more than sixty people attended even though the weather was appalling. They reworked a wassail song sung by the Waterstons to include local varieties such as Fred Webb, Kentish Fillbasket, Orange Goff, Cobham, Lady Sudeley's Apple, Lamb Abbey Pearmain. Jerry Ash of the Woodlands Group adds, 'We got in touch with the Lewes Bonfire Council to find out how to make safe flaming torches – and they really added so much drama and atmosphere on a dark night.'

The Westbury Friendly Society at Westbury-sub-Mendip started wassailing in this millennium on Old Twelfth Night and in style. In 2007 more than eighty people of all ages enjoyed an evening of mulled cider and juice from local apples, wassailing five orchards around the lanes led by a master of ceremonies with a Wassail King and Queen. The Langport Mummers performed a cautionary tale in a farmyard, and the evening concluded with a traditional burning of an ashen faggot and, of course, good food around a fire.

RECIPES

THE ENGLISH & THEIR APPLES: A COOK'S PERSPECTIVE

Philippa Davenport

'No fruit is more to our English taste than the Apple,' wrote Edward Bunyard in 1929. 'Let the Frenchman have his Pear, the Italian his Fig, the Jamaican may retain his farinaceous Banana, and the Malay his Durian, but for us the Apple.'

Life without apples is unthinkable. I love pears, figs and many other fruits, but the apple is the best beloved. I never tire of it. Noel Coward advocated 'a little eggy something on a tray' as the ideal comfort food. I propose instead good bread spread with good butter, a perfectly ripe apple and a glass of cold creamy milk. My desert island collation.

Britain is not the original birthplace of the apple, of course, but it is the adopted home of the fruit, where man has nurtured and developed an amazing diversity down the centuries. Britain became the proud epicentre of appledom – and remained so until commercial dictates insidiously began to delete apples from our list of national treasures.

Common Ground has done sterling work in alerting us to the perils: the destruction of orchards and the wildlife they support, the replacement of biodiversity with monocultural mediocrity, and the bludgeoning of local culture and cooking. Now, it is up to us. Every one of us. We are all responsible and each of us has the power to make a difference. Individually our voices and our purchasing power may be slight, but jointly we can halt and perhaps reverse the trend – if we are sufficiently vociferous and if we persevere.

To recognise ripeness, re-establish the seasonality of apples, rediscover local varieties, their uses in cooking and ways to preserve them, all these things need to go on the agenda. Above all, I suggest, we need to ask for our regional apples by named variety. Don't be daunted. Don't take no for an answer. Ask, ask and ask again until the day dawns when the distinctive and particular pleasures of a multitude of individual apples are available in their respective seasons, instead of an ever decreasing, ever more commercially watered down few.

It seems crazy to cultivate only a handful of different sorts when thousands of apples once thrived and can still flourish here. If we don't fight for their survival they will vanish completely and we shall have only ourselves to blame if there is no alternative to bland uniformity.

Campaigns to halt the ravaging of our orchards, and stem the invasion of cut-price imports, sometimes concentrate on trumpeting the Cox and the Bramley. This famous duo can be superb when well grown and properly ripened, of course, but they need no promotion, and their nomination for just about every apple recipe published in the 80s and 90s succeeded in pushing lesser known, but not necessarily less delicious, varieties further into the shadows. This, in turn, meant more Coxes and Bramleys were planted and other, rarer, varieties were dropped by growers: a crying shame.

As the recipes that follow indicate, appreciative chefs and food writers now advocate a far wider range of local seasonal apples, and take care to specify them on their restaurant menus and in their published works. I hope fervently that increasing numbers of home cooks will follow their lead. The more who do, and the more we all press for these less familiar but no less desirable apples, the more likely serious growers will become interested in growing them, and the more shops will want to stock them. A virtuous apple circle.

The market, however, is still dominated by the same few commercial varieties that are unnaturally omnipresent: on sale in June and December, in places as far flung as John O'Groats, Land's End and London, with sad disregard for seasonality and locality, often imported and often of second-rate quality.

English apples are not a constant twelvemonth staple. They are living fresh foods, and part of the charm of growing, eating and cooking them lies in the natural succession of textures, tastes and varieties that reflect the passing months and may capture the essence of particular places. An orchard planted with a judicious mix of early, mid-season and late eaters, cookers and keepers, should provide apples from late summer 'till rhubarb comes again in the garden' as the country saying goes, in other words for eight or nine months. Traditionally, some fruit was stored and matured in attic, outhouse or spare room, exuding an irresistible heady ripe scent. The rules were clear-cut. Store only unblemished fruits. Do not let them touch each other, or rot (when it starts) will spread faster than measles in a kindergarten. Last but not least, check stored apples and use them at their best, rather than hoard them until wrinkled and dulling.

Much of the crop would be squirrelled away in the larder, preserved with sugar or vinegar, juiced or transformed into cider. Bottling has now been replaced by freezing (chopped or sliced windfalls bagged up raw, or space-saving cooked apple purée) but the sight of shelves stacked with glowing jellies, chutneys, pickles, and dried apple rings as soft and pliant as chamois leather, is curiously reassuring even today, and would have provided earlier generations with valuable sources of vitamin C in months when fresh fruits and leafy vegetables were scarce. Our recipes reflect an undiminished taste for preserves and preserving, and the address book section includes suppliers of dehydrators, steam-juicers and presses. Good equipment can be expensive but own-dried apples and home brews can be delectable, they make dramatic inroads into superabundance, and make the maker glow with pride.

I rejoiced last autumn to watch a mother and child harvesting apples in a Community Orchard where families are reconnecting with real food and treating it with proper respect. The woman and her boy rolled windfalls over tentatively with their feet to check for wasps before gathering the fruit. 'Fine for puddings and preserves after the bad bits are cut out,' the mother explained.

Later, picking from the tree, she demonstrated how to cradle an apple lightly in a cupped hand, then lift and twist gently to see if the stalk was ready to part from the bough. I remembered my father teaching me this, and his delight in a little ritual peculiar to the Cox that his father had taught him. Shake the apple gently and listen: if the pips rattle inside, it is ready to eat.

Finding out about apples local to where we live, ferreting out traditional recipes for them, and creating new ones is a fascinating voyage of discovery. Apples that do brilliantly in some places frequently do poorly where terrain and microclimate are different. Hence the time-honoured recommendation to plant varieties known to do well in your area – and the observation that the qualities of local apples help to shape recipe variations and give distinctive tastes to local dishes. The character of Norfolk apples make a typical Norfolk apple pie very unlike a Somerset apple pie; each boasts its own uniquely flavoursome slant. Detective cooks may or may not know that Sweet Lark apples are Cornish, but the fact that an old recipe for Pickled Sweet Larks ends with the instruction 'eat with bread and butter and perhaps cream' clearly suggests that it comes from the lush cattle grazing West Country.

Old recipes handed down through generations of family cooks did not need to specify varieties by name, though sometimes they did. People just ate and cooked what was available locally in its season. Late summer recipes that team apples with, say, blackberries naturally used early season apples of fleeting berry-like fragrance because the harvests of the two fruits coincided. Later in the year, puddings combining apple with quince or medlar invariably employed later-maturing fuller-flavoured apples. And the manifold suet apple puddings, as warming as central heating, served in deepest midwinter could only have been made with what was available then: dessert apples left on the tree as long as possible then stored to achieve maximum aromatic ripeness, or mid-late season dual-purpose varieties that keep well and undergo gradual transformation from very sharp to just sweet enough to eat raw. Intriguingly the skins of some of these change from acid green to mellow yellow, and may develop a natural waxy protective coating in storage.

The biggest difficulty for apple lovers and keen apple cooks remains where to buy the choicest, most interesting and specifically local varieties. Greengrocers need encouragement to offer a wider selection than they usually do, though some make valiant efforts to source from local small-scale growers to supplement the more standardised offerings of regional wholesale markets. Buying from farmers' markets and scrounging from friends with orchards put us in better touch with apples rarely carried by shops. Garden gate boxes of windfalls with the scrawled invitation for passers-by to help themselves can throw up a time-honoured local treasure trove. Specialist fruit growers and nurseries and Apple Day events bring us another fruitful step closer to appreciating the extraordinary diversity of apples that once thrived and can still be grown in Britain. But planting your own orchard (even just one or two espaliers), or participating in a Community Orchard, is probably the best route to rediscovering the special pleasures of our best apples, grown and matured to perfection.

As H. V. Taylor wrote in *The Apples of England* in 1936, 'Only the private gardener will always put quality before quantity and will find a place for shy but choice varieties like Cornish Gillyflower, D'Arcy Spice and King's Acre Pippin. It would be a sad day for the apple lover if Blenheim Orange ceases to be planted because it takes so long to come into bearing.' Hear, hear. And let us go on planting new apples alongside the old. From little acorns mighty oaks grow, and from the pips in the core of the apple I am eating as I write, and the one you may be eating as you read, unique new varieties will emerge. Whether they will prove worth propagating for subsequent generations of cook-gardeners, only time will tell. Nothing ventured, nothing gained. Who can resist trying?

Philippa Davenport has been food columnist of the Financial Times *since 1973. From 1985 until 2001 she also wrote about food and cookery for* Country Living.

SOUPS & SMALL SAVOURY DISHES

• CELERIAC & APPLE SOUP **JULIET KINDERSLEY** • COLD CURRIED APPLE SOUP **SIMON HOPKINSON** • TOMATO SOUP WITH APPLE **CHARLES DOWDING** • MELON, APPLE & TARRAGON CREAM SOUP **LYNDA BROWN** • APPLE & STILTON TOASTS **CAROLINE WALDEGRAVE** • BLACK PUDDING & APPLE POTS **SUE LAWRENCE** • CHEESE & APPLE TARTLETS **CRAIG & CHRISTINE PILLANS** • CHOPPED HERRING **CLARISSA HYMAN** • ORCHARD TOASTED CHEESE **PHILIPPA DAVENPORT** •

Juliet Kindersley is a gardener, environmentalist and organic farmer. With the help of her son-in-law Eric Treuille (who runs Books for Cooks in London), she designs seasonal menus for the conference centre at Sheepdrove Organic Farm, using the produce from the farm, kitchen gardens and orchards.

I wanted to plant a selection of apples with varied tastes for specific uses. One of my first choices was Lord Lambourne, partly because he is such a good eater and partly because we live just outside Lambourn, but the noble lord doesn't seem to care for this high windy spot on the Berkshire Downs with its thin, chalky soil. I chose D'Arcy Spice because she is so richly aromatic and spicy, qualities that improve with storage, but she doesn't seem very happy here either. The real star for us has been the Reverend W. Wilks, a great dual-purpose apple that seems to rejoice in being at Sheepdrove, so we have planted more Wilkses recently. We also have Blenheim Orange, Bountiful, Winston (which used to be called Winter King but was renamed in 1945, after Churchill, presumably), the lovely little Pitmaston Pine Apple and Early Victoria; some of these should produce their first harvest this year.

Because we are organic and now grow our fruit biodynamically, we use no sprays. We grease the trunks before Christmas to discourage winter moth; and we put wood ash from our log fire into the compost, with a light seasoning of seaweed, to top-dress feed the trees occasionally.

Eric makes this soup at Books for Cooks and it is a favourite at home: a nicely seasonal combination of earthy root and fragrant fruit, enlivened both in looks and flavour by the addition of a bacon and cabbage garnish at the end of cooking.

Serves 4–6

25 g (1 oz) butter

1 tablespoon olive oil

1 onion, finely chopped

2 garlic cloves, finely chopped

1 carrot, chopped

2 well-flavoured apples, such as the Reverend W. Wilks,
   Howgate Wonder or Blenheim Orange, chopped

1 medium celeriac, chopped

1 medium potato, chopped

1 litre (1¾ pints) hot chicken stock or water

4 rashers streaky bacon, rind removed, chopped

A quarter Savoy cabbage, cored and finely shredded

Melt the butter with the oil in a pan over low heat. Add the onion, garlic and carrot and cook gently until softened but not coloured, about 10 minutes.

Add the apples, celeriac and potato with the hot stock or water, turn the heat to medium and bring to the boil. Adjust the heat and simmer steadily until the potato is cooked through, about 20 minutes.

Put the soup into a food-processor (you may have to do this in batches) or use a hand-held blender and whiz until silky smooth. Thin the soup with hot water as needed, reheat until simmering and season to taste.

Add the bacon and cabbage and simmer gently until the cabbage is bright green and tender, about 15 minutes. Ladle the soup into warmed bowls and serve hot.

COLD CURRIED APPLE SOUP

Simon Hopkinson is founding chef and co-proprietor of Bibendum and four-times Glenfiddich winner. His latest book is Week in Week Out. *Happy cook, cat lover and passionate smoker. This recipe is taken from* Gammon & Spinach.

I reckon I have eaten a raw apple perhaps … oh, say, once every two years. I love *cooked* apples – when they fit the dish: crumble, charlotte, tart, turnover and fritter. I think that the ubiquitous Golden Delicious makes the finest Tarte Tatin. Bramleys are only good for apple sauce – otherwise a waste of time. I loathe baked Bramleys, for instance, with all that puffy, tasteless sour flesh.

This exceptionally good cold soup I first came across when I was working at the Hat and Feather restaurant in Knutsford, Cheshire, some twenty years ago now. Some may think it sounds odd and rather, how should one say, dated? But it is a rare combination: sweet yet savoury, elusive, seductive and essentially English. The combination of the two apples make its sweet/acid ratio perfect.

Serves 4

25 g (1 oz) butter

1 onion, peeled and chopped

1 heaped tablespoon curry powder

900 ml (1½ pints) light chicken stock
   (I have made it very successfully using cubes)

450 g (1 lb) dessert apples and 450 g (1 lb) Granny Smiths,
   peeled, cored and chopped

the juice of ½ a large and juicy lemon, or more for a sharper-tasting soup

200 mls (7 fl oz) whipping cream

chopped mint (apple mint is best)

cayenne pepper

Melt the butter in a roomy pan and fry the onion gently until pale golden. Add the curry powder and cook over a very gentle heat for a couple of minutes. Pour in the stock, bring to the boil, add the apples and a little salt. Turn down to a simmer and cook for about half an hour, stirring occasionally; the apples must be completely soft and pulpy. Liquidise in batches until very smooth and pass through a fine sieve. Allow to cool, stir in the lemon juice and whisk in the cream. Check for seasoning and chill well in the fridge. Pour into cold soup bowls, sprinkle with chopped mint and dust with a little cayenne pepper.

TOMATO SOUP WITH APPLE

Charles Dowding has been growing organic vegetables since 1982. He set up one of the first vegetable box schemes in 1983 and has supplied local restaurants and shops for more than twenty-five years. He writes for RHS Magazine *and the* Blackmore Vale Magazine. *This recipe is taken from* Organic Gardening the natural no-dig way.

Cooking apples have higher acidity than eaters, and are often easier to grow because of better disease resistance. They also crop more heavily. The classic cooking variety is Bramley and it deserves its reputation, succeeding both as a small tree and as a large old one. If picked and stored, the fruits turn more yellow in late winter and can become just sweet enough to eat, if still acidic. Newton Wonder is another reliable cropper and better as a dual-purpose apple, good to eat in February and March. Bountiful is an exciting, relatively new variety (originating in 1960). It is a heavy cropper, ready to harvest in September and becomes edible by November, as it ripens. It stays crisper than many eating apples and is often large, especially when thinned out on the tree in summer.

This soup makes good use of a glut of tomatoes at the end of the season when the plants need to come out to make room for the next crop. It is also a time when the apple trees are groaning with fruit. Apple adds body to the soup and a bit of sweetness. If your tomatoes are very sweet and ripe you may want to choose an apple that is more acid than sweet. Conversely, if the tomatoes are underripe, you may want to counterbalance them with a sweet apple. Work on the basis of 1 onion and 1 apple to 1 kg (2.2 lb) of tomatoes. Garlic, celery and good stock help enormously.

Sweat the chopped onion in a little oil or fat in large saucepan. Add some chopped celery, then the apple and tomatoes, both cored and chopped (skins on or off, as you wish) and a couple of cloves of garlic. Then add the stock. Bring to the boil, then simmer for about 20 minutes. Liquidise before serving.

MELON, APPLE & TARRAGON CREAM SOUP

Lynda Brown is an award-winning food writer, broadcaster and author of several books including The Cook's Garden, Modern Cook's Manual *and* The Shopper's Guide to Organic Food.

This summer recipe offers the opportunity to experiment with some of the excellent locally pressed single-variety apple juices that are now available. Apple varieties that ripen early in the season are the natural choice here with their hint of summer fruits – say, Worcester Pearmain, Discovery or Norfolk Royal. Edward Bunyard put his finger on it when he wrote in *The Anatomy of Dessert* (1933 edition) 'the early apples mostly have what has been called the Strawberry or Raspberry flavour: Worcester Pearmain, Duchess of Oldenberg, Emperor Alexander being notable examples. The first-named fruit, however, must not be judged from barrow or shop examples, which are usually gathered before they are ripe, and in both texture and flavour are to be passionately avoided,' a compelling reason to try to grow your own or find a grower/vendor who understands and really cares about quality.

Serves 4

225 g (8 oz) ripe fragrant melon, e.g. Charentais, peeled,
   seeded and cut into chunks, plus extra for serving
300 ml (10 fl oz) apple juice
60–90 ml (2–3 fl oz) best double cream, or to taste
1–2 teaspoons finely chopped tarragon

Blend the melon chunks and apple juice to a smooth cream. Stir in the double cream and finely chopped tarragon to taste. Add the extra melon, cut into small cubes. Serve chilled, in pretty soup cups or small dishes.

APPLE & STILTON TOASTS

Caroline Waldegrave is co-owner and managing director of Leiths School of Food and Wine. She is also a cookery and health food writer and broadcaster. A former member of the Health Education Authority, and a past chair of the Guild of Food Writers, she is now on the editorial board of the BBC. This recipe comes from **Leith's Simple Bible** *by Viv Pidgeon and Jenny Stringer.*

Apples featured greatly in my childhood, we had an orchard with a large variety of apples my favourite of which was the Russet. There was, however, always a bit of a disappointment because my father was determined to make the apples 'last through' – through to what, I never quite understood but he diligently wrapped each apple in a piece of newspaper and kept them in an outside shed. By the time we were allowed to eat them the skins were always slightly wrinkled and the texture had lost some crispness. I now live in Somerset and have my own orchard and we eat the apples just as they are about to drop.

Apple and Stilton Toasts can seem like a succession of different treats each time you make it if you take the trouble to hunt out different apple varieties. For example, you may like to try it first with juicy fresh Discovery, Beauty of Bath or

George Neal, apples that come into season as early as August; then, successively, with Devonshire Quarrenden and soft, creamy James Grieve; followed by nutty Russet, gentle Lord Lambourne, versatile and handsome Peasgood's Nonsuch; and finally apples like honeyed Cornish Gillyflower, which should eat well from November through February.

Serves 4
Preparation time: 5 minutes
Cooking time: 5 minutes

4 medium-thick slices of bread
1½ eating apples, cored and thinly sliced
100 g (4 oz) Stilton cheese, crumbled
85 g (generous 3 oz) walnuts, roughly chopped
100 g (4 oz) strong Cheddar cheese, grated

Preheat the grill to a medium setting.

Toast one side of each of the bread slices. On the uncooked side of the bread arrange the apple slices, scatter over the Stilton and walnuts and finally the Cheddar.

Arrange the toasts under the grill so that the cheese melts and browns but takes about 3–5 minutes.

Serve immediately.

BLACK PUDDING & APPLE POTS

Sue Lawrence is a cookery writer and cookery demonstrator, lecturer and author of twelve books including Sue Lawrence on Baking, Scots Cooking, Sue Lawrence's Scottish Kitchen *and* A Cook's Tour of Scotland. *She is president of the Guild of Food Writers.*

I like to use Stornoway black pudding for this dish because, as a partisan Scot, I believe we produce some of the finest black pudding around. Sometimes I use haggis instead of black pudding: cut into a haggis and crumble some into the base of each ramekin, then continue as described in the recipe.

Naturally, my first choice of apple would be a Scottish variety – a tart one is needed here. James Grieve is probably most widely available, generally regarded as an eater in the sunny south but as a cooker here in its native Scotland. Then there is Hawthornden, White Melrose (a dual-purpose apple), Stirling Castle (an early cropper and very fertile), Tower of Glamis and Coul Blush. Who can resist names like these? George Neal and Bountiful are not Scottish but also worth considering.

Serves 6

500 g (1 lb 2 oz) cooking apples, peeled, cored and chopped
the juice of 1 lemon
25 g (1 oz) golden caster sugar
25 g (1 oz) butter
2 heaped teaspoons horseradish sauce
12 slices black pudding, skinned

Put the prepared apples into a saucepan with the lemon juice, sugar and 10 g of the butter. Bring to the boil, cover and simmer until soft. Mash with the horseradish sauce, then cool.

Butter 6 x 4-cm (1½ in) deep ramekins. Lay a slice of black pudding in each, spoon on some of the apple sauce, and lay another slice of black pudding on top.

Melt the remaining butter, brush this over the tops, and sit the ramekins on a baking tray. Bake in the oven at 200°C/400°F/gas mark 6 for 15 minutes or until piping hot. Serve at once.

CHEESE & APPLE TARTLETS

....

Craig and Christine Pillans built up a collection of more than seventy-five varieties of apples, including all the surviving pre-twentieth-century Scottish varieties, in their Lincolnshire orchard reflecting Craig's booklet Historic Apples of Scotland *(1987). On leaving it they infected the new owners with enthusiasm and happily make autumnal visits.*

Despite its northerly latitude, Scotland has a long tradition of apple-growing and, until quite recently, large areas of Clydesdale south-east of Glasgow, the Carse of Gowrie between Perth and Dundee, and Tweedside in the Borders were devoted to orchards. About twenty historic Scottish varieties are still in existence, most of which can be traced back to particular counties or districts.

This recipe is based on one from a *Good Housekeeping* book of 1955. It provides a good basis for experimenting with both apple varieties and different cheeses as the ingredients are few and uncluttered with other flavourings.

We would, of course, suggest Scottish apple varieties: James Grieve (an eater, but will cook well), Hawthornden, White Melrose, Tower of Glamis, Galloway Pippin, Stirling Castle, Bloody Ploughman and Coul Blush, depending on availability.

Line patty tins with shortcrust pastry and prick. Half fill the pastry cases with chopped apple, and sprinkle with sugar. Bake in a hot oven (220°C/425°F/gas mark 7) until the apple is tender and the pastry beginning to colour – about 10 minutes. Remove from the oven and sprinkle with a layer of grated cheese, then continue to bake until the pastry is cooked through and the cheese is golden brown – approximately 5 minutes. Serve hot or cold.

CHOPPED HERRING

....

Clarissa Hyman is a food and travel writer, contributing to a wide range of publications. She has also written three books: Cucina Siciliana, The Jewish Kitchen *and* The Spanish Kitchen.

In all Jewish homes, symbolism plays a key part in festive meals. In the early autumn, at Rosh Hashanah, the New Year (the exact date depends on the lunar calendar), apples are the main symbolic food. In many communities, the custom has grown up of starting the meal by ritually dipping newly harvested ripe apples in honey fresh from the hive. Both the apple's sweet taste and its round shape express the personal and communal wish for a sweet and happy year ahead.

Apples feature again at the ritual *Seder* meal at the freedom festival of Passover in spring, when apple stores might be running down. The dish served then is Apple Charoset, a sweet, paste-like dip that reminds the celebrants of the mortar they made while they were enslaved in biblical Egypt. It is made by mixing the peeled, cored and finely chopped flesh of a large sweet apple with chopped walnuts and ground cinnamon, bound with a few spoonfuls of sweet red wine.

Chopped Herring, on the other hand, is not associated with any particular occasion or ritual. It is an everyday *Forspeise*, or appetiser. The topping of chopped hard-boiled egg helps but does not disguise the dismal grey colour of the herring. And the taste, frankly, doesn't appeal to everyone – you either love or hate its almost savage pungency. It may be something genetically inherited. But you don't have to be Jewish to eat it. Novices are allowed to add some sugar but hardcore enthusiasts need no such refinement.

Serves 6

1 x 500 g jar or tub of pickled herring fillets
  (traditionally salt herrings are used, but this version is simpler and quicker)
4 hard-boiled eggs

half a mild white onion
1 small sweet apple, peeled
2 tablespoons ground almonds
1 tablespoon lemon juice
1 teaspoon or more sugar (optional)

Drain the herrings and rinse them well. Dry on kitchen paper.

Briefly pulse all ingredients, except for one of the eggs in a food-processor (although I sometimes still use my vintage *Hachmesser*, the two-handled chopper and curved board once kept specially for herring; the faint whiff of Bismarck No 5 that hangs around the knives, dishes and fingers for days explains why.) The chopped herring should not be too pasty; it needs some texture.

Taste for seasoning, adding white pepper – plus sugar, if wished. Leave to 'mature' for a few hours.

Scatter with the reserved, chopped hard-boiled egg before serving with rye or challah bread, bagels, matzoh or crackers as a *forspeise* (appetiser).

ORCHARD TOASTED CHEESE

....

Philippa Davenport has been food columnist of the **Financial Times** *since 1973. From 1985 until 2001 she also wrote about food and cookery for* **Country Living** *magazine. This recipe is adapted from* **Country Cook.**

Lighter than many rarebits, this makes a lovely quick lunch dish or snack and is pretty enough to serve at a party. Like all exceedingly simple dishes, its success depends almost entirely on using top-quality ingredients.

I recommend Kirkham's clean, fresh-tasting Lancashire cheese to balance a full-bodied farm-made Cheddar from James Montgomery in Somerset. I buy local Wiltshire cured ham from Sandridge Farm and mustard from Wiltshire Tracklements, and bread made from flour milled by Dove's Farm, a few miles over the border in Berkshire. My fruit supplies originate from neighbouring counties: Blenheim Orange (native to Oxfordshire) or Queen Cox apples (found in Berkshire) or Ashmead's Kernel (born and bred in Gloucestershire), and my favourite pear, Williams' Bon-Chrétien, raised in Berkshire. Muscat-scented white Italia grapes are the only import from overseas that I use for this dish. Patriotic cooks could substitute peppery bunches of watercress; the best is grown organically by John Hurd, another great Wiltshire producer.

Only a splash of cider or apple juice is needed for the recipe – I suggest Julian Temperley's Burrow Hill cider, or apple juice made at home or pressed by one of the small producers springing up round the country. Cider and apple juice are the right drinks to accompany Orchard Toasted Cheese; and I like to think that the ham has come from a pig that once roamed orchards and fed on windfall apples...

Serves 4 (or 8 as a snack)
3–4 each ripe dessert apples and pears
a bunch of fine grapes, or 2 bunches watercress
a few spoonfuls of cider or apple juice
the juice of half a lemon
4 large or 8 small not-too-thick slices of bread
a little mild mustard, preferably wholegrain
4 large slices of ham, just carved from the bone
100–150 g (4–5 oz) each Lancashire and Cheddar cheese, grated and mixed

Quarter the apples and pears, core them and cut into thick crescent moon slices. To prevent discolouration dip the slices in, or brush them with, the lemon juice mixed with 4 tablespoons of cider or apple juice. Shake off excess liquid, arrange on individual plates and garnish with clusters of grapes or clumps of watercress.

Toast the bread well on one side and very lightly on the other. Splash the lightly toasted side with cider or apple juice, just a teaspoon or so per slice.

Spread with mustard, cover with ham and top with the grated cheeses.

Cook under a medium-hot grill (avoid fierce heat: it spoils cheese making it stringy and tough). When the cheese is molten, hot and freckled golden-brown here and there, transfer the toasts to the prepared plates and serve. The idea is to nibble the fruit between mouthfuls of the hot toast, the clean tastes of the fruit providing an excellent foil for the richness of the ham and cheese.

SALADS & VEGETABLES

• CHICORY, WATERCRESS, APPLE & HAZELNUT SALAD **BARNY HAUGHTON** • APPLE & FENNEL SALAD WITH OR WITHOUT A SOFT CHEESE MOUSSE **PATRICIA HEGARTY** • WINTER SALAD WITH APPLE BALSAMIC VINEGAR **JOANNA BLYTHMAN** • ROLLMOP, APPLE & POTATO SALAD **HUGH FEARNLEY-WHITTINGSTALL** • AUTUMN COLESLAW **SKYE GYNGELL** • A SALAD OF RABBIT (OR CHICKEN) LIVERS WITH APPLES, HAZELNUTS & CHIVE FLOWERS **DARINA ALLEN** • APPLE, BEETROOT & BUTTER BEAN SALAD WITH HONEY DRESSING **ROSE ELLIOT** • CHESTNUTS BRAISED IN CIDER WITH APPLES **LYNDA BROWN** • PARSNIP & APPLE CAKES **HUGH FEARNLEY-WHITTINGSTALL** • ROAST BUTTERNUT WITH SHALLOTS, APPLES & OLIVES **PHILIPPA DAVENPORT** • BRAISED RED CABBAGE WITH APPLE **LAURA MASON** • APPLE & BACON MASH **SOPHIE GRIGSON** • HOT BEETROOT IN APPLE SAUCE **ROSE ELLIOT** • LEEK & COCKPIT FLAN **GEORGE & BARBARA MORRIS** •

CHICORY, WATERCRESS, APPLE & HAZELNUT SALAD

....

Barny Haughton has been chef-patron of a pioneering organic restaurant, Bristol's Quartier Vert (formerly Roccinantes), since 1988. He opened a cookery school for children and a bakery in 1998, and opened Bordeaux Quay restaurant, brasserie, bar, bakery, cookery school and deli in 2006. Bordeaux Quay is based on the principle that the best food comes from sustainable farming systems and that good food is, by definition, local, seasonal and organic.

Tartness is the first thing to look for in the taste of the apples you use here, sweetness the second, and the texture should be crisp. Either Worcester Pearmain, Cox's Orange Pippin, Ribston Pippin, Sturmer Pippin or Tydeman's Late Orange, all grown and ripened with care, would be perfect. This salad doesn't need the robust flavour of olive oil in the dressing: groundnut or hazelnut, or a mix of both, is best, but sunflower will do fine.

Serves 6 as a starter or as an accompaniment to ham or roast chicken
2 heads of chicory
2 bunches of watercress
4 medium-sized tart/sweet, crisp apples
a handful of whole unblanched hazelnuts
a small bunch of chives, cut into 2.5-cm (1-inch or so) lengths
cider vinegar
groundnut oil and/or hazelnut oil
Maldon salt

Toss the hazelnuts in a little oil and a sprinkling of Maldon salt and roast in a hot oven until toasty brown. Leave to cool. Break them into coarse pieces with a rolling-pin.

Make the dressing in a large bowl: mix 2 tablespoons of vinegar with a pinch of salt along with 10 tablespoons groundnut/hazelnut oil into an emulsion.

Remove the more fibrous stalks from the watercress and separate the leaves of chicory. Cut the apples into slim wedges, removing the core with a sharp knife.

Just before serving, gently toss the chicory, watercress and apple in the dressing and transfer to serving dish. Sprinkle liberally with the broken hazelnuts and chives, adding an extra pinch of Maldon salt.

APPLE & FENNEL SALAD WITH OR WITHOUT A SOFT CHEESE MOUSSE

. . . .

Patricia Hegarty is the author of An English Flavour *from which this recipe is taken. She and her husband, John, ran a small hotel, Hope End, near Ledbury, Herefordshire, for twenty years, growing and cooking organic fruit and vegetables from their rescued, mellow redbrick eighteenth-century walled garden. They have spent the last nine years at Llwynywormwood Park, in Wales, repairing a smaller stone-walled garden and planting an orchard – John's fifth.*

At Llwynywormwood we found a stone-walled garden, much breached – where trees had fallen and burst the walls or they had been deliberately broken open – waist high in brambles, facing south-east to the mountains. In one corner the only apple tree lay prone. Wonderfully, it still bore fruit: pale green, knobbly and exquisitely appley, Catshead, a very old variety. We have repaired the walls and planted a little apple orchard with some of our old favourites, including Pitmaston Pine Apple, Lord Lambourne and Ashmead's Kernel; a row of Welsh apples such as Pig y Derwyn, Cissy and Monmouth Green; and we have grafted the Catshead to continue for another generation. Not sure what would do well in this climate, with twice the rainfall of Herefordshire, we have been rewarded with some good, flavoursome harvests. Now, the Duchy of Cornwall has taken over the estate to be Prince Charles's seat in Wales, so the future of the garden looks rosy and restoration of the Park will continue.

For this salad, try to find an aniseedy or fresh-tasting apple, such as Ellison's Orange, or a crimson-coloured one like Belle de Boskoop to point up the emerald of the fennel fronds. Egremont Russet is also good here.

To turn the salad into an easy lunch dish, surround it with a ring of soft cheese mousse. I like to use goat's cheese partly because we used to keep goats at Hope End and partly because there is such splendid artisan goat's cheese being made here in Wales. The cider brings a deeper apple note to the dish.

Serves 6

2 Florence fennel bulbs
4 dessert apples

for the dressing:
1 garlic clove
1 teaspoon fennel seeds
5 teaspoons virgin olive oil
1 teaspoon cider vinegar
1 teaspoon Meaux mustard

for the mousse:
300 g (12 oz) soft cream cheese
2 dessert apples, cored, diced quite small and tossed in the juice of half a lemon
50 g (2 oz) pistachio nuts
4 small or 2 large sheets of fine leaf gelatine (6–7 g in total)
275 ml (10 fl oz) dry organic cider or pure apple juice
½ teaspoon fennel seeds, crushed

Make the mousse first as it needs time to set. Soak the gelatine in cold water for 5 minutes. Warm the cider, take it off the heat, drop the drained sheets of gelatine into it and stir until melted.

Lightly oil a 750 ml (generous 1¼-pint) ring mould and dot some pistachios and diced apple, skin side down, round the base.

Mash the cheese with a fork, add the remaining nuts, diced apple and fennel seeds, and stir in the cider. Leave in a cool place until beginning to set, then tip the mixture into the ring mould, level the top, cover and keep cool until ready to unmould.

For the salad dressing, first crush the garlic with a little sea salt. Whiz the fennel seeds in a liquidiser to release their aroma, then add the garlic and the remaining ingredients and whiz together.

For the salad, first cut the fennel bulbs in half lengthways, then cut across in thin slices. Depending on how much fennel frond there is, either mix it into the salad or reserve for decoration. Leaving the pretty peel on the apples, cut, core and slice them to match the fennel pieces.

Dress the salad, tossing well to prevent the apples from browning.

If serving the mousse, unmould it and pile the salad loosely into the creamy ring.

WINTER SALAD WITH APPLE BALSAMIC VINEGAR

....

Joanna Blythman is an influential investigative journalist and broadcaster who has won five Glenfiddich awards and the BBC Radio 4 Derek Cooper Award. Shopped: The Shocking Power of British Supermarkets, *and* Bad Food Britain, *both published by Fourth Estate are her most recent books.*

I first came across apple balsamic vinegar when I visited Vienna in 1999. It was all the rage in discerning food shops and in smart restaurants, where chefs were teaming it with that other Austrian favourite, pumpkin-seed oil. Seeing the word 'balsamic', I imagined it would be a sticky, dark brown vinegar. In fact, it is a thin, limpid, amber-coloured vinegar with an exceptionally clean, crisp apple bouquet that manages to capture some of the sweet, refreshing quality of the fresh fruit. It used to be almost impossible to buy this vinegar in Britain, but now Clearspring, a company whose products I rate highly, is importing an organic version from Italy. The difference between apple balsamic and traditional cider vinegar is that the former, after carefully blending concentrated apple must and cider, is fermented, then left to rest and mature in tuns (wooden casks) until it reaches its peak of flavour and aroma.

As winter sets in, I often make a salad on the fruit, cheese and nut theme, dressing it with apple balsamic and a nutty oil – walnut, hazelnut, brazil nut or pumpkin seed.

Start by assembling a selection of salad leaves to give a balance of bitter (chicory), peppery (rocket, red mustard) and juicy (Cos, Little Gem), red leaves (radicchio, red chicory) and green (watercress, spinach), and a good contrast between soft (lambs' lettuce, oak leaf) and crunchy (frisée, endive).

Combine three parts nut oil to one part apple balsamic with sea salt and lots of black pepper. Dress the leaves with it.

Slice a firm apple with a good sugar/acid balance (such as Sturmer Pippin, Orleans Reinette, King of the Pippins, Blenheim Orange and Tydeman's Late Orange) over the dressed leaves, then squeeze over the juice and seeds of a pomegranate.

Finally, add a sprinkling of fresh or toasted nuts and crumble over small pieces of cheese. I find that Stilton, or other blue cheese, goes well with freshly shelled walnuts and walnut oil, while a slightly matured goat cheese, such as Golden Cross or Ragstone, works particularly well with toasted, skinned hazelnuts and hazelnut oil.

ROLLMOP, APPLE & POTATO SALAD

....

Hugh Fearnley-Whittingstall is a writer, broadcaster and campaigner, widely known for his commitment to seasonal, ethically produced food. His River Cottage *TV series and books have earned him a huge following.*

This is a wonderful, refreshing starter to serve in late summer, when there are plenty of herring about and the first tart English apples are coming in too. Use Ashmead's Kernel or sharp, early Cox's for particularly pleasing results.

Serves 4 as a starter

2 tablespoons crème fraîche

1 teaspoon English mustard

6 rollmops, plus a little of their pickling liquid

a pinch of sugar

300 g (11 oz) cooked, cooled waxy salad potatoes such as Anya or Pink Fir Apple,
    thickly sliced

1 smallish red onion, peeled and thinly sliced

2 crisp, sharp eating apples

1 tablespoon chopped dill or flatleaf parsley

rye bread, to serve

Start by making the dressing. Combine the crème fraîche and mustard in a bowl with 1 tablespoon of the rollmop pickling liquid. Season to taste with salt, pepper and sugar (bearing in mind that the pickling liquid will be pretty salty). Set aside while you prepare the salad.

Cut the rollmops into thickish strips and place in a large bowl. Add the potatoes and onion, then core and very thinly slice the apples and throw them in too. Toss together lightly. Add the dressing and the chopped herbs, then toss again. Taste, and adjust the seasoning if necessary. Serve straight away, with rye bread on the side.

AUTUMN COLESLAW

* *

Skye Gyngell is an innovative Australian chef and food writer. She has worked in Sydney, Paris and London. Her latest role is as chef at the Petersham Nurseries Café, near Richmond in Surrey, which has rapidly acquired a reputation for superb food in an outstanding setting. She is the author of A Year in My Kitchen *and writes weekly for the* Independent on Sunday.

This strong, crunchy, earthbound salad embraces all that is best about autumn – apples, cobnuts, red cabbage and beetroot. My last meal on earth would have to be some sort of salad...and this just might be it! Pretty pink and white candy-striped beetroot looks amazing but the purple or golden variety will taste just as good. Our lovely organic cobnuts come from Allen's Farm, Plaxtol, in Kent.

Petersham's food-sourcing policy – headed by forager Wendy Fogarty – is to seek out the highest-quality ingredients, always respecting the seasons and supporting small farmers and producers, many of them local; and we look forward, every autumn, to rediscovering a wealth of forgotten apple varieties.

Many of our orchard fruits come to us from Brogdale Horticultural Trust, courtesy of the Knutsalls from England Preserves. Last year we had our first taste of Zabergau Reinette, Blenheim Orange and Caville Blanc d'Hiver. Apples find their way on to our menus in all sorts of sweet and savoury ways – and, of course, they are available to enjoy simply as the perfect pieces of fruit that they are. We also sell them by the kilo from a rickety old table outside the Café. They never last long as people find them hard to resist.

Serves 4
200 g (7 oz) cobnuts, shelled and very roughly chopped
1 pomegranate, quartered
a quarter red cabbage, cored
1 fennel bulb

4 raw beetroot, washed

3 carrots, peeled

4 apples (one of the Pippins would be perfect)

the leaves of a small bunch of tarragon, finely chopped

1 tablespoon extra virgin olive oil

the juice of half a lemon, or to taste

for the dressing:

2 organic egg yolks

1 tablespoon honey

1½ teaspoons Dijon mustard

1 tablespoon cream

1 tablespoon cider vinegar

1 teaspoon pomegranate molasses (optional)

200 ml (7 fl oz) mild olive oil

Preheat the oven to 180°C/350°F/gas mark 4.

Spread the cobnuts on a baking tray and toast them gently in the oven for 3–4 minutes, just to release their flavour. Set aside to cool. Carefully extract the seeds from the pomegranate, avoiding the bitter membrane; set aside.

Finely slice the red cabbage into thin ribbons. Cut off the base of the fennel bulb and remove the tough outer layer, slice the rest very finely. Cut the beetroot into very thin rounds. Shave the carrots into long ribbons, using a swivel peeler. Quarter and core the apples, leaving the skin on, then slice thinly.

Place the red cabbage, fennel, beetroot, carrots, apples and tarragon in a bowl and season with salt and pepper. Drizzle over the extra virgin olive oil and squeeze over the lemon juice. Toss gently together with your hands and set aside while you make the dressing.

Put the egg yolks into a bowl. Add the honey, mustard, cream, cider vinegar (and pomegranate molasses, if using) and whisk together to combine. Season with a little salt and pepper, then pour in the olive oil in a slow stream, whisking as you do so to emulsify. The dressing should have the consistency of a very loose mayonnaise.

Divide the salad between individual plates, piling it high. Drizzle over the dressing, then scatter the pomegranate seeds and cobnuts around the edges.

SALAD OF RABBIT (OR CHICKEN) LIVERS WITH APPLES, HAZELNUTS & CHIVE FLOWERS

Darina Allen is an author, journalist, broadcaster, teacher, and the owner of Ballymaloe Cookery School in Co. Cork, situated on an organically run farm and accredited by the IACP (International Association of Culinary Professionals). She is a member of Eurotoques, councillor for Ireland in the Slow Food movement, founder of the first farmers' markets in Ireland and currently involved in helping to set up new markets. This recipe is taken from **Easy Entertaining.**

In 1970 I married a farmer with an inheritance of more than sixty acres of apple orchards close to the sea at Shanagarry in East Cork. The orchards were dotted with beehives to help with pollination, so we had the most delicious apple-blossom honey every year. There were about fifteen apple varieties, including Lady Sudeley, Beauty of Bath, Grenadier, Cox's Orange Pippin, Miller's Seedling, James Grieve, Norfolk Royal, Golden Delicious, Laxton Superb and Laxton Fortune. It was already difficult then to compete with the import of French Golden Delicious but when my husband read that Brazil and Chile were planting large acreages of eating apples we knew that the writing was on the wall for Irish apple growers. Reluctantly, in the mid-seventies, we pulled out most of those beautiful trees, keeping just a five-acre block of Bramley's Seedling and Worcester Pearmain.

In recent years we have started to replant old apple varieties, not for commercial purposes but to enjoy choice at home, in the cookery school and at Ballymaloe House. The Irish Seed Savers in Scarrif, Co. Clare (00353 61 921866) – www.irishseedsavers.ie – have built up a wonderful collection and I have found many rarities in their catalogue. We now have Irish Peach, American Mother, Lane's Prince Albert, Arthur Turner, Pitmaston Pine Apple and Egremont Russet. The students love the variety and many have been inspired to plant an apple tree at home. I also remind them to look for any old apple trees in their parents' or grandparents' gardens; they should have them identified – they might find they have lost treasure that should be propagated.

Serves 4
4 rabbit or chicken livers
1 sweet, crisp dessert apple
2 tablespoons sliced hazelnuts
5 g (¼ oz) butter
1 tablespoon olive oil
a selection of salad leaves and herbs – e.g., butterhead lettuce, frisée,
    wild sorrel, oakleaf, radicchio, rocket, golden marjoram
chive flowers

for the dressing:
6 tablespoons hazelnut oil
2 tablespoons white wine vinegar
½ teaspoon Dijon mustard

First make the dressing by whisking all the ingredients together. Season with salt, sugar and freshly ground pepper.

Core and cut the apple into thin julienne strips, mix with the sliced hazelnuts and 1 tablespoon of the dressing.

Melt the butter and oil in a frying pan and cook the livers gently until just cooked.

While the livers are cooking, toss the greenery in enough dressing to make it just glisten and divide it between four plates.

Place a quarter of the apple julienne on top of each salad and finally the warm sautéed livers. Sprinkle with chive flowers and serve immediately.

APPLE, BEETROOT & BUTTERBEAN SALAD WITH HONEY DRESSING

*Rose Elliot is widely recognised as having revolutionised vegetarian cooking and played a major role in transforming its image, taste and popularity. She has written many books (*Veggie Chic *is the latest), broadcasts regularly and contributes to the new ecological monthly magazine,* Lifescape. *This recipe is adapted from* Rose Elliot's Complete Vegetarian Cookbook.

I grew up on the Hampshire–Sussex border, about fifteen miles from Petworth, where the Egremont Russet is said to have been raised. Coincidentally, this has always been one of my favourite apples. I love the way its modest matt-brown skin hides such sweet, juicy white flesh, and the nutty flavour, which mellows as the apple matures. While the season lasts I eat these apples almost daily: plain and unadorned, cooked in compôtes, or peeled and sliced into fruit or vegetable salads – they make a superb Waldorf, mixed with new-season walnuts and celery, bound with mayonnaise and served on watercress. I also like to mix them, as here, with cooked beetroot, firm, mealy butterbeans and a mustard and honey vinaigrette for a pretty pink and burgundy salad, which tastes as good as it looks. One of the joys of this salad is that you can whiz it up in no time at all if you use good quality ready-cooked beetroot (without added vinegar) and butterbeans (canned in water with no added sugar and salt). It's good heaped up on crisp lettuce leaves, with a spoonful of garlic mayo or some soft goat's cheese alongside.

Serves 4
400 g (14 oz) can of butterbeans, drained
300 g cooked beetroot, peeled and diced
2 Egremont Russet apples, peeled, cored and diced
small bunch of chives, chopped

for the honey dressing:
1 teaspoon ready-made English mustard
2 teaspoons honey
1 tablespoon red wine vinegar
3 tablespoons olive oil

Make the dressing straight into a large mixing bowl: put in the mustard, honey, vinegar, olive oil and some salt and pepper and mix well.

Add the butterbeans to the bowl along with the beetroot, apples and chives. Mix gently. Taste and add more salt and pepper as required.

CHESTNUTS BRAISED IN CIDER WITH APPLES

Lynda Brown is an award-winning food writer, broadcaster and author of several books including The Cook's Garden, Modern Cook's Manual, *and* The Shopper's Guide to Organic Food.

Interest in apple varieties naturally centres on their eating qualities but, having had the privilege for the last twenty years of enjoying apples we grew ourselves, I often reflect on how that is only half the story. Growing your own apples adds an unrivalled dimension to the cooking, eating and unabashed year-round delight to be derived from our nation's favourite fruit.

With an orchard you have a companion for life; and a life rich in what Edward Bunyard called 'hopeful voyaging', for traditional apple varieties speak of people, places and pride – not of indecipherable hybrids or a few soulless supermarket 'greens' and 'reds'. Thanks to dwarfing rooting stocks, an orchard of twenty-plus varieties needs occupy no more space than a medium-size lawn, and will reward you with apples to enjoy from August until the following spring. No lawn? Easy. Cordons up the wall of the house will do nicely.

Producing a succession of apples rarely found in the shops means recipes become uniquely yours, and will naturally change every time you make them. For this autumnal recipe, I would choose varieties with full-bodied, nutty/warm spicy notes, such as Cornish Gillyflower, Newton Wonder, D'Arcy Spice, King's Acre Pippin, Annie Elizabeth, Ellison's Orange, Blenheim Orange, Cox's Orange Pippin or Egremont Russet.

Serves 4
Allow up to 675 g (1½ lb) chestnuts in the shell,
    to yield 340 g (12 oz) peeled chestnuts
300 ml (10 fl oz) organic cider, e.g. Dunkerton's
1 teaspoon Demerara sugar
1 largish apple, peeled or not, as you wish, cored then chopped into small neat dice
15 g (½ oz) butter for frying

Score each chestnut around the middle, then simmer them in water to cover for about 10 minutes. Peel while hot, taking one chestnut out of the water at a time and keeping the rest in their hot bath. The shell and inner skin should slip off easily.

Put the peeled chestnuts in a single layer in a snug-fitting pan. Pour over the cider and add the sugar. Simmer gently, with the lid slightly ajar, until soft, about 20–25 minutes. Remove the nuts to a serving dish, breaking them into large pieces. Boil down the juices if necessary to 2–3 tablespoons, and pour over the nuts. Fry the diced apple in the butter for 2–3 minutes, and mix with the chestnuts. Serve with roast goose or game.

PARSNIP & APPLE CAKES

....

Hugh Fearnley-Whittingstall is a writer, broadcaster and campaigner, widely known for his commitment to seasonal, ethically produced food. His River Cottage *TV series and books have earned him a huge following.*

These are delicious with (or without) any kind of pork, from sausages to a full-scale roast. Use a fairly dry-fleshed apple variety, such as a Russet, so the mixture doesn't get too wet.

Makes 8 cakes
1 large parsnip, about 300 g (11 oz)
2 largish eating apples – about 300 g (11 oz) in total
1 medium egg, lightly beaten
15 g (2 level tablespoons) plain flour
sunflower oil, for frying

Peel the parsnip, quarter it and remove any tough core. Quarter the apples and cut out the cores, but don't worry about peeling them. Grate the parsnip and apples, combine them, add the egg, flour and plenty of salt and pepper and mix well.

Heat a non-stick frying pan over a medium heat and add enough oil to coat the base completely. When the oil is hot, take a handful of the parsnip and apple mixture and squash into a rough patty. Squeeze out any excess liquid (there may not be any – it depends on the juiciness of your apples). Put the patty into the pan and press down with a spatula to make a thin cake. Repeat with more of the mixture (you'll probably have to cook the cakes in two batches). Turn the heat down a little and fry for about 10 minutes, or until golden brown on the base, then turn over carefully and fry the second side until golden brown. Keep the heat fairly low and fry the cakes slowly to avoid burning. Serve them hot, as soon as they're cooked.

ROASTED BUTTERNUT WITH SHALLOTS, APPLES, OLIVES & FETA

. . . .

Philippa Davenport has been food columnist of the Financial Times *since 1973. From 1985 until 2001 she also wrote about food and cookery for* Country Living *magazine.*

This variation on roasted roots makes a nutritious main dish in its own right. Plainly cooked grains go well on the side: barley, spelt, rice, or a combination of all three. Dessert apples with a good ratio of sweet to acid are just right here: choose strongly aromatic, nutty or spicy, according to taste. Which variety is 'best' depends on where you live, what is grown there and what is properly ripe from the tree (or storeroom) when you come to cook the dish. The following varieties all spring to mind, but this list is far from exhaustive, of course: Kings Acre Pippin, Tydeman's Late Orange, Laxton's Exquisite, D'Arcy Spice, Kidd's Orange Red, Sturmer Pippin, James Grieve, Charles Ross, Cornish Gillyflower, Ashmead's Kernel, Court Pendu Plat and Blenheim Orange.

Serves 3–4
1 butternut squash
5–6 shallots
2 dessert apples
200 g (7 oz) feta cheese
50–75 g (2–3 oz) small black olives, such as Taggiasca
    or Niçoise, bottled in oil, rather than brine, if possible
fresh rosemary, oregano and thyme (preferably lemon thyme)
a couple of bay leaves
dried chilli flakes
olive oil and unsalted butter

Heat a roasting pan on top of the stove. Add a generous glug of olive oil and, when it is hot, slide into it the peeled and quartered shallots. Turn them once to coat with oil then leave to start cooking on the hob while you prepare the squash. Cut the butternut across into 2–2.5-cm (1-inch or so) thick slices: start at the stalk end and stop slicing when you think you have enough. Peel and de-seed the slices and cut the flesh into chunks. You need about 550 g (1¼ lb) net.

Add the squash to the pan, with a little more oil if needed. Turn the squash so it glistens with oil. Sprinkle on the leaves of several branches of rosemary and thyme and a little oregano, all roughly chopped to release their aromatic oils. Add chilli flakes to taste, the bay leaves and a parsimonious pinch of salt. Mix everything well then put the pan into an oven heated to 220°C, 425°F, gas mark 7. Roast for about 30 minutes until the squash is tender within and appetisingly spotted with slight scorching and browning on the surface.

Towards the end of this time, core the apples and cut them into chunks – I think it is a pity to peel them. Fry them in butter just long enough to gild them on all sides.

Add the apples to the roasting pan, mixing them and the olives with the butternut squash and shallots. (If the olives were bottled in brine, rinse them well, dry them, then roll them in olive oil before using.) Crumble the feta, scatter it over the top and return the pan to the oven for another 10 minutes or so until the cheese is molten and hot and it too has become streaked with gold.

BRAISED RED CABBAGE

Laura Mason grew up on a small farm in West Yorkshire. She ran away to live in a city as soon as she was able, but retains a strong interest in landscape, food and farming. She researched local foods in Britain for an EU project (published as **Traditional Foods of Britain***, with Catherine Brown, recently reissued as* **Taste of Britain***), and has also written* **Sugar Plums and Sherbet**, **Food Culture in Great Britain**, *and* **Farmhouse Cookery**.

On a day of clichéd golden autumn mellowness, we went for a drive to a few North Yorkshire beauty spots. Rounding a corner at Byland Abbey, we saw the top of a cottage-garden wall lined with boxes and baskets of apples, all named varieties and all for sale. While we were exclaiming over the multitude of shapes, colours and sizes, the owner came out and invited us to view the trees. In a little orchard to one side of the house there were about a dozen, several still laden with fruit, branches bowing towards the neatly mown grass.

We came home laden with bags of apples (the money they raised was donated to the local church). I can't remember all the different varieties, but one, with a curious name, Improved Cockpit, has lodged in my mind. A very Yorkshire apple, according to the lady who owned the orchard. Bright green, acid and slightly underripe, they were just right for my favourite braised red cabbage, which goes particularly well with roast pork, sausages, gammon and goose.

Serves 4 generously
half a medium red cabbage
1 medium onion, chopped
1–2 medium-size apples, peeled, cored and chopped
a little pork, goose or duck fat (or cooking oil)
about 4 tablespoons each cider vinegar and water
1 generous tablespoon soft brown sugar

Use an enamelled cast-iron casserole, which will go on the hob and into the oven.

Trim the cabbage, removing any tattered outer leaves, cut it in half and remove the central core. Slice finely.

Melt the fat and cook the onion gently until transparent, then add the apple and stir well. Add the cabbage and cook gently for a few minutes, stirring. Then add the liquids, sugar, a scant teaspoon of salt, and ground black pepper to taste.

Cover closely and transfer the casserole to a slowish oven 170°C, 325°F, gas mark 3 for about 2 hours. Stir the cabbage halfway through this time and add a little more water if it shows signs of drying out.

APPLE & BACON MASH

Sophie Grigson is an author, broadcaster, food writer and cookery columnist for **Waitrose Food Illustrated** *and* **BBC Good Food***, among others. Her most recent books are* **The First Time Cook** *and* **Vegetables***.*

There's a magic moment in the early autumn when the first of the garden's main-crop potatoes and the first of the apples coincide. The children disappear outside to gather produce and earthworms, and soon a basket of potatoes, topped with a few sour cooking apples, appears on the kitchen table. Occasionally the worms are included, but it is not something I encourage.

The apple and potato coincidence makes the German dish *Himmel und Erde* (heaven, for the apples, and earth, for the potatoes) inevitable. It is a surprising and welcome mixture, the apples imparting a mild fruity sourness to a rich buttery mash. We like it even better with plenty of crisp old-fashioned bacon stirred in. Great with sausages, chops, fish (particularly cod or salmon), and other elemental, plainly cooked main courses.

Arthur Turner, Bramley, Howgate Wonder or any good, tart cooking apple will combine well with a fluffy-fleshed potato, such as Kerr's Pink, King Edward or Maris Piper.

Serves 4

700 g (1½ lb) floury potatoes, peeled and cut into large chunks
310 g (11 oz) cooking apples, peeled, cored and cut into chunks
4 rashers streaky or back bacon, derinded and cut into strips
30 g (1 oz) butter
2 tablespoons chopped fresh chives

Put the potatoes into a pan with water to cover and salt. Bring to the boil, and simmer until the potatoes are almost done. Now drain off about two-thirds of the water and add the apple to the pan. Mix, then cover and cook gently until the apple is soft enough to mash into the potato. Add the butter and beat in well to make a smoothish purée.

While the potatoes are cooking, fry the bacon in its own fat, slowly at first until the fat runs, then raising the heat to crisp it up. Stir about a quarter of the bacon, with its fat, into the mash, together with most of the chives. Spoon into a big warm bowl and sprinkle with remaining bacon and chives.

HOT BEETROOT IN APPLE SAUCE

Rose Elliot is a writer, broadcaster and author of more than sixty books, she is widely recognised as having revolutionised vegetarian cooking and played a major role in transforming its image, taste and popularity. This recipe is adapted from **Rose Elliot's Complete Vegetarian Cookbook.**

I have lived in Hampshire for most of my life so it gives me special pleasure to use the Howgate Wonder apple, which was raised in Bembridge on the Isle of

Wight, scene of some happy holidays when my daughters were young. One of the joys of this apple is that, like its more famous cousin, the Bramley, it collapses into a soft, fluffy purée when cooked, so a sauce practically makes itself. Adding tender cooked beetroot to this sauce results in a wonderful sweet-and-sour marriage of flavours and textures. It's a vegetable dish that goes well with anything with which you'd normally serve with an apple sauce. It also works well as an accompaniment to cooked cheese dishes: a gratin, say, or bistro-style grilled goat's cheese or a well-flavoured cheese soufflé – and I often eat it just on its own or with some cooked Savoy cabbage.

Serves 4

500 g (1 lb 2 oz) Howgate Wonders (or Keswick Codlins or
    Dumelow's Seedlings, if they grow better in your area)
a small pinch of ground cloves
2–4 teaspoons mild honey
500 g (1 lb 2 oz) cooked beetroot, skin removed
1 tablespoon chopped dill (optional)

Peel, core and slice the apples; put them into a medium-sized saucepan with 2 tablespoons of water and cook over a gentle heat, with a lid on the pan, for about 10 minutes, until soft and mushy.

Cut the beetroot into smallish dice and add to the apple sauce. Stir in honey, salt, pepper and ground cloves to taste. Warm through over a gentle heat, stirring, and serve sprinkled with a little chopped dill if you like.

LEEK & COCKPIT FLAN

George and Barbara Morris are experts on apples surviving in Yorkshire. In the text that follows, (Y) denotes a native Yorkshire variety.

Our study has been of the local old orchards to try to reconstruct the part played by apples in the life and economy of farms and their workers. This was different from the part orchards played in the life of the country houses and larger rectories, although they were important there too. A farmer's wife with a team of men to cook for, or a worker's wife with a large family, had no time for sophisticated recipes. Each seems to have developed her own recipe for tarts, pies, roast apples and dumplings, and she would vary the filling according to the varieties in season and the kind of dish she was making. Orchards seem to have been the domain of women, an acre of ground might contain as many as sixteen varieties of apple, designed to ensure a season from August to May. Good storage was essential for many of these old varieties.

Among the first of the cooking apples would be the codlings – such as the Keswick Codling, sharp-flavoured, falling smoothly when cooked. They were used in the famous 'Codlings and Cream tarts' ordered by Parson Woodford for a 'good dinner' he gave at New College, Oxford, at the end of July 1774. During the early winter the selection available for use increased with distinctively flavoured apples becoming mature: Gooseberry, whose taste is, of course, reminiscent of gooseberries, Lemon Pippin, whose flavour and smell have a citrus quality, and Cockpit (Y), sharp-tasting and keeping its shape well in a pie. Some varieties keep their scent when cooked, like Gravenstein and Green Balsam (Y), widely grown locally. One unusual variety was Wellington (or Dumelow's Seedling), ripening in November: it is juicy and sharp, and popular for mincemeat. These are all moderate sized apples. Kept properly, all of these apples will mature and store till Easter, when the real keepers, like Northern

Greening, come to their best; earlier, these are hard and sour and often wasted by the later owners of orchards, who do not know how to treat them.

Yorkshire Greenings' alternative name, Yorkshire Goose Sauce (Y), suggests another use, but for apple sauce late in the season many people now use Keswick Codlings, cooked and kept in the freezer.

The large apples are best roasted or used in dumplings. Warner's King provides a change of taste from Bramley, and in this area, Lane's Prince Albert keeps very well, retaining texture and flavour till quite late. Striped Beefing is another good keeper, in Yorkshire rather outside its home area. But Yorkshire Beauty (which goes by different names in different places, such as Hawthornden) produces a fruit of a pound or more in weight. Who today would welcome a dumpling containing a pound of apple?

Some of the old apples are more interesting for their names than their flavour – Dog's Snout and Catshead (or Cat's Head). Others are frankly undistinguished, like Burr Knot, once widely grown in Yorkshire. Backhouse's Flowery Town (Y) was once popular but we find it ordinary, although its pink flesh is quite attractive.

These notes are based on our experience in using a few of the old apple varieties grown in Ryedale, North Yorkshire. We have learned the flavours of many, especially when properly stored to allow them to gain a true maturity. But selection is necessary. Some varieties fail to reach their best outside a limited area. Some have only antiquarian interest. However, carefully selected and grafted on to a stock appropriate to modern gardens, many could give a lively interest to apple dishes. Why serve 'apple pies' when you could offer 'Cockpit Pie with a Dash of Brownlees Russet'?

Serves 4–6
175 g (6 oz) shortcrust pastry
2–3 leeks
1–2 Yorkshire Cockpit apples (or what you will, in season)

2 eggs
275 ml (half pint) milk
a few sage leaves, finely chopped
a little grated Wensleydale cheese, to taste

Line a suitable dish or tin with the pastry. Clean and chop the leeks; parboil in slightly salted water, drain well and cool. Peel, core and chop the apples. Mix the leeks and apples and put them into the flan case. Beat the eggs with the milk, sage, salt and pepper; pour this into the flan and sprinkle with cheese. Bake on a pre-heated baking sheet at 160°C/325°F/gas mark 3 for 30–40 minutes.

Try different apple varieties in season and rename the flan accordingly.

FISH, FOWL, GAME & MEAT

• STEAMED BRILL WITH CIDER SABAYON **SHAUN HILL** • JOHN DORY WITH CIDER, APPLES & CREAM **SARA PASTON-WILLIAMS** • MONKFISH WITH LEEKS, APPLES & GINGER **CLAIRE MACDONALD** • POT ROAST GUINEA FOWL WITH SAUSAGE & APPLES **NIGEL SLATER** • A WHOLE ROAST GOOSE ACCOMPANIED BY APPLES COOKED IN QUINCE JELLY **JEREMY LEE** • PIGEON & APPLE CASSEROLE **TOM PARKER-BOWLES** • BRAISED PARTRIDGES WITH APPLE & FIGS **JILL NORMAN** • VENISON BURGERS WITH FRIED APPLE **HUGH FEARNLEY-WHITTINGSTALL** • BRAISED WILD RABBIT & PORK BELLY WITH CIDER, CARAMELISED APPLE & MARJORAM **BARNY HAUGHTON** • ROAST FILLET OF PORK WITH APPLES & CIDER **NIGEL SLATER** • SELF-MARINATING PIG **FERGUS HENDERSON** • SLOW ROASTED HAND OF PORK WITH APPLES, CIDER, CIDER VINEGAR & BAY LEAVES **MATTHEW FORT** •

STEAMED BRILL WITH CIDER SABAYON

Shaun Hill has held a Michelin star for the past twenty years. In London he cooked at Robert Carrier's, the Gay Hussar and at the Capital Hotel. He was head chef at Gidleigh Park in Devon for nine years, then chef-patron of the Merchant House in Ludlow for ten years. Lately, he has opened a brasserie, the Glasshouse, in Worcester. His books include Cooking at The Merchant House, How To Cook Better, *and* Archestratus, *with Professor J. Wilkins.*

The Welsh Marches, which track the England–Wales border, cover some serious cider- and perry-making territory. Herefordshire, especially, sports some of the biggest and best cider-makers in the country. Think of Bulmers in Hereford itself or Westons in Much Marcle. Cheesemaker Charles Martell, in nearby Dymock, makes Stinking Bishop, named after the perry variety he uses to wash its rind and to impart its distinctive flavour – much in demand since it featured in Wallace and Gromit's recent film adventure. Dunkertons in Pembridge name their ciders after the apples they use or list the varieties like the cepage of fine wine, Foxwhelp perhaps or Dabinett, Kingston Black or Breakwell's Seedling. Like good wine, cider is made for drinking, but is a similarly fine addition to an ingredients list. The smart cook may wish to open a larger bottle than strictly necessary for the recipe purposes. If you catch my drift.

White fish are good steamed so this dish would work as easily with sole, plaice or turbot. The sabayon is made in a similar way to Hollandaise sauce but is lighter and more fragile because no butter is added. I have also used this method with humbler fish to good effect and found that a heap of cooked mussels and cockles on sourdough toast was improved by the tang of dry cider in the sabayon sauce.

Points to watch:

Steamed fish is as dull overcooked as fish that has been fried or grilled too long. The time it takes to cook will vary according to its thickness of the fish. If in any doubt, separate the fish into sections or cut into the fillet to see how far cooked it is.

The volume of sabayon sauce produced is more dependent on the quantity of cider used than the number of egg yolks. Plenty of cider will give a light and voluminous sauce.

Yellow sauce on top of white fish can look dull so serve it on a bed of something bright and green, like spinach.

Serves 4
4 x200 g (7 oz) fillets of brill
3 egg yolks
150 ml (5 fl oz) dry cider
Tabasco
lemon juice

Season the fish fillets and then steam them until just done – the time taken will vary with the thickness of the fillet but 15 minutes would be a good guideline.

Heat a saucepan of water until nearly boiling. Whisk together the egg yolks and cider in a bowl – preferably one without too many corners, the more rounded the better – then whisk the yolks and cider mixture over the hot water. Use a lifting action as you whisk so that as much air as possible is incorporated into the sabayon. When the sabayon has risen, and thickened enough to coat the back of the spoon, season it with Tabasco and lemon juice to taste, then spoon it over the cooked brill.

JOHN DORY WITH CIDER, APPLES & CREAM

Sara Paston-Williams is a food historian, food writer for the National Trust and journalist for Taste Cornwall. *She has lived in Cornwall for nearly thirty-five years. This recipe is adapted from* Fish: Recipes From A Busy Island.

John Dory is an excellent firm-fleshed fish common in the warm waters off the Cornish coast. I buy from day-boats working out of Looe to get the freshest and best quality. Apples eat very well with many types of fish. A sweet, crunchy dessert variety like Ben's Red, first raised by Benjamin Roberts at Trannack in Cornwall around 1830, is suitable for this recipe and looks attractive with its wonderful bright red skin and slightly pink flesh. Alternatively, you could use Bread Fruit, a greenish-yellow dessert/cooker streaked with orange; it has very white flesh and an unusual strawberry flavour.

A medium farmhouse cider made by Cornish Orchards, a farm near me, is perfect for the sauce, giving it a lovely mellow appley flavour. The owner, Andy Atkinson, was inspired to replant his farm's old orchard by Cornwall's Orchard Project, which in turn was encouraged by Common Ground. It changed Andy's life: he went from dairy-farming to producing farm-pressed ciders and apple juices, using old varieties of Cornish apples.

For a final flourish, I like to finish the sauce with organic Jersey cream from Barwick Farm, where the cows graze on the rich pastures of the Roseland Peninsula.

Serves 4
4 medium or large John Dory fillets, skinned
a little seasoned flour
about 85 g (3 oz) clarified butter
2 dessert apples, cut into 8 wedges

a little caster sugar for sprinkling
1 tablespoon fresh fennel, chopped
1 tablespoon fresh tarragon, chopped
1 tablespoon fresh parsley, chopped
1 tablespoon lemon juice
150 ml (5 fl oz) medium cider
about 4 tablespoons thick cream

Coat the fish with a little seasoned flour, patting off any excess. Melt 25 g (1 oz) of the butter in a frying-pan, then fry the apple quickly for a minute or two until golden brown on both sides. Sprinkle with a little caster sugar and baste with the butter to give a slightly caramelised finish. Remove and keep warm.

Wipe out the pan, then heat the remaining butter until foaming. Add the fish skinned-side down and fry over a brisk heat for 2–3 minutes until golden brown, then flip over and cook the other side for about a minute. Remove the fish and place on four warmed plates.

Add the herbs, lemon juice and cider to the pan and bring to the boil. Simmer for a few minutes to reduce. Adjust the seasoning, if necessary, then stir in the cream. Cook for another minute until the sauce is smooth, then pour it over the waiting fish. Garnish with the fried apples and serve immediately.

MONKFISH WITH LEEKS, APPLE & GINGER

Claire Macdonald has been described as Scotland's foremost ambassador for the revitalised traditions of highland hospitality. Author, broadcaster, lecturer and cookery demonstrator, she and her husband, Godfrey Macdonald of Macdonald, have run their family home, Kinloch Lodge on the Isle of Skye, as a small luxury hotel for the past thirty or so years. This recipe comes from her latest book, Fish.

Apples belong in a savoury capacity every bit as much as they do in a sweet one. The obvious examples are apples with cheese, and apple sauce with rich meats and fowl, such as roast pork, baked ham, roast duck or goose – and I do like to make my apple sauce with a bit more to it than apple purée; I fry (such a deeply politically incorrect word, these days!) finely diced shallots till they are beginning to turn golden at the edges, then add them, with finely grated lemon rind, to the apples. Grated eating apples stirred into crème fraîche with a good dollop of horseradish makes the perfect, simple accompaniment to any smoked fish. You can add dill, too, if you like. But the combination of apples with fish is perhaps not as usual an encounter as I think it should be.

Either Galloway Pippin or White Melrose (an old Scottish variety introduced by the monks of Melrose Abbey) would make a fine patriotic choice of apple to use in this recipe. Any firm-fleshed white fish is suitable here but best of all is monkfish because it holds its shape when cooked; other species – such as cod, hake and megrim – tend to fall into large flakes. Leeks, apple and ginger go very well with all of them.

Serves 6

1 kg (a scant 2¼ lb) monkfish (or cod, hake, ling or megrim)

6 leeks, washed, trimmed and sliced diagonally into 4-cm (2-inch) pieces

4 tablespoons olive oil

6 good eating apples, quartered, peeled, cored and sliced

approximately 4-cm (2-inch) piece of fresh root ginger, skin pared off
    (I use a potato peeler) and the flesh either coarsely
    grated or finely chopped
2 fat garlic cloves, skinned and finely chopped
300 ml (10 fl oz) dry cider
2 tablespoons dark soy sauce

Lay the fish on a board, feel it with your fingertips and remove any skin and all bones. Cut the fish into 3-cm (1½-inch) pieces. You can do this in advance, but keep the prepared fish in a covered bowl in the fridge.

Heat the olive oil in a large sauté pan and add the leeks and ginger. Stir them around over medium heat so they cook evenly, then add the apples and garlic. Cook, stirring from time to time, for 2–3 minutes, then add the cider and soy sauce. Let this mixture simmer gently, for 2–3 minutes. Season generously with black pepper, then add the pieces of fish to the gently simmering contents of the pan, pushing them down into and amongst the leeks and apples. Cook gently for about 5 minutes until the fish is cooked through.

POT ROAST GUINEA FOWL WITH SAUSAGE & APPLES

. . . .

Nigel Slater is cookery columnist of the Observer *and author of* The Kitchen Diaries *and* Eating for England.

My own apple trees, the Blenheim Orange and the Court Pendu Plat, produce too few fruits to cook with yet. Being young trees, the handful of apples I get from them is mollycoddled, fussed over and eaten with the same sort of ceremony that the Japanese reserve for a perfectly ripe melon.

A medium sweet and nutty apple will work well with guinea fowl, perhaps Ashmead's Kernel, Court Pendu Plat, Orleans Reinette or any of the Russets.

There is no need for any accompaniment here, save perhaps some lightly cooked leafy greens.

Serves 2
1 guinea fowl
2 medium onions
a thin slice of butter
2 tablespoons olive oil
4 thick butcher's sausages
2 medium sized potatoes
3 medium-sweet apples – about 600 g (1 lb 6 oz)
a couple of bay leaves
50 ml (less than 2 fl oz) Marsala

Set the oven to 200°C/400°F/gas mark 6. Peel the onions, cut them in half and then into thick segments. Put them into a large, heavy ovenproof pan – one for which you have a lid – with the butter and olive oil and leave to colour over a moderate heat. Slice each sausage into three and add them to the pan, then stir from time to time to stop them sticking.

Peel the potatoes, cut them into large chunks and add them to the pan. Continue cooking until the onions are soft and golden, the potatoes are pale gold and the sausages have coloured nicely. Push everything to one side of the pan, put in the bird, breast-side down, and let it colour briefly. Turn it over and do the other breast, then the underside.

Meanwhile peel the apples, core them and cut them into thick chunks. Drop them in with the other ingredients then season with the bay leaves, some salt and coarsely ground black pepper. Tip in the Marsala and leave it to bubble furiously for a minute or two. Cover with a lid and put in the oven.

Leave for 40 minutes then remove the lid. The fowl should be golden on all sides. Check that it is ready by inserting a skewer deep into its thigh. If the juices run clear then it is ready. If there is any sign of blood, put it back into the oven for a few minutes.

Cut the bird in half down the backbone, then serve on warm plates with the potatoes, apples and sausages.

A WHOLE ROAST GOOSE ACCOMPANIED BY APPLES COOKED IN QUINCE JELLY

Jeremy Lee served an apprenticeship in Scotland, then moved to London where his natural talent was honed over years of immensely enjoyable cooking with Simon Hopkinson, at Bibendum, and Alastair Little, at his eponymous restaurant in Frith Street. He now cooks at Blueprint Café, in the Design Museum, using carefully chosen produce in a deceptively simple, vibrant and flavoursome manner. He contributes to newspapers such as the **Daily Telegraph** *and the* **Guardian** *and to BBC's television's* **Great British Menu.**

A great delight in seasonal cooking is the arrival of the first fruits from the early summer through to the great autumn harvests of quinces, medlars and such like. As a berrycentric Scot, the delights of apples as they came into season snuck up on me in a manner most subtle. In Scotland, as the last of the raspberries were dispatched, so started the apples, the lovely Discovery, Jonagolds and Cox's, of course, all thrilled but we must not forget the delightfully named Lass O'Gowrie, White Melrose, Grenadier, Seaton House and Tower of Glamis, among many more. When it comes to eating and cooking, though, I make little choice: mostly into the pot they go.

Needless to say, like olive oil and other good things, by taste is the truth found. A memorable lunch at Benoît in Paris gave a brilliant recipe for apples, as ever, simple and elegant. A compôte of stewed apple was spooned alongside a great slice from a terrine of foie gras. When I served a similar compôte with roast goose at the Blueprint, a discernible hum of pleasure was overheard. It has remained a firm favourite ever since.

This is the kind of cooking I enjoy most and which I have practised at the Blueprint Café, taking each ingredient as it appears and cooking it according to its merits, letting it taste of itself. Some of these dishes are simplicity itself, some deceptive in their preparation and cooking, but all are carefully chosen to make, rich, light eating, savoury or sweet, flavoursome and nourishing. From several wee farmers come bags of lovely things, but the hands always reach first to pluck out an apple as few things delight more than eating new-crop apples.

To Roast A Goose

1 oven-ready goose weighing 4.65 kg (10 lb) will feed 8 people handsomely

For many years I have assiduously followed the advice of the Symingtons, who rear splendid geese at Seldom Seen Farm in Leicestershire.

Heat the oven to 180°C/350°F/gas mark 4. Prick the goose all over to let the fat run with ease. Rub sea salt and pepper all over the bird. Sit it upon a rack in a roasting tray. Cover with tinfoil and let it cook for 3 hours. Remove the foil then continue cooking for a further 25 minutes or so until the skin colours and crisps to an even golden brown.

Let the bird rest for at least 25 minutes before carving. Serve with the apples (see below) spooned alongside and with clumps of watercress.

Apples Cooked In Quince Jelly

I like to make a large pot of this for it improves with a day or two, keeps well, and eats wonderfully with cheese, in sandwiches or with cold roast meats. For those fortunate enough to have crab apple or medlar jelly to hand, do use also or alternatively.

8 lovely apples, of a character similar to a Russet or Pippin
   (or, for the bold, try a sharp well-flavoured cooking apple)
1 lemon, freshly juiced
8 dessertspoons quince jelly
quarter of a vanilla pod, split and scraped

Peel the apples then cut them through the core into quarters. Cut away the core and toss each quarter in the lemon juice. When done, tip the apples into a heavy-bottomed pot, add the jelly and vanilla, stir, then place over a high heat. Once the apples begin to bubble, reduce the heat to a simmer and place the lid atop. Let the apples cook, stirring now and again, for at least half an hour until they are on the verge of collapse. Some varieties happily remain intact, some will pulp completely, the flavour being the prize.

Cooked on the day, they are lovely left to cool and served at room temperature.

WEST COUNTRY PIGEON

· ·

Tom Parker-Bowles writes a weekly food column for the Mail on Sunday *and a monthly one for* Tatler. *He is the author of* E is for Eating – an alphabet of greed, *and* The Year of Eating Dangerously.

My days at prep school were hardly exemplary, as I was awful at games and pretty slow in the classroom too. So I passed, like a ghost, through those five years leaving barely a trace. But the one legacy I did bequeath to the school was an apple tree. After one particularly – and typically – filthy lunch, I ate a Cox's Orange Pippin and kept the pip. Then I went down to the gardens (where we grew carrots and the like) and planted it. In the blessed relief of leaving the school, I forgot all about it. But recently, a wonderful teacher called the Reverend Willie Pryor sent me a parcel containing an apple. 'Nineteen years later,' he wrote, 'your pip has turned into a healthy tree.' Hardly the Victor

Ludorum but, somehow, a thousand times more satisfying.

I have borrowed this recipe from Theodora Fitzgibbon's lovely *West Country Cook Book*, and suggest teaming the birds with Profit, a cooker from Dorset.

Serves 4

4 young wood pigeons

1 lemon

2 onions

450 g (1 lb) cooking apples – maybe Profit, a good Dorset variety, or Lord Derby, Glass Apple or Bountiful, depending on where you live and what is available

175 g (6 oz) butter

4–5 tablespoons dry cider

150 ml (5 fl oz) single cream

a pinch of ground mace or a grating of nutmeg

Wipe the birds clean inside and out. Season them with salt and pepper and rub half a cut lemon over them. Set aside while you slice the onions; and quarter, core and cut the apples into thick crescent-moon wedges.

Heat a frying pan big enough to take all four birds. Heat half the butter in it and brown the pigeons all over. Remove them. Add the rest of the butter and, when the butter foam dies down, stir in the apples and onions. Let them cook gently for a few minutes until slightly softened. Season with nutmeg or mace.

Spoon half of the apples and onions into a casserole. Lay the pigeons, breast down, on top and spoon the rest of the apples and onions around them. Put the cider into the frying pan, stir and scrape up all of the meaty sediment and juices. Add the cream, salt, pepper and a squeeze of lemon juice, and pour the whole lot into the casserole.

Lay a circle of greaseproof paper directly on top of the birds and cover with a well-fitting lid. Slip the dish into the oven and cook at 180°C/350°F/gas mark 4 until tender, probably 2 hours.

BRAISED PARTRIDGES WITH APPLE & FIGS

....

Jill Norman is an internationally acknowledged authority on herbs and spices, and an award-winning author. Her latest books are The New Penguin Cookery Book *and* Winter Food, *from which this recipe is taken.*

Their subtle, delicate flavour makes partridges my favourite game birds. If you are sure you have young partridges they are superb plain roasted; if you aren't, it is better to braise them. Most often paired with cabbage, partridges go well with fresh and dried fruit and nuts, and a dish of lentils makes a good accompaniment.

I use different apples for this dish, depending on the season. James Grieve is a favourite, because it is soft and creamy; later in the autumn I use Egremont Russet because it too is creamy, and has a hint of spice which marries well with the figs. Cox's Orange Pippin, another soft and aromatic apple, is also a good choice. If I lived in cider country, I would try to adapt the recipe to use cider apples and cider instead of white wine.

Serves 2
2 tablespoons olive oil
2 partridges
2 medium onions, peeled and chopped
1 apple, peeled and cut into quarters
4 dried figs, sliced
a grating of nutmeg
200 ml (7 fl oz) white wine
80 ml (1 tablespoon) double cream
1 teaspoon lemon juice

Heat the oil in a flameproof casserole and brown the partridges. Remove them from the pot and fry the onions until soft. Put back the partridges, tuck the apple and figs around them, season and pour over the wine. Simmer for 10 minutes. Add enough water just to cover the birds, cover the casserole tightly and simmer for 1 hour. Check to see if the partridges are tender, if they are old they may need up to 30 minutes longer.

Transfer the birds to a serving dish and keep warm. Blend the cooking juices in a food-processor or blender, stir in the cream and lemon juice, heat through and pour over the birds.

VENISON BURGERS WITH FRIED APPLES

Hugh Fearnley-Whittingstall is a writer, broadcaster and campaigner, widely known for his commitment to seasonal, ethically produced food. His River Cottage *TV series and books have earned him a huge following.*

Apple slices, simply fried in butter until golden, make a wonderful accompaniment to all kinds of meat dishes, including chops, stews and sausages. They're also delicious sandwiched into a bun with a homemade burger – venison seems a particularly appropriate choice since it comes into season when the apple harvest is in full swing. You could cook any eating apple in this way, but we particularly like Ashmead's Kernel or Orleans Reinette.

Makes about 10 burgers
1 teaspoon juniper berries
3 bay leaves
1 tablespoon sage leaves
2 teaspoons white peppercorns
1 tablespoon salt
1.5 kg (generous 3½ lb) venison meat
500 g (generous 1 lb) fatty pork, i.e. belly
1 small glass white wine, if needed

olive oil
a large knob of butter
4 dessert apples, cored and sliced
10 good baps

Put the juniper berries, bay leaves, sage, peppercorns and salt into a coffee or spice grinder and reduce to a fine powder.

Combine the venison meat with the pork and put them through a mincer on a coarse (8 mm or ⅓ inch) plate. If you don't have a mincer, you can get your butcher to do this for you. At a push, you could mince the meat in a food-processor, but be very careful not to reduce it to a paste.

Add the spice powder to the minced meat and mix well, moistening the mixture with a little wine if you think it needs it.

Before making your burgers, heat a little oil in a frying pan, make a patty out of the mixture and fry it for about 5 minutes on each side or until cooked through. Taste to check the seasoning. Don't be tempted to add too much more in the way of spices, as the flavour will develop as the burgers cook – what you're really checking for is the salt level. When you're happy, form the minced, spiced meat into patties about 2 cm (¾ inch) thick. Heat 1–2 tablespoons olive oil in a large frying pan over a medium heat and fry the burgers for 3–4 minutes each side, until nicely browned and cooked through.

Meanwhile, heat the butter in a separate frying pan over a medium heat. Add the apple slices and cook, turning them over from time to time, until golden.

Stuff each burger into a bap, add a few slices of hot, butter-fried apple, and serve.

BRAISED WILD RABBIT & PORK BELLY WITH CIDER, CARAMELISED APPLE & MARJORAM

Barny Haughton has been chef-patron of a pioneering organic restaurant, Bristol's Quartier Vert (formerly Roccinantes), since 1988. He opened a cookery school for children and a bakery in 1998, and opened Bordeaux Quay restaurant, brasserie, bar, bakery, cookery school and deli in 2006. Bordeaux Quay is based on the principle that the best food comes from sustainable farming systems and that good food is by definition, local, seasonal and organic.

There is a tiny orchard, called Barleywood Garden Orchard, next to the walled Victorian garden where my brother Phil grows organic produce for the Better Food Company (which provides Bordeaux Quay's kitchen with much of its fresh produce). In this little corner of Somerset, the sun rises over a heavy blanket of mist that covers the whole valley. The Mendip hills are barely visible in the distance. The air is still and cold and fragrant with the earthy, bruised, almondy sweetness of windfall apples. For me no other place and no other time of day or month more clearly evokes that 'season of mists and mellow fruitfulness'.

This orchard is a miniature library of old apple varieties, whose names, with echoes of old French and glimpses of forgotten patches of rural England, read like a John Betjeman poem: Pomeroy of Somerset, Lucombe's Pine, Old Somerset Russet, Court of Wick, Court Pendu Plat, Hoary Morning, George Cave, Nine Square, Ribston Pippin.

This is a perfect autumn supper dish. Start cooking the meats a day ahead of serving.

Serves 4
1 wild rabbit (farmed will do, but lacks the subtle gaminess of wild)
1 kg (2.2 lb) skinned and boned (but with all fat left on) pork belly, cut into bite-size chunks

1 celery stalk
1 onion
1 carrot
3 garlic cloves
275 ml (10 fl oz) medium-dry cider
4 sweet dessert apples
a knob of butter and some olive oil
1 teaspoon fennel seeds
a couple of bay leaves
a little bunch of marjoram
the zest of an orange

On day one:

Season the pork belly with pepper and salt. Heat a good slug of olive oil in a casserole. Lay the pork belly fat side down in the casserole and cook over a gentle heat for about 20 minutes. Drain off the fat as it renders down and turns brown. Turn the meat over, cook for a further 5 minutes just to brown it, then drain off all fat. Add the fennel seeds, cook for a few seconds longer, then pour in the cider. Cover and leave to simmer gently.

Meanwhile cut the celery, scrubbed carrot and onion into rough chunks and brown them off in a little olive oil in a frying pan. Transfer them to the casserole. Slice the garlic cloves wafer thin, fry briefly and add to the casserole. Now joint the rabbit into legs, saddle and shoulders and brown off the meat in the frying pan, seasoning as you go with a little salt and pepper. Transfer the rabbit to the casserole.

Add a bay leaf or two and enough water (or chicken stock if you have some) to cover the meats, put the lid back on the casserole and leave to simmer very gently... blip, blip, blip... until the rabbit is tender and almost falling off the bone. This will take about 1 hour. (You could put the casserole into the oven at

150°C/325°F/gas mark 3 to achieve the same result.) The pork should also be ready by this time, since it was probably cooking for half an hour or so before the rabbit joined it.

Leave to cool until just tepid. Then transfer the pork and rabbit to separate bowls. Strain the broth through a fine sieve into another bowl. Now pick the meat off the rabbit in as large pieces as you can; put the broth, the rabbit meat and the pork belly into the fridge, and bin the bones and the strained vegetables (as food waste/compost of course) – they have done their work.

This is probably beginning to sound like a lot of work. It's worth it. Carry on.

The next day:
The broth will have a layer of congealed fat on the top; remove and discard, transfer the broth to a saucepan. Reduce by boiling until it becomes a sweet, well-seasoned, viscous liquid. Put the rabbit and pork meats into a serving dish, pour over the liquid, cover with parchment paper and put in the oven to warm through gently and thoroughly. Allow 25–35 minutes at 150-175°C/325-350°F/ gas mark 3–4.

To caramelise the apples, cut them into wedges, and remove the core. Heat a generous knob of butter with a little olive oil in a frying pan and add the apple wedges, laying them neatly on their sides. Cook them gently over a very low heat for as long as it takes to brown them, then turn them over and repeat the process. Resist the temptation to turn them before the flesh is golden brown and don't worry about the apples disintegrating – they won't.

Meanwhile, chop the marjoram and mix it with the orange zest. When the apples are cooked, add the aromatic mixture to the pan. Fry for a few seconds longer then scatter the mixture over the meat.

Serve with creamy mashed potato or celeriac and a good strong cabbage – *cavolo nero* is perfect.

ROAST FILLET OF PORK WITH APPLES & CIDER

Nigel Slater is cookery columnist of the Observer *and author of* The Kitchen Year *and* Eating For England.

Which variety of apple I use in the kitchen will depend partly upon the other ingredients in the recipe, and partly on what treasures I have found at the farmers' market. The nuttier apples, such as Ashmead's Kernel, work best for me with a firm, sharp cheese of some sort, while the 'acid-drop' apples, such as Rosemary Russet, are exceptionally good in a salad, particularly if fennel is involved too. Pork and game seem to get on better with tart fruit, such as the plump Peasgood's Nonsuch, and I am forever looking out for interesting apples with a bit of a snap to them.

I don't often use a cut as lean as fillet, preferring something more fatty, but here it seems to work well. It would be a good dish to double or even treble if you were cooking for four or more, and there are no bones to slow down carving. I use an organic cider, because of its clear and deep apple flavour, and a tart apple for this recipe: Dumelow's Seedling, Warner's King, Peasgood's Nonsuch are good. As a side dish, celeriac and potato cooked in equal quantities then mashed together are extraordinarily good with the sweetness of the pork.

Serves 2
400 g (14 oz) pork fillet
olive oil or butter
2 medium-sized onions
a small bunch of thyme
50 g (2 oz) ginger
3 largish apples
350 ml (12 fl oz) cider

Set the oven to 200°C/400°F/ gas mark 6.

Season the pork fillet all over with salt and black pepper. Put a roasting tin over a fairly high heat and pour in 2 tablespoons of olive oil. When the oil is hot, lower in the pork fillet and let it sizzle and brown lightly on one side. Turn it and colour the other side, then lift it out and set aside.

Peel the onions, halve them and cut them into thick slices then put them into a mixing bowl. Pull the leaves from the thyme stems, chop them roughly then add them to the onions. Peel the ginger and cut it into thin strips about the size of a matchstick. Core and roughly chop the apples, toss them with the onions, thyme, ginger and a little oil, then add a good grinding of pepper and salt. Tip the lot into the roasting tin and let it soften over a moderate heat.

Once the onions are starting to turn pale gold, lay the fillet of pork back in the tin and put in the oven to roast for 25 minutes.

Check the pork for doneness then lift it out on to a warm plate to rest. Cover it lightly with foil and leave it in a warm place. Put the roasting tin, with the apples and onions, over a moderate heat and pour in the cider. Bring to the boil, then let it reduce to about half its volume, stirring from time to time to scrape up any pan-stickings.

Cut the pork into thick slices, place on two warm plates and surround with the onion, apples and cidery pan juices. Serve with mashed celeriac.

SELF-MARINATING PIG

Fergus Henderson trained as an architect, was distracted by kitchens, opened St John, wrote Nose To Tail Eating, *and is still happily distracted by kitchens. He opened St John Bread and Wine in 2004.*

We had four gentlemen come into St John who were proudly wearing jackets with '1999 Illinois Pork Convention' on their backs. They were asking for the pig that ate the apples. Those friends of the pig are an inspiration for this sort of recipe. Find an orchard of your favourite apples and place your pig in there to eat the fallen apples: self marinating pig. When content with pig's size, roast!

One breed has even earned the name 'the orchard pig' – the Gloucester Old Spot, described by Dorothy Hartley in *Food in England* as 'a decorative pig … having the acumen to fatten rapidly during the short orchard harvest, where they save their bacon on the fallen fruit (which would produce belly grouting in other breeds)… [Their] motley accords pleasantly with the dappled shadow dance of the Gloucester apple orchards.' Traditionally the Gloucester Old Spot (whose few black splodges on its pinky-white coat are, according to legend, bruises acquired from falling fruit) was let loose in the cider orchards of the Berkeley Vale to snuffle and gorge on windfalls. It still enjoys such bounty in some places, encouraged by rarities such as Charles Martell, an indefatigable champion of the pigs, cattle, cheeses, apples and pears of his native Gloucestershire.

SLOW ROASTED HAND OF PORK WITH APPLES, CIDER, CIDER VINEGAR & BAY LEAVES

. . . .

Matthew Fort has been food and drink editor of the Guardian *since 1988. His books include* Rhubarb and Black Pudding *and* Eating Up Italy. *He is currently working on a book about Sicily,* Lunching with Leopoldo, *due to be published in 2008. He has also appeared in* The Great British Menu *(BBC 2) and* Market Kitchen *(UK Food).*

I love a cheap cut, and cuts don't get much cheaper than hand of pork. The hand is the lower bit of the shoulder, on the bone, usually with the upper bit of the leg attached. It's a part of the animal that's done quite a bit of work in its time, especially if the pig it comes from has been roaming around outside, as it had in this case. The vinegar cuts any fatty richness of the dish, but gently, as cooking reduces its acidity. It's a bugger to carve, so don't bother. Cook it until it falls off the bone in juicy, succulent lumps.

Serves 6–8
1 hand of pork
8 bay leaves
250 ml (9 fl oz) sweet cider
100 ml (3½ fl oz) cider vinegar
1 teaspoon black peppercorns
1 teaspoon juniper berries
1 kg (2.2 lb) sweetish apples with a firm structure
    (e.g. Cox, Ashmead's Kernel, Ellison's Orange)

Turn on the oven to 140°C/275°F/gas mark 1.

Put the juniper, bay leaves and peppercorns into the bottom of a casserole or roasting tray. Place the hand of pork skin-side up on top. Pour the cider and vinegar, over the pork. Put the roasting tray into the oven and leave it there for 2½–3 hours. Check occasionally and top up the liquid with up to 100 ml (3½ fl oz) water if it is evaporating too much. The skin will protect the meat from drying out.

While this is going on, peel, core and slice the apples into eighths.

About 30 minutes before the end of cooking, add the apples to the casserole or roasting tray.

When the meat is ready, you can cut the skin off, turn up the oven to 200°C/400°F/gas mark 6 and turn the skin into crackling, keeping the meat warm elsewhere. Taste the juices, and, if necessary, reduce them.

All you need with this is some crushed potatoes to soak up the juices and some leeks, just softened in butter.

PUDDINGS

• BAKED APPLE & ALMOND PUDDING WITH MASCARPONE VANILLA CREAM **DELIA SMITH** • APPLE COMPÔTE **RAYMOND BLANC** • APPLE FRANGIPANE TART **LINDSEY BAREHAM** • APPLE SORBETS **FRANCES BISSELL** • APPLE DAPPY **SARA PASTON-WILLIAMS** • POMMES AU BEURRE **ELIZABETH DAVID** • LA TARTE AUX POMMES NORMANDE **ELIZABETH DAVID** • AUTUMN PUDDING WITH WILDING APPLES **RICHARD MABEY** • FLYING SAUCERS **BOB FLOWERDEW** • APPLE & TREACLE PUDDING **HATTIE ELLIS** • CHARLOTTE RUSSE **ANDREW WHITLEY** • APPLE & GUINNESS FRITTERS **MARK HIX** • APPLE GALETTE **TAMASIN DAY-LEWIS** • APPLE SNOW **ROSE PRINCE** • CARAMELISED APPLES WITH LANCASHIRE CHEESE ON PUFF OR FLAKY PASTRY **PATRICIA MICHELSON** • APPLE BROWN BETTY **SALLY CLARKE** • BAKED APPLE CREAM **SOPHIE GRIGSON** • BAKED APPLE & QUINCE DUMPLINGS **SIMONE SEKERS** • A DEVONSHIRE CHARLOTTE OF APPLES & PLUMS **ALICE WOOLEDGE SALMON** •

BAKED APPLE & ALMOND PUDDING WITH MASCARPONE VANILLA CREAM

....

Delia Smith is Britain's best-selling cookery author. This recipe is taken from Delia's Kitchen Garden: A Beginner's Guide to Growing and Cooking Fruit and Vegetables, *by Gay Search and Delia Smith. More Delia recipes can be obtained from www.deliaonline.com.*

I think of all the apple recipes this one has proved the most popular over the years, and as soon as I see the windfalls in the autumn I know it is time to make it yet again. Bramley's Seedling (from Nottinghamshire) has an enviable reputation but there are lots of other traditional local apple options to consider when planning your garden and food shopping. For instance, Lady Henniker was first grown here in Suffolk where I live. Emneth Early originated in neighbouring Cambridgeshire, and Golden Noble comes from Norfolk. Lady Henniker was discovered in cider must at Thornham Hall, near Eye, in the 1840s. A dual-purpose apple, suitable for cooking and eating, it was equally appreciated by the Victorians for its lovely appearance on candlelit dessert tables and for the 'pale yellow, quite strongly flavoured purée (but not a fluff) that it cooks to, retaining acidity but hardly needing much sugar'.

Serves 4–6

450 g (1 lb) Bramley or other variety of cooking apple,
    peeled, cored and sliced
110 g (4 oz) ground almonds
50 g (2 oz) soft brown sugar
110 g (4 oz) butter, at room temperature
110 g (4 oz) golden caster sugar
2 large eggs, beaten

for the mascarpone vanilla cream:
250 g (9 oz) mascarpone, at room temperature
1 teaspoon vanilla extract
200 ml (7 fl oz) fromage frais
1 rounded dessertspoon golden caster sugar

You will also need a buttered dish, approximately 850 ml (1½ pints) capacity.

Preheat the oven to 180°C/350°F/gas mark 4.

First of all, place the cooking apples in a saucepan with the soft brown sugar and approximately 1 tablespoon of water. Simmer the apples and sugar gently until soft, and then arrange them in the bottom of the prepared dish.

Meanwhile, in a mixing bowl, cream together the butter and golden caster sugar until pale and fluffy, and then beat in the eggs a little at a time. When all of the egg is in, next carefully and lightly fold in the ground almonds. Now spread this creamed mixture over the apples, and even out the surface with the back of a tablespoon. Then bake on a 'highish' shelf in the oven for exactly 1 hour. Meanwhile, mix together all the ingredients for the mascarpone vanilla cream until smooth, and chill until needed.

This pudding is equally good warm or cold. It will keep in the fridge for 3 or 4 days. Serve with the mascarpone vanilla cream.

APPLE COMPÔTE

. . . .

Raymond Blanc is chef patron of Le Manoir aux Quat' Saisons, which has held two Michelin stars for more than twenty years. One of the finest chefs in the world, he uses only the freshest and most wholesome of ingredients. His organic kitchen garden produces food for the table for eight months of the year, with ninety types of vegetable and seventy herbs. His books include Foolproof French Cookery *(BBC Worldwide).*

As the saying goes 'an apple a day keeps the doctor away,' and for good reason: apples are a good source of soluble fibre, which helps to keep the digestive system healthy, and their carbohydrates help to regulate blood-sugar levels.

Apples are the source of so many great recipes. We have been using this fruit for thousands of years and we should not forget what a remarkable ingredient it is. It is a fruit that fascinates me: there are so many wonderful varieties, each with its unique blend of flavour and texture. Oxfordshire used to be a prolific county for growing apples and we have nearly lost all of its beautiful local varieties. With the guidance of Will Sibley, we will reintroduce an orchard at Le Manoir aux Quat' Saisons where we will grow seventeen or eighteen varieties that originated in Oxfordshire, our local heritage, including Blenheim Orange, Old Fred and Oxford Yeoman.

Serves 6
500 g (1 lb 2 oz) Braeburns
500 g (1 lb 2 oz) Bramleys
30 g (1 oz) fructose
1 teaspoon lemon juice
scant 5 tablespoons water

Peel, core and chop the apples into approximately 2-cm (1-inch) dice. Put all of the ingredients into a medium pan over a high heat, and bring to a gentle simmer. Turn down the heat and simmer for 5 minutes until the apples are just cooked.

Leave to cool, then store in a covered container in the fridge until required.

APPLE FRANGIPANE TART

....

Lindsey Bareham is an author, broadcaster and cookery columnist for The Times *and* Saga *magazine. Her most recent book is* The Fish Store.

I grew up in Kent, where the cookers Beauty of Kent and Warner's King originated, surrounded by apple orchards, on a diet of windfalls. The best apples were wrapped in newspaper and stored in the rafters for later in the year when the harvest was over. My mother's speciality was apple pie, which she made with big, blowsy apples with shiny, smooth yellow-green skin. I loved the way the apples turned fluffy in the cooking, leaving occasional sour chunks that hadn't soaked up the butter and sugar she added to sweeten the pie. Years later, when I started making apple puddings for my own family, I copied the French way of arranging thin slices of eating apples over puff pastry to make dainty tarts. This is an elaborate version of those early experiments, the thinly sliced apple 'halves' poking through golden frangipane. Any properly ripened eating apple is suitable but early-season raspberry-scented Discovery or strawberry-scented Worcester Pearmain is particularly good. If I could find George Neal, I would try it – a Kentish dessert apple introduced in 1904, reputedly greeny-yellow with patches of russet and of excellent flavour.

Serves 6–8

200 g (7 oz) self-raising flour, plus extra for dusting

200 g (7 oz) soft butter, plus extra for greasing

100 g (3½ oz) caster sugar, plus 1 tablespoon

2 large eggs

100 g (3½ oz) ground almonds

1 tablespoon finely chopped lemon zest

4 Discovery, Worcester Pearmain or other soft eating apples

1 tablespoon smooth apricot jam

Preparation time: 30 minutes

Cooking time: 45 minutes plus 15 minutes resting

Sift the flour into a bowl and dice half the butter directly into it. Add a pinch of salt and, using your fingertips, quickly rub the butter into the flour until it resembles heavy breadcrumbs. Using a knife (or fork, if superstitious), stir in 1–3 tablespoons of water a little at a time, until the dough seems to want to cling together. Knead lightly to make a ball, dusting with extra flour if it seems too wet. Chill for 30 minutes before rolling.

Preheat the oven to 180°C/350°F/gas mark 5.

Generously butter a 24-cm (9-inch) flan tin with a removable base and dust with flour, shaking away the excess. This makes it reliably non-stick. Roll the pastry to fit and trim the edge. Cover loosely with foil and half fill with dried beans to stop the pastry rising. Bake for 10 minutes, carefully remove the foil and bake for a further 5 minutes.

Meanwhile, beat together 100 g (3½ oz) each butter and sugar, preferably in an electric mixer, until light and fluffy. Beat in one egg at a time. Fold in the almonds and lemon zest, then tip the mixture into the hot pastry case. Halve and peel the apples, then carefully cut out the cores. Place flat-side down and slice thinly across the width. 'Plant' the apple 'halves', spreading them out slightly, rounded side uppermost, towards the edge of the pastry case, with the last one in the middle.

Melt a knob of butter and paint the exposed apple, then dredge with the tablespoon of sugar. Bake for 40–45 minutes, until the frangipane is puffy, golden and springy to the touch and the apples just cooked through. Paint the apple with the apricot jam and leave in the warm, switched-off oven with the door ajar for 15 minutes. Remove the flan tin collar and serve warm or cold.

APPLE SORBETS

....

Frances Bissell's long-awaited book on cooking with flowers, The Scented Kitchen, *was published in 2007. When she is not travelling the globe lecturing on a diversity of food-related subjects, she might be found, especially on Apple Day, in the orchard of Fenton House in London's Hampstead, an event she has supported since its inception.*

Tropical fruit sorbets are fashionable, but one can tire of their insistent flavours and vivid colours. For the very best sorbets, apples are hard to beat. In their infinite variety they provide a palette of colours, textures and aromas, as well as a sorbet for every season. Even if you can't find the apples to serve a Cornish Aromatic, a D'Arcy Spice, a Melcombe Russet or a Green Balsam sorbet, consider the perfumed sweetness of an Egremont Russet. A Granny Smith makes a marvellously tart, mouth-tingling sorbet and a really ripe flushed Golden Delicious a mouthful of icy sweetness.

To prepare apples for a sorbet, quarter and core them, then roughly chop, and put in a food-processor or blender with a couple of tablespoons of water and a teaspoon or two of lemon juice to prevent discolouring. I like to keep a little of the peel on for the flecked effect it gives. Blend to a purée, then mix with the syrup as described. I find it worthwhile keeping a bottle of syrup on hand for making sorbets. It is a sad fact that the smoothest-textured sorbets contain the most sugar.

for the syrup:
1.1 kg (2½ lb) sugar
580 ml (1 pint) water

Dissolve the sugar in the water over a low heat, then bring to the boil and boil for 1 minute. Leave to cool, then bottle and refrigerate.

To make the sorbet:

dilute the syrup with an equal quantity of water, and add fruit pulp in equal volume to the liquid. Stir in the juice of half a lemon. Blend thoroughly and freeze, either in an ice-cream maker or sorbetière, according to the manufacturer's instructions. The mixture can also be frozen in a container put in the freezer or ice-making part of the refrigerator. As the mixture freezes and crystals form, it will need to be stirred from time to time. To ensure a smooth sorbet, it is quite a good plan to give it a final stir in a food-processor before putting it back into the freezer. Sorbets are best eaten within a few hours of being made.

I prefer to use raw apples, but interesting sorbets can be created with different varieties cooked into a purée and then flavoured with cinnamon, cloves or cardamom. For another version, simply freeze cider into a sorbet or a coarser granita.

APPLE DAPPY

. . . .

Sara Paston-Williams is a food historian, food writer for the National Trust and journalist for Taste Cornwall. *She has lived in Cornwall for nearly thirty-five years. This recipe is adapted from* The National Trust Book of Traditional Puddings.

Unlike Devon and Somerset, Cornwall has never been a major apple-producing area yet it has a diversity of excellent local varieties. The county's isolation ensured that most farms and homes were self-sufficient in apples with at least a few trees, if not an orchard, of good keepers, good eaters and good cookers – the names and qualities are still well remembered by older locals. One end of our ancient farmhouse was once an apple store and it wasn't long after we moved in that we came across the corner of a massive granite cider-press sticking out of the hedge that had once protected a productive apple orchard from the Cornish gales.

There are many simple West Country recipes for much-loved apple puddings like this one. I like to use a cooker/eater called Hockings Green, once very common in my part of east Cornwall and also excellent for baking, or a large green cooker called Lord of the Isles.

Don't forget to save an extra large apple to put under your pillow on Hallowe'en so that you dream of your sweetheart.

Serves 4–6

for the lemon syrup:
1 large lemon
1 tablespoon golden syrup
15 g (½ oz) butter
110 g (4 oz) sugar

for the pudding:
225 g (8 oz) self-raising flour
1 level teaspoon baking powder
60 g (2 oz) butter, cut in small pieces
150 ml (5 fl oz) full-cream milk
450 g (1 lb) cooking apples
1 tablespoon Demerara sugar
½ teaspoon ground cinnamon or allspice

Preheat the oven to 190°C/375°F/gas mark 5.

To make the lemon syrup, peel the lemon as thinly as possible and squeeze out the juice. Place the lemon rind, juice, 200 ml (7 fl oz) water and the other syrup ingredients in a pan and heat gently, stirring until the sugar has dissolved. Leave to stand until needed.

To make the pudding, first sieve the flour and baking powder into a large mixing bowl and rub in the butter until the mixture resembles breadcrumbs. Mix to a dough with the milk, then roll out the dough on a floured board to about 20 cm (8 inches) square and about 5 mm (¼ inch) thick.

Peel, core and chop the apples, then spread them over the pastry. Sprinkle with the sugar and spice, and roll up like a swiss roll. Cut into 2.5-cm (1-inch) slices and arrange the slices in a buttered 1.2-litre (2-pint) ovenproof dish.

Strain the lemon rind from the prepared syrup and pour over the pudding. Bake for about 30 minutes, or until puffed up and golden.

Serve hot, with plenty of Cornish clotted cream.

POMMES AU BEURRE

. . . .

Elizabeth David was a self-taught cook and the most influential food writer in the twentieth century. Following the austerity of the Second World War and its aftermath, her European perspective and passion for good, local food set British interest on the path towards good ingredients and seasonal cooking. Her beautifully written books include **Mediterranean Food, Summer Cooking, English Bread and Yeast Cookery,** *and* **Harvest of the Cold Months** *(published posthumously). See also her essay 'Big Bad Bramleys' in* **An Omelette and a Glass of Wine.**

I have never very greatly appreciated cooked apple dishes, but from the French I learned two valuable lessons about them. First, choose hard sweet apples whenever possible instead of the sour cooking variety, which are used for English apple dishes. And secondly, if the apples are to be eaten hot, cook them in butter instead of in water. The scent of apples cooking in butter is alone more than worth the small extra expense.

For 1 kg (2.2 lb), then, of peeled and cored sweet apples (I always use Cox's Orange Pippins), evenly and rather thinly sliced, melt 50 g (2 oz) of butter in a frying pan. Put in your apples, add 3 or 4 tablespoons of soft white sugar (vanilla-flavoured if you like), and cook gently until the apples are pale golden and transparent. Turn the slices over very gently, so as not to break them, and if very closely packed, shake the pan rather than stir the apples. Serve hot; and I doubt if many people will find cream necessary. The delicate butter taste is enough.

LA TARTE AUX POMMES NORMANDE

. . . .

Elizabeth David is the author of French Provincial Cooking *(Michael Joseph 1960), from which this recipe and the previous one are taken.*

Cook 750 g (1½ lb) of sweet apples as for 'pommes au beurre' (see previous recipe). Make a *pâté sablée* or crumbly pastry by rubbing 75 g (3 oz) of butter into 175 g (6 oz) of plain flour, a quarter-teaspoon of salt and 3 teaspoons of white sugar. Moisten with 2–4 tablespoons of ice-cold water. If it is still too dry, add a little more, but the less water you use the more crumbly and light your pastry will be.

Simply shape the pastry into a ball and immediately, without leaving it to rest or even rolling it out, spread it with your hands into a lightly buttered 20-cm (8-inch) flan tin. Brush the edges with thin cream or milk; arrange the apples, without the juice, in overlapping circles, keeping a nicely shaped piece for the centre. Bake in the tin on a baking sheet, in a preheated hot oven at 200°C/400°F/ gas mark 6 for 30–35 minutes, turning the tin round once during the cooking. Take it from the oven, pour in the buttery juices, which have been reheated, give another sprinkling of sugar, and return to the oven for barely a minute.

Although it is at its best hot, this pastry will not go sodden even when it is cold.

AUTUMN PUDDING WITH WILDING APPLES

....

Richard Mabey is Britain's foremost nature writer. Author of the seminal Food for Free, Flora Britannica, *and* Nature Cure, *he won the Whitbread Biography Prize in 1986 for* Gilbert White: a biography of the author of 'The Natural History of Selborne'. *His latest book is* Beechcombing. *He is a long-standing trustee of Common Ground.*

Wild apples don't really deserve their reputation for forbidding sourness. True crab trees (distinguishable by their spiny branches) do indeed have small, acrid, bullet-hard fruits that are only really useful as providers of pectin in jam-making. But most feral apples are commonly known as 'wildings', sprung from the seed of discarded domesticated apples. They carry all the genetic variety of the family, and are often mild and bulky enough to be edible raw. Among them you can find apples whose flavour is touched with gooseberry, lemon and pear, in colours from straw yellow to plum red, and with a range of textures to match. The most seductive are those occasional fruits which are scented with quince, and which can fill the autumn air with their savour a hundred yards away.

A good way of catching the fruity tang of these wilding apples is to use them in an autumn pudding. Make this like a summer pudding, but substitute dark, autumnal fruits for the bright red raspberries and redcurrants.

Core, but don't peel half a kilo (a pound or so) of wilding apples and mix with about the same weight of blackberries, elderberries, stoned sloes, or whatever dark fruit is about. The precise ingredients and proportions aren't important: these seasonal fruit puddings should have the happenstance variety and spontaneity of a stockpot.

Cook for about a quarter of an hour, or until soft. Stir in dark honey to taste, and perhaps a pinch each of ground cumin and anise, as recommended by the French cook Gisèle Tronche in her wild fruit, '*humeur-noir*' jam recipes.

Transfer the pulp to a deep pudding basin lined with slices of wholemeal bread and use further slices until the pulp is absorbed and covered. Put a weight on top and leave in the refrigerator overnight, but remove half an hour before serving.

FLYING SAUCERS

Bob Flowerdew is well known as the organic expert on 'Gardener's Question Time', 'Gardener's World' and 'Muck and Magic'; he grows and cooks almost every gourmet esculent. He has other lives as **Mastermind** *question setter, pilot, inventor, scuba diver and sculptor. With more than a dozen books in print, this recipe is from* **Bob Flowerdew's Complete Fruit Book.**

Early apples are best eaten off the tree. They rarely keep for long, going pappy within days. Most mid-season apples are also best eaten off the tree as they ripen, but many will keep for weeks if picked just underripe and stored in the cool. Late keepers must hang on the trees till hard frosts are imminent, or bird damage is getting too severe; then, if they are deliberately picked and kept cool in the dark they may keep for six months or longer. Thus apples can be had most months of the year, providing early- and late-keeping varieties and a rodent-proof store are available. They are best picked with a cupped hand and laid gently in a tray, traditionally provided with dry straw. Straw may taint if dampened so it is better to use shredded paper. Dried stinging nettles help stored fruit keep. Wrapping apples individually in paper is also recommended for long keeping. Do not attempt to store early varieties, and be sure to keep apples well apart from pears, onions, garlic and potatoes. Apples to be stored must be free of bruises, rot and holes, and the stalks must remain attached. Apples can also be preserved by freezing, juicing, drying, and making into cider or vinegar.

Cooking apples are different from desserts, much larger, more acid and less sweet raw. Many break down to a frothy purée when heated and few retain their texture, unlike most of the desserts. Bramley, Norfolk Beauty and Reverend W. Wilks are typical, reducing to a lovely froth when cooked. Lane's Prince Albert, Lord Derby and Encore stay firm and are the sorts to use for pies rather than sauces.

per person
1 large cooking apple
approximately 3 dessertspoons mincemeat
a knob of butter
1 heaped teaspoon sesame seeds
cream or custard to serve

Wash, dry and cut each apple in half horizontally. Remove the tough part of the core but leave the outside intact. Stuff the hollow with mincemeat, then pin the two halves back together with wooden cocktail sticks. Rub the outside with butter and roll in sesame seeds, then bake in a preheated oven at 190°C/375°F/ gas mark 5, for half an hour or until they 'lift off' nicely. Serve the Flying Saucers immediately, with cream or custard.

APPLE & TREACLE PUDDING

Hattie Ellis is the author of Eating England, Sweetness & Light, the mysterious history of the honeybee; Planet Chicken, *and* Mood Food, *from which this recipe comes. A contributor to the Herbivore column in* Kew Gardens *magazine, she is interested in the natural and social history of food.*

This pudding was inspired by a visit to Ampleforth Abbey orchard in Yorkshire, where, alongside their many kinds of eating apples, they grew fifteen varieties of cookers. Father Anthony, one of the monks who ran the orchard, picked me a Howgate Wonder that was four times the size of a standard apple and had to be to held in two hands. Such beauties are a British speciality and the way they collapse to a soft fluffiness has given rise to a number of our delicious puddings. This recipe combines the sweet, sticky topping of a treacle tart with the sharpness of such fruit. Back at my home in Sussex, I would use the Alfriston, but, depending on where you live, try the Keswick Codlin (in Lancashire and the Lake District) Early Victoria or Emneth Early (from Cambridgeshire), Hawthornden (in Scotland).

Serves 8
4 large cooking apples
150 g (6 oz) crustless white bread
half a small tin golden syrup – about 225 g/8 oz
grated rind of ½ lemon

Preheat the oven to 180°C/350°F/gas mark 4. Quarter, core, peel and roughly chop the apples. Cook with 100 ml (a small wineglass) of water in a pan with the lid on over a medium heat for about 5 minutes, or until the apples collapse. (You could add a little sugar at this stage but I prefer the contrast between the sharp apple and the sweet topping.) Put the purée in a shallow ovenproof dish.

Whiz the bread in a food-processor to make crumbs. Gently heat the golden syrup to make it more liquid. Add the breadcrumbs and grated lemon to the pan and mix well. Spread the sweet crumbs over the fruit. Cook for 20 minutes or until lightly browned. Serve hot or warm with cream or custard.

CHARLOTTE RUSSE

* *

Andrew Whitley runs baking courses under the title Bread Matters *(see www. breadmatters.com) and works for the improvement of public health through good food, in part as chair of the Soil Association's Processing Standards Committee. This recipe comes from his book* Bread Matters: the state of modern bread and a definitive guide to baking your own, *winner of the André Simon Award.*

Generally credited to the famous French chef Antoine Carême, and probably dedicated to Queen Charlotte, wife of King George III, this delicious apple pudding is known in Russia by the charming diminutive *Sharlotka*.

Some recipes for Charlotte Russe call for slices of bread or effectively cake (in the form of 'ladies' fingers') to line the mould, but I think that a lining of crumbs makes for a more delicate pudding. I suggest using Borodinsky breadcrumbs because of their malty coriander flavour, but a plain rye (or mixed rye/wheat) bread would be a perfectly acceptable substitute.

In Russia the apples used would almost certainly be the much-loved Antonovsky variety, a crimson-skinned eater/cooker. When I planted an orchard at the same time as I founded the Village Bakery, Melmerby, in 1976, I chose Grenadier and Early Victoria as my main cookers. The latter had a habit of dropping all its fruit at once as soon as frost threatened – just the weather for a pudding like this.

As a baker I measure all ingredients by weight out of habit. Home cooks will find 5 g of spice is equivalent to 5 ml or 1 teaspoon, while 150 g/6 oz liquid is the same as 150 ml/6 fl oz.

Makes 1 plump Sharlotka

300 g (12 oz) Borodinsky (or other) rye bread, at least 4 days old

150 g (6 oz) butter

2 g ground cloves

5 g ground cinnamon

150 g (6 oz) raw cane sugar

150 g (6 oz) white wine

6 medium-size apples

50 g (2 oz) ground almonds

50 g (2 oz) currants or raisins

Grate the bread to make crumbs.

Use a little of the butter to grease a large pudding basin or mould. Dust this thoroughly with some of the breadcrumbs, making sure that there are no blind spots. If the apple mix seeps through, Sharlotka may be reluctant to come out of her shell.

Fry the remaining breadcrumbs with the spices and 50 g (2 oz) of the sugar in the rest of the butter. When they have caramelised slightly, remove them from the heat and pour on two-thirds of the white wine.

Peel, core and finely slice the apples. Add the rest of the sugar, the almonds, the currants and the rest of the white wine.

Put a layer of breadcrumb mix in the bottom of the mould, followed by a layer of apple mix, and so on until finishing with a layer of breadcrumb mix. Bake in a slow oven (150°C/300°F/gas mark 2) for about an hour. Turn the mould upside down onto a serving dish and hope for the best. Serve warm with cream or crème fraîche.

APPLE & GUINNESS FRITTERS

Mark Hix is the chef-director of the Ivy, Le Caprice and the new Scott's fish res-taurant. He has written a number of books, and has a regular column in the Independent on Saturday *magazine. He has won a Glenfiddich Newspaper Cookery Writer of the Year award and two Guild of Food Writers' awards. This recipe is taken from* British Regional Food.

Apples are probably the fruit that crops up most in Irish recipe books. I suppose the apple is the potato of the fruit world and it is so user-friendly, in pies, dumplings and the traditional Irish cake. Guinness, or Smithwicks, stout makes a good batter – and why not make good use of traditional regional drinks in a pudding? It seems equally appropriate to choose Irish apples for this recipe, if possible. Irish Seed Savers are helping to revive traditional varieties such as Sam

Young, a small fruit with intense peardrop flavour, once a favourite in Kilkenny, Offaly and Cavan; Reid's Seedling, sometimes described as Ireland's answer to Charles Ross; the pale-skinned Kill Apple, which flowers late, so is good for areas prone to frost; and White Russet, large, round and lumpy-looking but boasting juicy peach/pineapple flavour. Why did these fruits get ignored, I wonder, because they make good eating with cheese and are perfect for Irish-stout frittering.

Serves 4–6
150 ml stout
110 g (4 oz) self-raising flour, plus a little extra for dusting
1 tablespoon caster sugar
vegetable oil for deep-frying
4 well-flavoured eating apples (perhaps Sam Young, Reid's Seedling, Kill Apple, White Russet or Charles Ross), peeled, cored and sliced
caster sugar for dusting
thick cream to serve

Whisk the stout into the flour to form a thick batter. Add the sugar and leave to stand for an hour.

Preheat about 8 cm (3–3½ inches) of oil to 160–180°C (325–350°F) in a large heavy-based saucepan or an electric deep-fat fryer.

Dust the apple slices in flour and shake off the excess, then dip 4 or 5 slices at a time into the batter, shake off the excess and drop them into the hot oil. After a minute or so, turn them with a slotted spoon so they colour evenly. When they are golden all over, remove them from the oil and drain on kitchen paper. Repeat with the rest of the apples.

Dust with caster sugar and serve with thick cream.

APPLE GALETTE

···

Tamasin Day-Lewis is a food writer, journalist, broadcaster and film-maker. Her most recent book is Tamasin's Kitchen Classics. *This recipe is taken from* The Art of the Tart.

Each region of Lorraine and Alsace has its own version of quiche, and the name is sometimes used for sweet custard tarts, too. Old-fashioned Quiche Lorraine was made with a yeasted bread dough, and likewise the galette, a deliciously crisped, doughy crust harbouring a juice-sodden layer of apples, plums, green-gages, apricots or any of the scented fruits. You can scatter chopped nuts into the dough and over the fruit if you desire. This is not a dish that will good-temperedly reheat; it is to be eaten straight from the oven, or warm. However, you can keep the fruit and the rolled-out dough in the fridge, and finish off the pudding when you need it.

Crisp, juicy eating apples with a good balance of sweet and acid work best here: one of the Pippins (King's Acre Pippin, Queen of Pippins, Sturmer Pippin or Cox's Orange Pippin, for example) or a Reinette.

Serves 8

for the dough:

200 g (7 oz) strong white flour

2 teaspoons dried yeast

1½ teaspoons salt

2 eggs

5 tablespoons melted unsalted butter

about 150 ml (5 fl oz) water or milk at blood heat

a handful of chopped toasted hazelnuts, almonds or walnuts (optional)

for the top:
8 Pippins
150 g (5 oz) unsalted butter
100 g (3½ oz) vanilla sugar, mixed, if you like, with 1 teaspoon ground cinnamon
    and 1 teaspoon ground allspice
150 ml (5 fl oz) double cream
1 egg
extra sugar
extra nuts (optional)

First make the dough. Mix together the flour, yeast and salt, then add the eggs, butter and liquid to make a soft, coherent and unsticky dough. Knead by hand or in a food-processor. Put the dough into a bowl inside a plastic bag and seal tightly; leave to double in size for at least an hour.

Turn out and punch down the dough, throwing in a handful of nuts if you feel like it. Lightly oil the bowl, roll the dough in it gently, and seal in a plastic bag for a second rise – 30 minutes should be enough this time. Punch down again and refrigerate: this dough will not roll out properly if it isn't chilled – it will shrink back temperamentally each time you try.

Roll out the chilled dough into a 30 cm (12-inch) circle and place it on a well-greased baking sheet or pizza plate.

Peel and core the apples, then cut them into wedges. Fry them in the butter until gently coloured, then sprinkle them with the sugar and spice mixture. Let them begin to caramelise, then remove from the heat and cool to tepid.

Preheat the oven to 200°C/400°F/gas mark 6.

Leaving 3 cm (about 1 inch) free at the edge, arrange the fruit and juices over the dough. Put it in a warm place for 20 minutes, then bake for 25 minutes.

Beat the cream, egg and a little sugar together and pour over as much of it as you can – the edge will have risen slightly. Scatter over the nuts if you are using them and return the galette to the oven. Cook until the top has set, roughly 10 minutes.

APPLE SNOW

....

Rose Prince writes about food for the Daily Telegraph, Telegraph Magazine, *the* Independent, *the* London Evening Standard, *the* Spectator, *the* Tablet *and* Resurgence *magazine. Her books,* The New English Kitchen *(from which this recipe is taken) and* The Savvy Shopper *are published by Fourth Estate. In 2006 she was listed in* Harpers Bazaar *as one of the thirty most influential women in Britain.*

Planting our own orchard in an unfenced grassy area close to the woods in a Dorset village was not easy. The greatest threat to the fruit is the wild deer, which will rip through an orchard like a plague of locusts. They always visit when the trees are in full blossom, so an attack means the trees will be barren and forlorn until next year; a harsh reminder that fencing is the only answer. We have fenced in the trees individually; I like the architectural lines of a six-foot high tree guard – they add beauty to the orchard, rather than detracting from it. The sculptor Belinda Rush Jansen wove me a stag from twisted wood and wire, which now stands among the trees. The best sight of all is to see the fallow deer grazing among the trees, not feasting on them, with the ghostly sight of the wire sculpture behind them. We have lost two trees to disease. We never treat them, and prune only lightly. This is not down to a pursuit of organic purity but sheer laziness.

Nine years ago my mother bought me a quince sapling – a twig with roots would be better description. I stuffed it into the ground in a place I hoped was nowhere near the drains. Inexplicably it is now an enormous tree that not only yields 200 fat quinces each year but has a crop of babies that we snip off and plant or give away. The quinces go to my sister's restaurant, in return for dinner. I feel very good about orchard fruit.

Here is an easy, whisked-up pudding that shows off the glorious flavours of the old apple breeds that appear in shops after the September harvest. I'm not fussed about which variety I use, providing it is English grown. Serve this pudding in glass tumblers with sweet biscuits. Any remainder can be frozen to make a simple sorbet.

Serves 4
2 egg whites
120 g (4 oz) golden caster sugar
375 ml (12 fl oz) unsweetened apple sauce, puréed
1 pinch cinnamon
4 teaspoons golden muscovado sugar

Whisk the egg whites until stiff and fold in the caster sugar. Whisk again until shiny and smooth. Mix the apple with the cinnamon, then fold into the egg-white mixture. Divide the mixture among the glasses and sprinkle muscovado sugar on top of each.

CARAMELISED APPLES WITH LANCASHIRE CHEESE ON PUFF OR FLAKY PASTRY

Patricia Michelson lectures on cheese and wine pairing and is the author of The Cheese Room, *from which this recipe is taken. Her love of cheese was inspired by a skiing holiday in Méribel. She returned to London with a wheel of Beaufort Chalet d'Alpage, which she sold from her garden shed, and then a stall in Camden market. La Fromagerie now comprises two award-winning shops and a wholesale business.*

Cheese with apples – a sensorial memory from childhood. You start with tiny cubes of mild crumbly cheese and slivers of apple when you are a toddler, graduate to a grab-and-go chunk of cheese with an apple as a teenager, then reach the glorious moment of indulging in the pleasure of mingling savoury and sweet with a glass of claret.

Served at the end of a meal, this dish makes an interesting alternative to the usual cheese course. In Lancashire they say, 'An apple pie without the cheese is like a hug without the squeeze' – unthinkable. This easily assembled tart guarantees no such disappointment. A variety of apples can be used as they ripen and come into season: Braeburn, Norfolk Royal, St Edmund's Pippin and Blenheim Orange, for example. The cheese should have a lovely nutty taste and crumbly texture, which breaks down well when heated in the oven – unpasteurised gives added depth of flavour. If you don't fancy making your own flaky pastry, look out for Dorset Pastry's excellent organic puff pastry, hand-made in the traditional way with butter: no shortcuts and no cheating.

Serves 6

250 g (9 oz) flaky or puff pastry

200 g (7 oz) unsalted butter

3–4 fine, large dessert apples, cored and sliced, but not too thinly

a little ground cinnamon or mixed spice

a thin slice of quince cheese – fruit paste (optional)

2 teaspoons Demerara or fine muscovado sugar

200 g (7 oz) Shorrock's or Kirkham's farmhouse Lancashire, on the young side

120 g (4 oz) fromage blanc or fromage frais, low or full fat

Preheat the oven to 200°C/400°F/gas mark 6.

Roll out the pastry in a 20-cm (8-inch) circle, then score an inner circle, around 2.5-cm (1-inch) from the edge, with the tip of a knife. Place the pastry on a lightly oiled baking sheet. (Alternatively, you can use the pastry to line a shallow tart tin.)

In a heavy frying pan melt the butter until it is foamy then fry the apples until they are golden but still firm, not collapsing. Add the spice, and the quince cheese if using, then sprinkle over the sugar and continue to cook until everything is nicely caramelised. Take the pan off the heat, remove the apples and let them cool to room temperature. Reduce any juices in the pan to a thick syrup, then add this to the apples.

In a bowl crumble the Lancashire cheese and mix in the fromage blanc or fromage frais until it is smooth but retains some texture. Spread the mixture over the pastry, lay the apples and their thickened juices on top, and bake on the middle shelf of the oven for about 15 minutes until the pastry is golden and the filling is evenly cooked. Serve warm, maybe with a glass of Somerset cider brandy.

APPLE BROWN BETTY

Sally Clarke opened her restaurant, Clarke's, in Kensington Church Street, London, in 1984, following studies and work experience in Paris, and four years working in California. She opened her shop and wholesale bakery next door to the restaurant soon afterwards. **Sally Clarke's Book: recipes from a restaurant, shop and bakery** *won the Glenfiddich award for Best Food Book of the year in 2000.*

Our first family home, in Surrey, was called Apple Tree Cottage and I have very happy memories of it – in the garden, up the tree and in the house. Every year the tree burst into blossom that seemed to last for weeks. The apples had smooth, shiny skins: pale red with a pink blush that faded into pale green. The flesh was sweet, juicy and bright pink under the skin, fading to a very pale pink at the core. Although I have never discovered the variety's name, they were moreish and just the right size for small fingers and hands.

Secrett's Farm Shop, near Godalming in Surrey, is our normal supplier for apples at the restaurant, although we have a few very well-trained customers who gather their windfalls for us each autumn and deliver them to the door.

Apple Brown Betty is probably my very favourite apple pudding: I love the contrast of the sharp, acidic but buttery apple purée and the crisp, sweetened, spicy crumb topping. Bramley's Seedlings, originally from Nottinghamshire, are widely available and the obvious choice to use here, but it does seem a pity to overlook lesser-known varieties that may be more local to you. Traditional regional alternatives to look out for, and ask for by name, include Early Victoria (in Cambridgeshire), Lord Suffield (raised by a Lancashire weaver), Queen (from Essex), Encore (from Berkshire), Baker's Delicious (from Wales), Wellington or Dumelow's Seedling (from Leicestershire) and George Neal (from Kent) to name but a few.

Serves 6

for the topping:

50 g (2 oz) butter

150 g (6 oz) fresh breadcrumbs

50 g (2 oz) brown sugar

2 teaspoons ground cinnamon

1 teaspoon mixed spice

for the apple:

1.6 kg (3½ lb) cooking apples, with a good acid kick to them, peeled, cored and roughly chopped

150 g (6 oz) sugar

25 g (1 oz) butter

First, make the topping. Heat the butter in a shallow heavy-based pan. Add the breadcrumbs and stir continuously over a medium-high heat as they become crisp. When they have turned golden remove them from the heat and stir in the sugar and spices. Leave to cool.

Place the apples in a heavy-based stainless-steel pan with a splash of water and the sugar. Heat gently, cover with a lid and stir occasionally. A smooth purée with a few lumps will result after 10–15 minutes. Remove from the heat, stir in the butter and taste for sweetness, although the apples should retain most of their inherent sharpness.

Serve the warm apple in warm bowls sprinkled with a generous amount of crumbs, and offer lots of whipped cream or crème fraîche.

BAKED APPLE CREAM

Sophie Grigson is an author, broadcaster, food writer and cookery columnist for **Waitrose Food Illustrated, BBC Good Food,** *the* **Independent on Sunday,** *and the* **London Evening Standard.** *Her fifteenth book is* **Sophie's Sunshine Food.** *This recipe is adapted from* **Sophie's Table.**

A marvellously rich and devastating pudding that is simple to make. It is based on a dish I first tasted in Normandy, but since British apples and apple brandy are as good as (if not better than) any French ones, it sits just as prettily on an English table. A small portion should be quite enough to satisfy each person after an ample meal, but if it is to follow a very light meal, you may find that there is only enough for four.

King Offa Cider Brandy is available from Hereford Cider Museum, The Cider Mills, 21 Ryelands Street, Hereford. Julian Temperley's Somerset Royal Cider Brandy, launched on Apple Day 1991, is made at Burrow Hill, Kingsbury Episcopi.

Serves 6
450 g (1 lb) scented eating apples
   (Cox's Orange Pippin or Kidd's Orange Red)
4 tablespoons Somerset Royal Cider Brandy, King Offa Cider Brandy or Calvados
30 g (1 oz) butter
6 tablespoons caster sugar
3 egg yolks

300 ml (10 fl oz) whipping cream
2 tablespoons flaked almonds

Peel and core the apples. Chop roughly and toss in the apple brandy or Calvados. Set aside for 1 hour.

Drain off the liquor and reserve. Either divide the apple pieces between 6 small ramekins or put them all into a single ovenproof dish. Dot with butter and sprinkle with half the sugar. Bake at 200°C/400°F/gas mark 6 for 20 minutes.

Mix the reserved liquor with the remaining sugar, the egg yolks and the cream. Take the apples out of the oven, and pour this mixture over them. Scatter the flaked almonds over the top. Stand the dish(es) in a roasting tray, filled to a depth of 25 mm (1 inch) with hot water, and return to the oven. Bake for a further 20–30 minutes, until the cream is almost set, but not quite solid. Serve hot, warm or cold.

BAKED APPLE & QUINCE DUMPLINGS

Simone Sekers used to write for the **Sunday Telegraph.** *She now writes for the* **Blackmore Vale Magazine,** *which does more than the average local paper to promote local food and local distinctiveness. This recipe is taken from* The **National Trust Book of Fruit and Vegetable Cookery** *(National Trust, 1991).*

It is said that the apple which, in falling from its tree, inspired Sir Isaac Newton and was then named after him, was a variety called Flower of Kent. It is also said that Newton's favourite dish was baked quinces. When I was writing for the National Trust on fruit and vegetable cookery, I cobbled together a recipe to combine both fruits. Flower of Kent apples are not native to Lincolnshire, where Newton lived at Woolsthorpe Manor, near Colsterworth, but Peasgood's Nonsuch is, and is perfectly suited to this recipe. Or you can cheat a little and use Bramleys, since they come from Southwell, just over the border in Nottinghamshire.

Serves 4

2 ripe quinces

honey to taste

25 g (1 oz) butter

350 g (12 oz) sweet shortcrust pastry

4 small cooking apples

1 egg, beaten

Peel and core the quinces, cut them up and stew with a little water over a low heat until soft. Purée them, together with enough honey to sweeten to your taste, taking into account that this mixture must sweeten the apples too, then beat in the butter. Roll out the pastry and divide it into 4 squares. Peel and core the apples and put one in the centre of each square of pastry. Fill the cavities generously with the quince purée, then fold the pastry up and around to enclose the apples, pinching the edges together firmly with the help of a little water, or some of the beaten egg. Brush with more egg and arrange on a baking sheet before baking in a hot oven (200–225°C/400–425°F/gas mark 6–7) for 25–30 minutes. Serve hot, warm or cold, with thick cream and extra sugar if necessary.

NB If quinces are unobtainable use the fruit of the japonica or Japanese quince (*chaenomeles*) instead, but you will need four times the quantity as they are so much smaller.

A DEVONSHIRE CHARLOTTE OF APPLES & PLUMS

Alice Wooledge Salmon, who writes in Britain and America, was a founder-member of the British Guild of Food Writers. This recipe was first published, in a slightly different form, by House & Garden *in March 1991. As Susan and 'Bo' Bosence are now dead, her charlotte is offered in affectionate tribute to their memory.*

I devised this charlotte in praise of Susan Bosence, the Devonshire crafts-woman-artist whose resist-dyed, hand-printed cottons and silks unite colour, pattern, and fabric in rare mutual affinity.

Susan and 'Bo' Bosence inhabited eight undulating acres at the edge of Dartmoor, growing domestic bounty of organic fruits, vegetables, flowers, and herbs, tending a long-established orchard of dessert and cooking apples mixed in with various ciders. 'It's likely,' said Susan, 'that we have the traditional Devon varieties – Allspice, Quarrenden, Oaken Pin, Crimson Costard, Star of Devon, Michaelmas Stubbard – but hardly any of the trees have been properly identified!'

Among the apples is a lone plum stock whose fruit, said Susan, 'looks like a cross between Damson and Dittisham: its taste is on the sharp side, but ripening into "fruitiness" with a hint of Victoria'. Theirs is too high and exposed to be 'true plum country', but several decades back, Susan and Bo would drive, each August, 'down the long lane beside the Dart estuary to Dittisham' where the riverbank shelters a 'warm, almost maritime "dip"', formerly filled with orchards of the rich, dark crimson Dittisham Ploughman plum that has now become a rarity.

If Susan were making an Apple Charlotte, she would probably have chosen an early Blenheim ('I *think* I have one!'), as recommended by Joan Morgan. When pressed, by me, to select a Devon variety from among her trees, she picked, for baking this mixture of apples with plum, the 'sharp, Bramley-like' Michaelmas Stubbard with, to provide the sweet density which I like to find in a charlotte, a couple of pounds of Charles Ross, the Berkshire-bred 'slightly peachy' dessert and cooking variety, of which Susan had one tree at the bottom of her kitchen garden. This is a charlotte for Michaelmas (late September/early October), when Susan's 'Damson-Dittisham' plums were ripe.

Serves 4

1 kg (2 lb) Charles Ross apples

750 g (1½ lb) Michaelmas Stubbard cooking apples

750 g (1½ lb) late-ripening red or dark crimson-skinned plums – 'Damson-
    Dittishams', or Laxton's Delicious, or one of the 'pure' damsons
150 g (5 oz) butter
about 125 g (4 oz) golden granulated sugar
juice of 1 large lemon
half a loaf of brown sandwich bread, 2 days old
icing sugar
crab-apple jelly, home-made if possible
double cream

Peel, core, slice the apples; quarter and stone the plums (leaving skins on). Place the fruit, with a little water, 25 g (1 oz) butter, the sugar, and lemon juice in a large, heavy saucepan. Cook the contents, first with and then without a lid, into a very stiff purée, stirring often to prevent burning. Cool; the result should be rather tart.

Preheat the oven to 200°C/400°F/gas mark 6.

Clarify the remaining butter and lightly brush a 1.2-litre (2-pint) charlotte mould with some of the resultant yellow oil; cut a circle of greaseproof paper to fit the base of the mould and press this into place. Thinly slice three-quarters of the bread, remove the crusts, cut each slice in half lengthwise and lightly toast on both sides. Brush the slices with clarified butter and run the toast upright, slices slightly overlapping, round the inside of the mould. Fill the bread case as full as possible with purée, cut and toast some wider, crustless slices to make a lid, and brush with the remaining clarified butter.

Place the charlotte mould on a heavy baking sheet and bake at 200°C/400°F/gas mark 6 for 20–25 minutes, until the toast is well browned. Let the charlotte cool for 20 minutes, turn it out on to a plate and peel away the greaseproof paper. Dust the sides lightly with icing sugar sifted through a tea-strainer, and present with crab-apple jelly and cream.

BAKING, PRESERVES & MISCELLANEOUS

• APPLE BREAD **JOAN MORGAN** • APPLE & ROSEMARY HEARTHBREAD **PHILIPPA DAVENPORT** • DORSET APPLE CAKE **ANNA PAVORD** • TOFFEE APPLE CAKE **JULIET KINDERSLEY** • DRYING APPLES **FRANCESCA GREENOAK** • SWEET GERANIUM JELLY **DARINA ALLEN** • SPICED APPLE CHUTNEY **SHONA CRAWFORD POOLE** • SWEETLY SPICED CRAB APPLES **GRACE MULLIGAN** • PICKLED SWEET LARKS **TRADITIONAL** • DEVONSHIRE APPLE & CUCUMBER PICKLE **MARGARET WILSON** • WASSAIL CUP **HENRIETTA GREEN** • LOCAL APPLES & CHEESES **SIMONE SEKERS** • THE BLENHEIM ORANGE **GAIL DUFF** •

APPLE BREAD

....

Joan Morgan is a fruit historian and pomologist. She is the author, with Alison Richards, of The Book of Apples *and its revised edition* The New Book of Apples, the Definitive Guide to Apples *including over 2000 varieties.*

A bread formed of 'one third boiled apple pulp baked with two thirds flour having been properly fermented with yeast' was 'excellent, full of eyes and extremely palatable' wrote the eminent horticulturalist John Claudius Loudon in his Encyclopaedia of Gardening in 1824.

The addition of apples to the dough makes a savoury bread that is good eaten with cheese. Experiment through the season with different varieties, which will give different results.

For 1 loaf
350 g (12 oz) wholemeal flour
175 g (6 oz) apples, weighed after peeling and coring
12 g (½ oz) fresh yeast (fresh is easier than dried)

Cook the apples to a purée or to soft slices depending upon the variety. Blend the yeast to a smooth liquid with a little warm water – about half a teacupful. Add this to the warm, but not hot apple. Stir this into the lightly salted flour and the resulting dough should be fairly moist. Leave it to rise and double its volume – about 1–2 hours. Then dust with flour, gather it together and work it into a ball. Put this into a greased bread tin and leave to rise. When the dough reaches the top of the tin put it into an oven heated to 210°C/400°F/gas mark 6. Bake for 20 minutes, then for 20 minutes more at 190°C/375°F/gas mark 5. Turn the loaf out of the tin and let it cool.

APPLE & ROSEMARY HEARTHBREAD

....

Philippa Davenport has been food columnist of the **Financial Times** *since 1973.*

My search is on to find Roundway Magnum Bonum. I read about it recently in *The Apples of England* by H.V. Taylor. First published in 1936, reprinted and revised almost annually in the 1940s, Taylor sets the apple lover's heart alight with his listings. Varietal names roll off the tongue like a lovely litany. His historical notes, botanical details and taste descriptions make compulsive reading. Names may proudly reflect an apple's birthplace (Stirling Castle, Claygate Pearmain, Blenheim Orange), invite questions (why 'The Glass Apple'? Why 'Cissy'?), spur exotic speculation (D'Arcy Spice must be a ballerina, surely; while Jersey Beauty should be a butterfly or a royal mistress), serve as poignant reminders (Widow's Friend, so sweet in blossom; Annie Elizabeth, named after an infant who died) or proclaim real or imagined grandeur (Court Pendu Plat, Gloria Mundi, Wealthy – and Roundway Magnum Bonum).

There must still be Roundway Magnum Bonums flourishing – or struggling to survive – in gardens somewhere near where I live. Taylor records that it was raised in Roundway Park near Devizes, less than twenty miles away. He says it was first exhibited at the RHS in 1864 when it received a first class certificate, and it sailed into national fruit trials twenty years later. Said to have yellow-green skin flushed with crimson, the white-green flesh is described as crisp and juicy with aromatic flavour. One black mark against it, I suppose, is its apparently short eating season: the four weeks of December.

I want to find it because I love the grandiose boom of its name, because it is a bona fide local Wiltshire apple, and because I like to try to use a different variety each time I bake this flatbread.

Greengrocers generally offer sadly little choice. There is special pleasure to be had from delving into the bran tub dip of a box of surplus windfalls left outside a garden gate with the scrawled invitation to help yourself (the offerings are usually anonymous but you never know what treasure trove you might find). Buying from farmers' markets and scrounging from friends with orchards puts us back in touch with yet more apples rarely carried by shopkeepers. And visits to specialist growers and Apple Day events bring us yet another fruitful step closer to appreciating the extraordinary diversity of apples that once thrived and can still be grown in this cradle of appledom called Britain.

This is good food for a fireside picnic, to eat with, say, chestnuts roasted in the grate, farm-made territorial cheeses and/or dry-cured ham freshly carved from the bone.

Makes 2 small loaves

550 g (1¼ lb) white bread flour, preferably unbleached and stoneground

1 x 7 g sachet of easy-blend yeast, mixed with 1 tablespoon salt

300 ml (generous 10 fl oz) warm water, one part boiling to two parts cold

140 ml (5 fl oz) virgin olive oil

2–3 apples, weighing no more than 450 g (1 lb) in total

several sprigs of rosemary

a little butter for frying the apples

Maldon or Halen Mon salt, for sprinkling over the loaves

Using your hands, a food-processor, or a food-mixer with a dough hook, mix and knead the flour, yeast, salt, warm water and 4 tablespoons of the olive oil to a dough. Cover with oiled polythene and set aside to rise until doubled in size. A slow rise in a cold place is best.

Peel the apples or not as you wish. Core and dice them then sauté the apples briefly in a modicum of butter until streaked with gold, and set aside to cool.

Knock back the risen dough and divide it into two. Knead briefly and work in the apple together with the bruised leaves stripped from a sprig or more of rosemary, then roll each piece of dough into a ball and flatten it slightly. Place each round on a separate greased baking sheet or in a pizza tin, then press and shape it with your hands to make a thin circle about 25 cm (10 inches) in diameter. Dimple the tops all over with your fingertips, cover and prove for about 45 minutes.

Drizzle a tablespoon or so of olive oil over the top of each puffed-up loaf. Spread the oil gently with your fingers, add a scattering of whole rosemary leaves and a scrunch of Maldon or Halen Mon salt. Bake at 220°C/425°F/gas mark 7 for 15 minutes, then at 200°C/400°F/gas mark 6 for 5–10 minutes more.

Slide the golden loaves on to a cooling rack. Drizzle another 1–2 tablespoons olive oil over each to give the fragrant bread its characteristic finish and heighten the rich fruity flavour. Leave for half an hour before tucking in (you'll get hiccups if you don't).

DORSET APPLE CAKE

Anna Pavord is gardening correspondent of the Independent, *and the author of* The Tulip, *and* The Naming of Names. *She gardens in Dorset.*

This recipe for Dorset Apple Cake is one of my favourites. I would recommend using the Reverend W. Wilks, creamy-white, cooking to a pale yellow froth. It's a small tree, useful for gardens that can't accommodate a Bramley. It was introduced at the beginning of the century and named after the vicar of Shirley in Surrey, who invented the Shirley Poppy.

If you cannot find the Reverend W. Wilks, you might like to make this cake using Arthur Turner, Howgate Wonder, Lane's Prince Albert or Peasgood's Nonsuch instead. Quite honestly any apple will work here but cookers and dual-purpose varieties give a contrast that is more tart than an eater would.

Makes 1 cake

225 g (8 oz) flour

50 g (2 oz) butter

50 g (2 oz) lard or other cooking fat

500 g (1 lb) cooking apples, peeled, cored and chopped

100 g (4 oz) sugar

1 egg

2 teaspoons baking powder

a little milk

Mix all the ingredients well and bake – in a greased and base-lined cake tin measuring about 20 cm (8 in) across and 4 cm (1½ in) deep – for 45 minutes in an oven preheated to around 180°C/350°F/gas mark 4.

TOFFEE APPLE CAKE

Juliet Kindersley is a gardener, environmentalist and organic farmer. With the help of her son-in-law Eric Treuille (who runs Books for Cooks in London), she designs seasonal menus for the conference centre at Sheepdrove Organic Farm, using the produce from the farm, kitchen gardens and orchards.

When so many apples are harvested at once that it becomes obvious we can't eat or cook them all straight away, we put a lot of them into store – not a romantic old-fashioned thatched-cottage-like store shaded by woodland, and certainly not the sort of gas chamber store used by big commercial growers to arrest apple development and allow the fruit to be held in limbo for up to a year. We just space out our apples on trays and put them into a large walk-in fridge where they can mature gently. We use these not-too-cold fridges for storing vegetable crops, such as potatoes, red cabbages and onions, as well.

We juice some of our surplus apples – and windfalls, minus the damaged parts of course – using a Scandinavian steamer or (better, I think, because it involves no application of heat) a small apple press we bought recently. Surplus and windfalls also go to make chutneys, jellies and an unsweetened purée that can be packed in polythene bags and frozen.

This unsweetened apple purée is invaluable for serving with pork, and using to make an easy and very popular cake.

At Sheepdrove we grind our own grain for wholemeal flour and we prefer the deeper flavour of muscovado sugar to make a 'wholefood' cake, but the recipe also adapts perfectly to lighter sugars for Apple Crunch Cake. To make this variation on the theme just use natural Demerara sugar instead of dark muscovado in the topping, and golden caster sugar instead of dark muscovado in the base.

Makes 1 cake

for the crumble topping:
50 g (2 oz) wholemeal or plain flour
50 g (2 oz) cold butter, diced
100 g (4 oz) dark muscovado sugar
1 teaspoon cinnamon

for the batter base:
125 g (5 oz) wholemeal or plain flour
2 teaspoons baking powder
100 g (4 oz) cold butter, diced
50 g (2 oz) dark muscovado sugar
1 egg
3 tablespoons milk

for the apple layer:
350 g (12 oz) apple purée made from any windfalls; we generally use the
    Reverend W. Wilks, Howgate Wonder or Blenheim Orange (if the purée has been

frozen, let it drain in a sieve over a bowl for several hours; the liquor that collects in the bowl is the cook's perk – an intensely appley pick-me-up drink)
½ teaspoon ground cinnamon

In a food-processor, whiz the topping ingredients to an even crumble mix. Set aside.

Then prepare the base in the food-processor. Whiz the flour, baking powder, butter and sugar until evenly combined. Add the egg and milk and whiz again to make a thick batter. Spread this in an even layer in a buttered and lined 23 cm (9 in) cake tin.

Mix the apple purée with the cinnamon and spread it evenly over the batter. Scatter the topping over the fruit and bake at 160°C/325°F/gas mark 3 for seventy-five minutes or until a skewer pushed into the cake comes out clean.

Leave to cool for 15 minutes in the tin, then unmould onto a wire rack. Serve warm or at room temperature with yoghurt (it's very sweet so the yoghurt goes well). Don't dust with icing sugar or the brown-sugar topping will look mouldy!

NB. Fresh apples can be used instead of apple purée. You will need 450 g (1 lb) of them. Just peel, core and slice thinly. Arrange the raw slices in an even layer over the batter and sprinkle with the ground cinnamon, then finish with the crumble topping.

DRYING APPLES

. . . .

Francesca Greenoak has a small mixed orchard and a high rise apple store in the old coal shed by her house in the Chilterns. Her books include **Forgotten Fruit: the English Orchard and Fruit Garden, All the Birds of the Air: the names, lore and literature of British Birds, The Natural Garden** *and* **The Gardens of the National Trust for Scotland.** *Francesca is also an Alexander Technique teacher, and edits the* **Alexander Journal.**

Not even the most fruit-avid children can deal with the quantity of apples given by a few productive trees in a good year. Perfect ones can be picked and stored for the winter, but some other method has to be employed for keeping blemished apples and windfalls. Poaching or puréeing, and then freezing works well but takes up a lot of room in the freezer, and it means you have to cook.

Drying is an old method of preserving apples, and has the advantage of conserving and concentrating the flavour of the original variety. Dorothy Hartley's *Food in England* describes how peeled and cored apples can be threaded on a string to make a long necklace which is dried in a dry, warm, well-aired store-room.

Nowadays it is customary to dry cored and sliced apple rings on trays in a warm oven. Another way is to use a custom-made drying machine or dehydrator, which consists of perforated circular trays which are loaded with fruit and stacked above or below a small fan-heater. When the machine is switched on, the fan gently draws warm air through the trays. The standard five-tray version takes roughly a basketful of windfalls which will dry overnight.

The fruit dryer is worth its keep just for the smell. The resulting dried apple rings are very tasty and distinctive. They make a delicious sweetmeat, or they can be reconstituted by adding water. Pears and quince can also be dried; pear flavour is less good than apple and the texture is interestingly gritty. Quince is grainier still, though not unpleasant and drying brings out the sweetness and tang of the fruit. It is possible to tell our Ribston Pippin rings from the Rosemary Russet and Lane's Prince Albert. The Lane's, quite sharp before drying, are possibly the best.

A particularly nice variation is to pour a thin layer of apple purée on to a flexible plastic mat which will fit on the trays in the fruit dryer. The puréed apple dries to a delicious leathery parchment which peels off when dry and can be stored rolled or flat. Cloves, nutmeg, cinnamon and different kinds of fresh chopped nuts can also be added. Apple parchment cones or rolls make interesting containers for all kinds of savories or sweetmeats – including ice-cream.

For domestic or commercial machinery for transforming apples or other fruit and vegetables the best first stop is Vigo (see page 292). They sell dehydrators and driers, steamers, crushers, presses, pasteurisers and more.

SWEET GERANIUM JELLY

Darina Allen is an author, journalist, broadcaster, teacher and the owner of Ballymaloe Cookery School in Co. Cork, which is situated on an organically run farm. She is a member of Eurotoques, councillor for Ireland in the Slow Food movement and founder of the first farmers' markets in Ireland. This recipe is taken from **Darina Allen's Ballymaloe Cookery Course.**

In May the fragrance of apple blossom wafts into our house. Since the children were tiny we have picnicked under the trees during apple blossom and we continue the tradition to this day with our grandchildren. The orchard is organic. Some years we have a huge crop of apples and others virtually none. When we have an abundance, we fill big wooden apple bins. We sell some at the farmers' market in Midleton, some are stored for the winter and some are sent to Tipperary to be pressed into organic apple juice. Last year we made cider for the first time, using some of this juice. I learned the almost-forgotten skill from Dick Keating, a farmhouse cheesemaker from the foothills of the Knockmealdown mountains in County Tipperary. He thinks he may be the last person making home-made cider in that area, and remembers a time when every house and cottage had an orchard and cider was made on every farm as part of the yearly cycle. Apples were introduced by the Normans to South Tipperary when they came to Ireland in the twelfth century.

Crab apple trees grow in the hedgerows around the farm. We pick them every year during our autumn foraging. Sometimes we mix them with sloes, elderberries, japonica and rowan berries to make jellies to serve with game and cheese. We've also got two decorative crab-apple trees in the garden, Yellow Hornet and Red Sentinel. The tiny red fruit of the latter make beautiful pickles. Those that aren't used in cooking are tied into Christmas wreaths and garlands or used for table decorations.

Fills 6–7 jars

2.7 kg (6 lb) cooking apples, such as Grenadier, Arthur Turner, Lane's Prince Albert or Early Victoria, or crab apples (windfalls may be used but be sure to cut out the bruised parts before weighing)

6–8 large sweet geranium leaves (preferably *pelargonium Graveolens*) for cooking plus extra for potting

2 organic or unwaxed lemons

sugar

Wash the apples and cut into quarters. No need to peel or core them. Put them into a large saucepan with 2.7 litres (4¾ pints) of water, the geranium leaves and the thinly pared rind of the lemons. Cook over a medium heat until the apples have dissolved to a mush, about 2 hours.

Turn the pulp into a jelly bag and allow to drip until all the juice has come through – usually overnight.

Measure the juice into a preserving pan and weigh out 450 g (1 lb) sugar for each 600 ml (1 pint) of juice. Put the sugar into a low oven (150°C/300°F/gas mark 2 to warm. Squeeze the lemons, strain the juice and add it to the preserving pan, with a few more geranium leaves if the flavour is still very mild. Bring to the boil and add the warm sugar. Stir over a gentle heat until the sugar has dissolved. Then boil rapidly without stirring for 8–10 minutes. Meanwhile sterilise the jars in the oven at 180°C/350°F/gas mark 4 for 5–8 minutes. Remove the geranium leaves from the pan and test for a set. Put a little jelly on to a chilled plate, let it cool for a minute or two, then press with your finger: if the mixture wrinkles slightly the jelly will set. Alternatively use a sugar thermometer: setting point is reached when the thermometer registers 220°C/425°F.

Skim off any scum, put a fresh geranium leaf into each sterilised jar and fill with the hot jelly. Cover and seal immediately. Label, then store in a cool airy place.

NB. Mint or cloves may be used as an alternative flavouring.

SPICED APPLE CHUTNEY

....

Shona Crawford Poole has written eight cookery books including The New Times Cook Book, The Sunday Times Cook's Companion, *and the best-selling* Ice Cream. *Food and drink editor of* Country Living *magazine for the past nine years, her most recent book is* Modern Country Cooking.

Apples apart, this recipe is evidently Indian in origin, as is the word 'chutney', from *chatni*. Anglicised chutneys don't usually include oil as this one does, and it is an unbeatable medium for transporting the rich tastes and smells of the spices. Try Spiced Apple Chutney with a piece of mature Cheddar, or to accompany a smoked haddock kedgeree – ah, there's another relic of the Raj.

Any crisp, tart apple that does not fall apart when cooked is good in this recipe, so use dessert or cooking apples, even windfalls. Egremont Russets are the best-known local apple in my part of West Sussex and contribute their own subtle spiciness. Falstaff is another aromatic apple that I first tasted on Apple Day at West Dean Gardens, now an unmissable annual event. One of the draws for me is the circular flint-built apple store, a little bit of other-worldly magic in a shady corner of the walled kitchen garden.

Chillies are the other important fresh chutney ingredient, both for their heat and their flavours. I use one hot habañero or Scotch bonnet, three bird's eye and two jalapeño chillies, and the result is warmth, not blistering heat.

Makes about 2.5 kg (5½ lb)

2 kg (4½ lb) tart apples, peeled, cored and
  cut into 1-cm (½-in) cubes
4 tablespoons salt
2 whole heads of garlic, peeled
5 cm (2 inches) ginger, peeled
6 fresh green chillies, stems and seeds removed
250 ml (9 fl oz) sunflower oil
4 tablespoons mustard seeds
2 tablespoons black peppercorns
1 tablespoon fenugreek seeds
1 tablespoon ground cumin
2 teaspoons ground turmeric
450 g (1 lb) dark muscovado sugar
600 ml (1 pint) cider vinegar

Combine the chopped apples with the salt and set aside for an hour or more. The salt draws moisture from the apple, helping the pieces to keep their shape when cooked.

In a food-processor or blender, combine the garlic, ginger and chillies and whiz to a paste with up to 7 tablespoons of the oil.

Heat the remaining oil in a large, heavy-based pan and, over a medium heat, fry the mustard seeds, peppercorns, fenugreek, cumin and turmeric until the mustard seeds start to pop, being careful not to burn the ground spices. Add the garlic, chilli and ginger paste and fry, stirring, for 5–10 minutes without allowing the paste to catch.

Add the salted apple, sugar and vinegar. Bring slowly to the boil, making sure that the sugar has dissolved completely before simmering the mixture for 2–3 hours so that it thickens slightly.

Transfer to hot, sterilised jars making sure that each has its share of the spicy oil. Le Parfait jars with their rubber-ring seals are ideal for pickles and chutneys containing vinegar, which will corrode the metal lids of standard jam jars.

SWEETLY SPICED CRAB APPLES

Grace Mulligan is probably best known as the presenter of ITV's **Farmhouse Kitchen.** *After ten years of television, Grace continues as a food writer and has added to the many cookery books she published during the series.*

According to Jane Grigson in her wonderful *Fruit Book*, God gave us the crab apple and left the rest to man. More than two thousand varieties of apple are known to have been grown in Britain – very varied in looks, size, texture and flavour, and very versatile in their uses. Some of the more acid sorts fall into a glorious snow when cooked; others hold their shape. Some apples improve when stored and ripened, others are best eaten fresh from the tree.

In my garden I have an old Bramley and the Reverend W. Wilks. My Newton Wonder is a good sharp cooker when harvested early in the season but if left on the tree it makes a really nice eating apple. I also have an Irish Peach, which ripens earlier than any other; like my Worcester Pearmain, it is aromatic and perfumed. I used to use them for toffee apples – their rosy cheeks shone through the toffee, the flesh soft and juicy within.

In our village school, the children used to make 'easy sausages', mixing coarse sausagemeat (from a traditional butcher – not pink paste) with a scattering of finely chopped dessert apple, rolling it up like a swiss roll with very well-floured hands, and going on rolling until the sausage was suitably thick. This was chopped into pieces, chilled a bit in the fridge, then fried in a little oil in a non-stick pan or baked in a hottish oven. Sometimes we made sausage and apple turnovers, adding onion and herbs to the pork and apple mixture, and wrapping the combination in triangles of shortcrust pastry.

Here is something very different. It is difficult to imagine that rock-hard crab apples will soften enough to make a pickle, but they do. The result is excellent with ham, duck and pheasant, and jars of it make lovely and unusual presents.

1 kg (2 lb) white granulated sugar
600 ml (1 pint) white malt vinegar
2 small strips of pared lemon peel
a small piece of cinnamon stick
4 cloves
3 black peppercorns
a tiny piece of dried red chilli
1.5 kg (3 lb) even-sized crab apples (yellow or red)

Put the sugar, vinegar and lemon peel in a roomy pan. Tie the cinnamon, cloves, peppercorns and chilli in the square of muslin or similar cloth. Drop this into the pan. Stir over a low heat until the sugar has dissolved. Wash the crab apples, remove the stalks and clean the stalk dent (I use a cotton bud). Prick each apple three or four times and add to the vinegar mixture.

Simmer until the fruit is soft but not breaking up. Remove the fruit with a slotted spoon and pack into clean warm jars. Discard the lemon peel and muslin bag. Raise the heat under the vinegar left in the pan. Boil hard until the liquid is a light syrup – when it has reduced in quantity by about half. Pour this over the fruit to cover completely. Seal while still hot with whatever lid you choose. Store in a cool dark place. Pickles are traditionally left to mature for two months before using.

NB. Be sure to use vinegar-resistant covers for your jars: metal twist tops with plastic linings, soft plastic snap-ons or hard plastic screw-on types.

PICKLED SWEET LARKS – TRADITIONAL

'Take a stone of Sweet Larks...' Colin Hawke could only remember the beginning, but this simple, yet terrifying statement, etched itself into our memory. You will be as pleased to know as we were that Sweet Larks are a Cornish variety of small apples. In the early 1990s, Colin was working for Cornwall County Council and picked up the challenge to revive interest in Cornish apples. He arranged for funding to support fruit trees and orchards, and helped start Cornwall's first Apple Day. Interest was aroused and the public began to share their knowledge. However, though your imagination might be sparked, it is vital to write things down.

We searched high and low for the particular recipe that came to Colin by word of mouth. Philip McMillan-Browse, horticultural advisor and fruit tree expert, remembers it from long ago, but we have Barry Champion, head gardener at the National Trust's Trelissick Garden to thank for the more restrained recipe below. Quantities may be varied to taste, as is usually the case with recipes passed down the generations. Margaret Wilson's recipe which follows elaborates on this tradition, but her recipe has precise weights, which may give you confidence to experiment.

The West Country has a rich orchard heritage dominated by apples. Cider is one way of extending their life, pickling is another, it seems rarely practised now but it is worth experimenting especially in years of abundance. Cornwall has specific varieties, such as Sweet Larks and Chacewater Longstem, which are small apples with long stalks, perfect for pickling.

Requirements:
1 quart of Malt Vinegar
2lbs of sugar
Cloves
1 clean sample of sweet larks

Scoop the eyes out of the apples and replace with one or two cloves in each socket.

Gently heat the vinegar adding the sugar until it is dissolved and then bring it to the boil.

Add the apples and simmer until the flesh is just softening.

Place the apples gently in the pickling jar and cover with the remaining syrup.

Store with a closed top.

Eat with bread and butter and perhaps, cream.

DEVONSHIRE APPLE & CUCUMBER PICKLE

Margaret Wilson is the author of The New Cornish Cookbook, *and* Vegetarian Recipes from the West Country. *She has over thirty years experience as a chef, and runs Tinhay Mill Guest House and restaurant in Lifton, Devon. This recipe is taken from* The Devonshire Cookbook *(Bossiney Books).*

Fills 6–8 jars

2 kg (4 lb) cucumber, peeled and thinly sliced

25 g (1 oz) salt

450 g (1 lb) shallots, peeled and finely chopped

2 thin green chillies (take out seeds if you want to reduce the heat)

1 kg (2 lb) Devonshire cooking apples, which will hold a little of their shape

2 tablespoons lemon juice

2 teaspoons whole grain mustard

1 teaspoon ground turmeric

1 teaspoon freshly grated ginger

1 teaspoon freshly grated nutmeg

600 ml (1 pint) white wine vinegar

225 g (8 oz) muscovado sugar

Prepare the cucumbers and sprinkle them with the salt. Leave them in a covered colander with a heavy weight on top for one and a half hours. While they are draining, chop the shallots and chillies. Peel, core and finely chop the apples, then drizzle them with the lemon juice to stop the apples going brown.

In a large pan put together all the spices, vinegar, apples and sugar, and bring to the boil. Stir with a wooden spoon until all the sugar has dissolved and then continue cooking for 2 minutes. Add the cucumbers, shallots and chillies, bring back to the boil and continue boiling for 2 minutes. Put the pickle into the hot, sterilised jars. Cover and seal straight away, then store in a cool, dark place for 3 weeks.

WASSAIL CUP

Henrietta Green has led the way in championing quality local and regional, sustainably and traceably produced food and drink. The success of her award-winning Food Lovers' Guide to Britain *has led to a website: www.foodloversbritain.com. This recipe is taken from* The Festive Food of England.

At one time in England and Wales most houses kept a wassail bowl ready throughout the Christmas festivities for unexpected guests. Carol singers carried their own cups to dip into the drink after they had sung.

Wassail comes from the Old English 'wes hal', meaning 'be thou whole', and drinking from the wassail bowl was an expression of friendship; the custom of drinking your neighbour's good health probably came to be called toasting after the 'sippets' or pieces of toast floating in the wassail bowl.

Even the apple trees were wassailed to ensure a good crop. In Devon, on Twelfth Night, some farmers and their families still gather around the trees with shotguns or pots and pans. They make a tremendous noise to raise the sleeping Tree Spirit and to frighten away the demons. Then a toast is drunk and, for extra luck, some of the branches are dipped into the wassail bowl.

Pitmaston Pine Apple – a tiny juicy apple with a hint of pineapple – is my favourite of the thousands of British apples. With its yellow-hued skin and miniature shape, it looks so appealing piled high on the Christmas table or bobbing up and down in the wassail bowl.

Serves 8
8 small eating apples
32 cloves
1.5 litres (2½ pints) brown ale
300 ml (10 fl oz) sweet sherry
a pinch each of ground cinnamon, ginger and nutmeg
the grated zest of 1 lemon
2 slices of bread, toasted

Slit the skin around the centre of the apples and stud them with cloves. Put them in to a baking tin with 150 ml (½ pint) brown ale and bake in the oven at 200°C/400°F/gas mark 6 for about 30 minutes, basting occasionally.

Heat the remaining brown ale with the sherry, spices and lemon zest and simmer for about 5 minutes.

Cut the toast and the baked apples into small pieces, and serve the punch very hot, in a punchbowl, with the pieces floating on top.

LOCAL APPLES & CHEESE

Simone Sekers used to write for the Sunday Telegraph. *She now writes for the* Blackmore Vale Magazine, *which does more than the average local paper to promote local food and local distinctiveness.*

Since I wrote about the pairing of local apples and cheese for the first edition of *The Apple Source Book*, I have moved from Surrey to the Somerset/Dorset border. This is an area of lush pasture producing one of the best cheeses in the world, and of orchards bravely resisting development.

The local apples are mainly cider varieties; you can kid yourself that some might be considered for stewing or baking, but bite into an apple fresh from the tree and it puckers your mouth. The making of cider transforms these apples into something that has a natural affinity with the traditional farmhouse Cheddar – nutty, fragrant, deeply satisfying – which is perfect, too, with one of the area's few eating apples, Beauty of Bath.

Of all the Cheddar-makers I still rate Montgomery's highest; I've been buying their cheese for almost forty years, and I remain loyal, apart from occasional flirtations with Westcombe's and Green's.

There are plenty of new cheeses too, especially those made by the Bath Soft Cheese Company (try the mellow Wife of Bath) and their disciples Whitelake Cheeses, who make a semi-soft goat's cheese puzzlingly named after a Cheshire landmark, called White Nancy. This is very good with a piece of Dorset Apple Cake and a glass of Pomona, Julian Temperley's rich blend of cider brandy and apple juice, made at Burrow Hill, Kingsbury Episcopi.

Heck's Cider, near Street, are now making perry too, light and sophisticated and delicious with the revived Dorset Blue Vinny cheese, brought back from extinction by Mike Davies on his farm at Stock Gaylard.

Best of all, go to Sturminster Newton's Cheese Festival, held in September, and taste cheese and cider all day long.

THE BLENHEIM ORANGE

Gail Duff was once a writer and broadcaster involved in food and country matters. Now she runs Traditional Arts Development South East (TRADS), basing education and community arts projects on the music, dances and traditions of England.

In late November, I start looking for a supplier of Blenheim Orange apples for Christmas. They are rarely available in the shops but there are still farms near us in Kent where one or two Blenheim Orange trees flourish in the corner of an orchard.

The Blenheim Orange is one of the largest dessert apples. It can sometimes be quite difficult to hold in one hand. It is usually round and regularly shaped, yellow and streaked with red on the side that faced the sun – a perfect picture-book apple. The flesh is crisp and juicy, sweet, yet with a refreshing tang, rather like sweet cider.

This quality has made Blenheim one of the few dual-purpose apples. Its flesh will cook down rather like a new-season's Bramley, and in 1831 it was described as a 'large noble sauce apple'.

Why do I like Blenheim at Christmas? Because Christmas and the days afterwards tend to bring with them very large lunches. The only thing I can usually face in the evening is an apple and some cheese. I like that apple to be special, and also substantial. I never cut apples up. I always munch them as though I have scrumped them from an orchard. Eating two small apples means you get too much core: a large one is a much better treat, especially if it is of a variety unavailable at other times of the year.

At Christmas it is a tradition in our house to buy a small truckle of Cheddar and large amounts of Stilton and Blue Cheshire. So, on Christmas night, after everyone has gone home or to bed, I curl up in an easy chair with a large Blenheim apple, a piece of each of my three cheeses and a glass of port. Bliss.

PICK YOUR OWN

BRAMLEY

COX   RUSSET

KIDDS ORLEANS

PEARS   J GRIE

CHS ROSS JONAGO

ASHMEADS KERN

ALL AT £1.00 K

GAZETTEER OF LOCAL VARIETIES

Apples do not breed true, which is why grafting is used to keep a variety in existence. Each pip brings something new. Apples found by the wayside, crossed by scientists or dabbled into existence by gardeners and horticulturalists may have a commercial or domestic future. We know where many apples hail from or where they were popularly grown, and for the sake of both nature and culture it is important to keep them, and the knowledge that surrounds them, alive and well in their place.

Perhaps two and a half thousand dessert and culinary varieties, and hundreds more cider apples, have been documented as growing in Britain and Ireland. The following list is not comprehensive: histories are in progress, geographies are contested, names are multiplied or confused, 'lost' varieties are still turning up, new apples are being created. Court Pendu Plat is thought to be a Roman apple; Catshead has no known birthplace but is first mentioned in 1629. They are both probably very old, which suggests that they should be cared for. Tom Putt is claimed by various south-western counties and sometimes has local names – and it is not alone.

We have referred here to historic counties because they have been around for a long time and help to link with pre-1970s references, but there may be inconsistencies. Consider: Colnbrook, birthplace of the Cox's Orange Pippin, was traditionally in Buckinghamshire but since the 1970s has found itself variously described as being in Middlesex, Surrey and Berkshire. Our first attempt in 1990 to discover the provenance of apples by county turned up a few sources, but little local activity. Now there are projects across the country, and many old varieties have been tracked down.

This gazetteer owes much to the work of the Victorians, as exemplified by Drs Hogg and Bull and their *Herefordshire Pomona*, and more recently to Joan Morgan and Alison Richards whose books, especially *The New Book of Apples*, have inspired as well as comprehensively informed. We hope that they, and those whose names follow, will take our unidentified quotation as the homage it signifies: Harry Baker; John Bultitude; Edward Bunyard; Raymond Bush; G.R.D. Child; Liz Copas; Roy Genders; the Irish Seed Savers Association; George Morris; Craig Pillans; Virginia Spiers, Mary Martin and James Evans; Phil Rainford; Roseanne Sanders; Muriel Smith; H.V. Taylor; R.R. Williams, whose books and help have been invaluable.

Thank you to the Armagh Orchard Trust; Brogdale Horticultural Trust; Cornwall County Council; Kevin Croucher, Cumbrian Fells and Dales Leader; Cheshire Landscape Trust; Cheshire Orchards Project; Cornwall Orchards Project; East of England Apples and Orchards Project; Gloucestershire County Council; Gloucestershire Orchard Group; Keith Goverd; Marcher Apple Network; Charles Martell; National Orchards Forum; Northern Fruit Group; Orchard Link (Devon); Orchards Live, North Devon; R.V. Rogers, Yorkshire; June Small, Charlton Orchards; Somerset County Council, Staffordshire Orchards Initiative; Symondsbury Apple Project; Andrew and John Tann, and many more.

The Gazetteer is not intended to be comprehensive: it is offered to excite your interest, provoke you into searches of your own, and as a challenge to care for the local distinctiveness of orchards. Keeping varieties in their own place, with the working knowledge that they demand, is the surest way to ensure their continuity.

KEY

Dessert, eating apples (e)
Culinary, cooking apples (c)
Cider apples (ci)
Dual use (d)

ENGLAND

BEDFORDSHIRE

Ballard Beauty (e) • **Bedfordshire Foundling** (c) • **Desse de Buff** (c) • **Earl Cowper** (c) • **Hambling's Seedling** (c), *Dunstable* • **Neild's Drooper** (d), *from Woburn Park 1915* • **Pam's Delight** (e) • **Queenby's Glory** (e), *probably from Wrest Park, Silsoe 1949.*

The famous Laxton Bros nurseries of Bedford raised many varieties in the late-nineteenth and early-twentieth centuries: **Beauty of Bedford** (e) • **Duchess of Bedford** (e) • **Laxton's Advance/Advance** (e) • **Laxton's Early Crimson** (e) • **Laxton's Epicure/Epicure** (e) • **Laxton's Exquisite/Exquisite** (e) • **Laxton's Favourite** (e) • **Laxton's Fortune/Fortune** (e), *raised in 1904 from Cox's Orange Pippin x Wealthy; light*

green mottled red, with creamy white, soft, sweetly scented flesh and a hint of banana • **Laxton's Herald** (e) • **Laxton's Leader** (e) • **Laxton's Pearmain/Bedford Pearmain** (e) • **Laxton's Peerless** (e) • **Laxton's Pioneer/Pioneer** (e) • **Laxton's Rearguard** (e) • **Laxton's Reward** (e) • **Laxton's Royalty** (e) • **Laxton's Superb** (e) • **Laxton's Triumph** (e) • **Laxton's Victory** (e) • **Lord Lambourne** (e), *considered the best-flavoured apple the nurseries produced, Worcester Pearmain x James Grieve; no good for damp districts; attractive – greenish-yellow flushed with broken red stripes; sweet, juicy and delicious* • **Owen Thomas** (e), *named after Queen Victoria's gardener, a fruit enthusiast* • **September Beauty** (e) • **Epicure, Fortune, Superb, Triumph**, *all noted by Lawrence D. Hills as having frost-resistant blossom.*

BERKSHIRE

Breedon Pippin (e), *raised by the Rev. Dr Symonds Breedon around 1801 at Bere Court, Pangbourne, from cider pomace* • **Delectable** (e) • **Frogmore Prolific** (c), *Windsor, popular in London market gardens in nineteenth century* • **Guelph** (e) • **John Standish** (e), *raised by John Standish of Ascot around 1873. Attractive fruit, scarlet dotted with russets on pale green; flesh white, juicy and firm; little flavour* • **John**

Waterer (c), *Twyford* • **Miller's Seedling** (e), *once widely grown in Berkshire, raised by James Miller at Speen Nursery, Newbury in 1848; attractive pale greenish-yellow fruit three-quarters mottled with pink; crisp, juicy, sweet and refreshing; bruises easily* • **Shinfield Seedling** (e), *from Reading University, Shinfield in 1944* • **Sunrise** (e) • **Welford Park Nonsuch** (e) • **Winston** (e), *raised by W. Pope, nurseryman at Welford Park in 1920; aromatic and sweet* • **Charles Ross** (d), *best known of this head gardener's thirty varieties raised at Welford Park, Newbury; cross between Peasgood's Nonsuch and Cox's Orange Pippin, good on chalky soils; a very handsome fruit, yellowish-green, light red flush of broken red stripes; crisp, sweet and flavoursome. Other varieties raised by Charles Ross include:* **Charles Eyre** (c) • **Encore** (c), *keeps until May; Warner's King x Northern Greening: bright yellowish-green with red flush; slices remain intact when cooked* • **Hector MacDonald** (c), *named after Ross's friend the war hero 'Fighting Mac'* • **Houblon** (e) • **Mrs Phillimore** (e) • **Paroquet** (e) • **Peacemaker** (e) • **Renown** (e) • **Rival** (e), *reputedly the juiciest of all the older varieties; Peasgood's Nonsuch x Cox's Orange Pippin; attractive, with pale yellowish-green flushed with brilliant scarlet and a slight bloom.*

BUCKINGHAMSHIRE

Arthur Turner (c), *raised by Charles Turner of Slough and first exhibited in 1912; a large handsome fruit with a very attractive blossom; polished green with pinky-orange flush; creamy white flesh, soft and juicy; better than Bramley for a small garden* • **Ball's Pippin** (e), *introduced 1923 by nurseryman J.C. Allgrove of Langley* • **Cox's Orange Pippin** (e,) *was planted as a pip from Ribston Pippin x Blenheim Orange in 1825 by Richard Cox, retired brewer in Colnbrook, and introduced by Small & Son in 1840; three-quarters of all dessert fruit grown commercially in Britain today are Cox's; the original tree, which grew in Cox's garden, blew down in a gale in 1911; difficult to grow – susceptible to disease; likes well-drained soils and doesn't thrive north of a line from Birmingham to the Wash; richly aromatic, very juicy; 'All characters so admirably blended and balanced as to please palate and nose as no other apple can do', .H.V. Taylor* • **Cox's Pomona** (d), *raised by Richard Cox around the same time as Cox's Orange Pippin* • **Feltham Beauty** (e) • **Grenadier** (c), *origin unknown, recorded in 1862, exhibited by nurseryman Charles Turner but promoted later by nurseryman George Bunyard of Maidstone, Kent; excellent for baking* • **Langley Pippin** (e), *raised in the late 1800s by the family firm of James Veitch, a*

Chelsea nurseryman; Veitch's son opened a nursery at Langley, near Slough • **Reverend W. Wilks** (c), *raised in the Veitch nurseries in Langley, Slough, by J. Allgrove, from a Ribston Pippin x Peasgood Nonsuch; in 1904 named after the vicar of Shirley, Surrey, who was secretary of the Royal Horticultural Society, from 1888–1919; 'A universal winner on the show bench'; fruits often weigh over 2lbs; flesh creamy-white, quite sweet and well-flavoured; cooks to a pale yellow froth.* • **Small's Admirable** (c), *raised in about 1859 by Mr F. Small, nurseryman at Colnbrook.*

CAMBRIDGESHIRE

Chivers Delight (e), *'Well-known for its good nature and excellent flavour'; raised by John Chivers at Histon, north of Cambridge, around 1920; attractive yellow-green, mottled with red; creamy white juicy flesh, slightly acid and sweet* • **Cockett's Red/Marguerite Henrietta/One Bite**, *from 1910 or earlier, once grown around Wisbech; used by toffee-apple manufacturers* • **Cottenham Seedling** (c) • **Emneth Early/Early Victoria** (c), *raised by William Lynn of Emneth, recorded 1899; once grown around Wisbech for jam production; earliest of the cookers; pale yellow when ripe; superb flavour; juicy, sharp but mild; cooks to a golden froth; good baked but too insubstantial for pies* • **Green Harvey** (d),

recorded 1930 from W.G. Kent in Wisbech, but may be from 1813 • **Histon Favourite** (e), *raised by John Chivers of Histon in mid-nineteenth century and widely grown later in the century throughout the county* • **Jolly Miller**, *rediscovered in a roadside survey by the East of England Apples and Orchards Project in 2005* • **Morley's Seedling** (c) • **Haggerstone Pippin** (e) • **Lady Hollendale** (e), *grown in East Anglia for Wisbech markets in 1920s and 1930s* • **Lord Peckover** (e), *Wisbech before 1926* • **New Rock Pippin** (e) • **Red Victoria** (c) • **St Everard** (e) • **Thoday's Quarrenden** (e), *found in 1949 by Ralph Thoday at Reedground Farm, Willingham, Cambridge* • **Wayside** (e), *a seedling of Charles Ross, from the garden of Miss Cunningham's home, Wayside, on Huntingdon Road, Cambridge in 1930.*

CHESHIRE

Arthur W. Barnes (c), *raised by N.F. Barnes, head gardener to the Duke of Westminster at Eaton Hall, Chester, in 1902* • **Bee Bench** (e) • **Bostock Orange** • **Burr Knot** (c), *named after the burrs at the base of branches, which can root (this type of tree is known as a 'pitcher'); its history is not clear but the variety was recorded in 1818 in England; also known as Bide's Walking Stick, after a Mr Bide who cut a branch in or around 1848 from a tree in Cheshire as a* walking-stick, which he stuck into the ground in his garden in Hertfordshire where it rooted. • **Celia** • **Chester Pearmain** • **Chester Pippin** • **Eccleston Pippin** (d), *raised or found before 1883 by N.F. Barnes, head gardener at Eaton Hall, Chester* • **Elton Beauty** (e), *raised in Ince Orchards, Chester by N.W. Barritt, introduced 1952* • **Gooseberry Pippin** • **Grange's Pearmain** (d), *raised before 1829 by James Grange, a market gardener of Kingsland, Middlesex, then introduced by Dickson's of Chester* • **Hazelby's Seedling** • **Lord Derby** (c), *raised by Mr Witham, first recorded in 1862; grows well on wet, clay soils; bright green, turning yellow when ripe; slices stay intact when cooked; 'Flesh cooks to an attractive deep claret colour, and is especially delicious sweetened with brown sugar.'* • **Millicent Barnes** (e), *raised around 1903 by N.F. Barnes, head gardener at Eaton Hall, Chester* • **Minshull Crab/Lancashire Crab** (c), *from Minshull village, original tree described in 1777; grown in Lancashire for cotton towns, including Manchester* • **Moston Seedling** • **Open Heart** • **Rakemaker** • **Rose of Sharon** • **Royal Seedling** • **Rymer** • **Shaw's Pippin** • **Sure Crop** (d), *from nurseryman, Clibrans, in 1905* • **Wareham Russet** • **Watlingford Pippin** • **Windsor Castle** • **Withington Welter**.

COLLOGET PIPPIN

CORNWALL

Ben's Red (e), *Helston, seedling of Devonshire Quarrenden; will grow on its own roots; such trees are known as 'pitchers'* • **Blackmoor Pippin** (c) • **Blackamoor Red** (c) *Tamar Valley* • **Blackrock** (c) • **Bottlestopper** (c) • **Box Apple** (e) • **Breadfruit** (d), *Rezare* • **Captain** (John) Broad (ci), *once popular in Cornwall; old trees found at Golant, near Fowey, in 1982* • **Captain Smith** (d), *Golant* • **Chacewater Longstem** • **Colloggett Pippin/Lawry's Cornish Giant** (d ci), *Tamar valley, Colloggett Farm, near Botus Fleming; as a single variety makes good 'champagne' cider and fine dumplings* • **Coombe Rough Cooker** • **Cornish Aromatic** (e), *first recorded in 1813, but thought to be much older; tolerates wet climate, good cropper; greeny-yellow flushed with orange-red, slightly russeted; excellent quality apple, crisp, nut-like aromatic flavour* • **Cornish Garden** • **Cornish Gilliflower** (e), *thought to have* been discovered in a cottage garden near Truro about 1800; first described in 1813 but may be older; remarkable for its rich aromatic, honey-like flavour; 'Gilliflower' may derive from 'Girofle' in old French, meaning 'clove-apple' as it is supposed to give off a clove-like fragrance when cut • **Cornish Honeypin** (e) • **Cornish Longstem** (c) • **Cornish Mother** (e), *traditionally grown in Wadebridge; perhaps American Mother from Massachusetts, USA, 1844* • **Cornish Pine** (e), *raised in Exminster, Devon, before 1920; tender, pineapple-flavoured flesh; grown in Devon and Cornwall in 1920s and 1930s* • **Cornish Spice** • **Cornish Wine Apple** • **Dufflin** (ci), *grown in West Country, may be from Taunton in Somerset* • **Duke of Cornwall** • **Early Bower** (e) • **Fairfield/ Millet** • **Glass Apple/Snell's White** (e), *raised before 1934 by Mr Snell, market gardener in Radland Mill, St Dominick, Tamar Valley* • **Grow-bi-nights** (ci) • **Gulval Seedling** • **Hamlyn** (ci) • **Hocking's Green** (d), *raised by Mr Hocking around 1860 at Illand Farm, Coad's Green* • **Hocking's Yellow** (d) • **Hodge's Seedling** (c), *attributed to J. Vivian, Hayle, in 1876* • **Improved Keswick** (d), *Tamar Valley* • **Jimmy Oliver** • **John's Delight** • **John's Early Eater** • **King Byerd** (d) • **Lady's Fingers** (d), *Calstock* • **Lawry's No. 1/Lord Grosvenor** (c) • **Lizzy** (ci) • **Long Keeper** (e), *Luckett* • **Lord of the Isles** (ci) • **Manaccan**

Primrose (d), *Lizard* • **Meil D'Or/Dawe Apple/ Door/Miles Dawe/Male D'Or/Mary Dawe** (e), *thought to be an old Cornish variety; may be same variety as Oslin (aka Arbroath Pippin), Scotland; pale greenish-yellow with orange flush, russet dots and patches; very sweet, honey-flavoured* • **Onion Moonstreak** • **Onion Red-streak** (c), *Tamar Valley* • **Pascoe's Pippin** (e) • **Pear Apple/Pig's Nose** (e) • **Pig's Nose I** (e), *West Cornwall* • **Pig's Nose III** (e), *Coad's Green* • **Pig's Snout** (e ci), *Callington* • **Pitcher** (e) • **Plympton King** • **Plymton Pippin** (d), *Tamar Valley* • **Queenie** (e), *Tamar Valley (St Dominick); dark red with faint darker stripes and pale dots; flesh stained red, sweet and aromatic* • **Polly/ Polly White Hair** (d) • **The Rattler** (d) • **Scilly Pearl** (d), *Isles of Scilly* • **Sidney Strake/Tom Putt** (c ci), *grown throughout West Country in nineteenth century; also known in West Midlands* • **Sops in Wine/Pendragon** (e) • **Snell's White/ Glass Apple** (d), *Tamar Valley* • **Sweet Larks** (c), *an apple for pickling* • **Sweet Merlin** (d) • **Tan Harvey** (ci), *Tamar Valley; trees found in 1980 by James Evans* • **Tommy Knight** (e ci), *St Agnes; described in 1946* • **Tregonna King** (d), *Wade-bridge* • **Trenance Cooker** • **Tresillian Seedling** • **Turnip** • **Venus Pippin** (d), *thought to have been known as Plum Bidy around Launceston* • **White Quarantine** • **Wintergreen** (c).

CUMBERLAND

Autumn Harvest (d), *recorded in 1950 as coming from Westmorland, but may be the same variety as recorded in Cumberland in 1934* • **Carlisle Codlin** (c) • **Forty Shilling** (e), *Thirsby; around 1800* • **Greenup's Pippin/Green Rolland** (c), *(may also be Yorkshire Beauty/Cumberland Favourite and Red Hawthornden) discovered in the garden of a Mr Greenup, shoemaker, in Keswick, in eighteenth century; widely grown in the Borders 100 years ago and in Yorkshire* • **Harvest Lemon**, *rediscovered in a farm orchard near Carlisle in 2004, dates from 1934* • **Keswick Codlin** (c), *introduced commercially by John Sander, nurseryman of Keswick; widely grown in Yorkshire where it was the farmer's favourite; can be used for tarts as early as July. See* Lancashire • **Margil** (e), *planted around Crosthwaite in 1800s but probably from France; taken to south east in seventeenth century* • **Nelson's Favourite** (c), *Kendal, first recorded 1958, but sounds older.*

DERBYSHIRE

Beeley Pippin (e) • **Belledge Pippin** (e), *Derby* • **Lamb's Seedling** (d), *raised around 1866 by Joseph Lamb, head gardener at Meynell Langley* • **New Bess Pool** (e), *Stanton-by-Dale before 1850; thought to be a seedling from Bess Pool* •

Mrs Wilmot, *named after resident of Langley Mill in the nineteenth century; the twentieth-century bus station was built on the old orchard* • **Newton Wonder** (c), *very late flowering, escapes most frosts and a prolific apple; popular until recently for its shiny golden-yellow skin with attractive red stripes and flush; 1840 pounds once recorded from one tree; one account suggests it was discovered growing out of the thatched roof of the Hardinge Arms, a pub in King's Newton, but another that it was raised by Mr Taylor of King's Newton, from Dumelow's Seedling x Blenheim Orange in about 1887; traditionally used in mincemeat and stuffings at Christmas; cooks to yellow fluff; good in salads as not overwhelmed by dressing; keeps until Easter when acceptable as dessert fruit.*

COURT PENDU PLAT

DEVONSHIRE

All Doer (d), *Lapford* • **Allspice** • **Barum Beauty** • **Beech Bearer** (ci) • **Beef Apple** (c), *Dunsford*

• **Bewley Down Pippin/Jackson's/Crimson King/ John Toucher's** (c ci), *East Devon/Somerset* • **Bickington Grey/Gray** (ci) • **Billy Down Pippin**, *Membury* • **Billy White** • **Bluey Sweet** (ci) • **Bowden's Seedling**, *may be same as the 1826 US apple Jonathan* • **Brown's Apple** (ci), *Staverton* • **Butterbox** (ci) • **Cerit** • **Coleman's Seedling** (ci) • **Court Royal/Sweet Blenheim/Improved Pound** (ci), *from Somerset/Devon border* • **Crediton Fair** • **Crimson Costard** • **Crimson Victoria**, *from Shute, Axminster* • **Dawe** • **Devon Crimson Queen/Queenie** (e), *from Launceston, Cornwall, 1953, once popular in the Tamar Valley* • **Devonshire Buckland** (c) • **Devonshire Court Pendu** • **Devonshire Quarrenden** (e). *a very old variety mentioned in 1678; may take its name from Carentan, an apple-growing district in France; it was extensively grown in the West Country where it tolerates the rain; beautiful polished dark crimson flush; refreshing flavour of straw- or loganberries* • **Devonshire Queen** • **Devonshire Redstreake** • **Devonshire Striped** • **Devonshire White Sour** • **Docker's Devonshire** • **Dufflin** (ci) • **Ellis Bitter** (ci), *Crediton area, perhaps Newton St Cyres, in the nineteenth century* • **Endsleigh Beauty,** *Torquay, 1906* • **Fair Maid of Devon** • **Farmer's Glory Devon** (d) • **French Long Stem** (ci) • **Golden Ball** (ci) • **Golden Bittersweet** (e ci) • **Goring** (ci), *Tedburn*

St Mary • **Great Britain** (ci) • **Green Bittersweet** (ci) • **Halstow Natural** (ci), *Tedburn St Mary* • **Herefordshire Pippin**, *Axminster* • **Hollow Core** (d), *Exeter, 1880* • **Improved Keswick** (d), *Tamar Valley* • **Johnny Andrews** (ci), *Tedburn St Mary* • **Johnny Voun** (e), *Barnstaple* • **Killerton Sharp** (ci) • **King Manning** (ci) • **Langworthy/Sour Natural/Wyatt's Seedling** (ci) • **Limberland**, *Landkey* • **Lincoln Horn** • **Listener** (e ci), *Landkey and East Buckland* • **Long Bite** • **Lucombe's Pine** (e), *raised at Lucombe Pince & Co, Exeter, in about 1800* • **Lucombe's Seedling/Newquay Prizetaker** (e), *raised at Lucombe Pince & Co, Exeter, in 1831* • **Major** (ci) • **Michaelmas Stubbard** • **No Pip** (c), *East Morley, Whiteway, Chudleigh, in 1913* • **Northwood** (ci), *Crediton eighteenth century* • **Oaken Pin/Taylor** (e), *Exe Valley pre-1876, grown widely on Exmoor in 1920s* • **Paignton Marigold** (ci), *Paignton pre-1834* • **Payhembury** (c ci) • **Pear Apple** (e) • **Pear Pine** (ci) • **Peter Lock** (d), *found in Dean Woods, Buckfastleigh, in early 1800s by villager Peter Lock* • **Pine Apple Russet of Devon** (e), *1920; indistinguishable from Sussex Peach/Pomeroy of Herefordshire* • **Plum Vite**, *pre-1800* • **Plympton Pippin** (d), *Tamar Valley* • **Pocket Apple/ Hangdown/Horner's Handydown** (ci), *may be from Glastonbury, Somerset, but widely grown in north Devon where it is known as Pocket Apple* •

Ponsford (c ci) • **Pound** (ci) • **Pyne's Pearmaine** • **Quarry Apple**(c) • **Queen's** (e), *Veitch nursery, Exeter, 1883* • **Quench** • **Rawlings** (ci) • **Red Jersey/Loran Drain/Loyal Drain/Loyal Drong** • **Red Ribbed Greening/Cornish Pine** • **Red Robin** • **Reine des Pommes** • **Reynold's Peach**, *1880s* • **Saw Pit**, *Cornwall or Devon, Tamar Valley* • **Sercombe's Natural** (ci) • **Slack Ma Girdle** (ci) • **Sops in Wine/Pendragon** (c ci), *Devon/Cornwall* • **Spicey Pippin** (ci) • **Spotted Dick** (ci) • **Star of Devon** (e) • **Stockbearer** (c), *Landkey* • **Stone Pippin** (ci) • **Sugar Bush** (e ci), *Lapford* • **Sugar Loaf** (e) • **Sugar Sweet** (ci) • **Sweet Alford** (ci) • **Sweet Bay** (ci) • **Sweet Bramley** (ci) • **Sweet Cleave** (d), *may be same as Flanders Pippin, from Barnstaple, pre-1831* • **Sweet Cluster** (ci) • **Sweet Coppin** (ci), *early eighteenth century, particularly Exeter area* • **Tale Sweet** (ci), *Tale* • **Tamar Beauty** • **Tan Harvey** (ci), *Tamar Valley, trees found in 1980 by James Evans* • **The Rattler** (d) • **Thin Skin** • **Tom Potter**, *may be same as Tom Putt and Devonshire Nine Square; thought to have come from Gittisham near Honiton in 1700s* • **Tremlett's Bitter** (ci), *late nineteenth century, Exe Valley* • **Upton Pyne** (d), *raised by nurseryman Pyne of Topsham, introduced in 1910; excellent baked, cooks to a purée* • **Veitch's Perfection** • **Venus Pippin/Plumderity/Plum Biddy** (c), *around 1800, Tamar Valley* • **Welling-**ton (ci), *perhaps from Killerton* • **Whimple Queen** (ci) • **Whimple Wonder** (ci) • **White Close Pippin** (ci) • **White Sheep's Nose** (ci) • **Whitesour** • **Winter Peach** (d) • **White Quarrenden** (e), *raised in about 1918, Hanniford Nursery, Paignton* • **Winter Queening/Winter Pearmain** (d) • **Woolbrook Pippin** (e), *raised at J.H. Stevens & Son 1903, Woolbrook Nursery, Sidmouth* • **Woolbrook Russet** (c), *Woolbrook Nursery. See also* Cornwall *for other varieties of the Tamar Valley.*

DORSET

Bewley Down Pippin/Jackson's (c ci), *propagated in the late nineteenth century by John Toucher of Bewley Down, Chardstock; once popular in neighbouring farms of Somerset and Devon* • **Buttery d'Or** (c ci), *a sharp apple from west Dorset* • **Golden Ball** (ci), *also known as Polly, Netherbury area* • **Iron Pin** (d) • **Melcombe Russet** (e), *nineteenth century, Melcombe Bingham; delicious, tangy, pineapple-like* • **Mollyanne** (e), *raised in Bournemouth* • **Profit Apple/Poor Man's Profit** (c), *recorded in about 1826, and thought to be extinct until rediscovered by Harry Baker at Kingston Maurward Apple Day, Dorset, 2001; a mid-season cooking apple with a unique flavour, no sugar needed; once grown widely in the Cranborne Chase area; origin Devon* or Dorset • **Syme's Seedling** (c) • **Tom Putt/ Sidney Strake** (c ci), *contested Dorset, Somerset or Devon; also planted widely in the West Midlands* • **Tyneham Apple** (c ci) • **Warrior** (d), *from eighteenth or nineteenth century; once thought extinct.*

WARRIOR

DURHAM

Barnard's Baker • Gateshead Lemon Pippin • Hebburn Red • Teesdale Nonpareil • Woolaton Pippin.

ESSEX

Acme (e), *raised by Seabrook & Sons, Boreham, with many other varieties in the 1930s and 1940s* • **Amber** (e), *Seabrook & Sons, Boreham* • **Braintree Seedling** (e), *raised in Braintree by Mrs Humphreys 1930* • **Chelmsford Wonder** (c), *raised by William Saltmarsh, a mechanic, near Chelmsford, 1870* • **D'Arcy Spice** (e), *discovered in a garden at the Hall, Tolleshunt d'Arcy, south west of Colchester around 1785; cultivated by nurseryman John Harris in 1848; well-known in East Anglia, it does best in sandy soil and dry areas; needs a hot, dry summer to gain its richly spicy flavour, which improves with storage; not a beauty, but well worth growing; yellowish-green with pale brown-grey russet; firm, sweet, nutty, aromatic and juicy* • **Discovery** (e), *raised by Mr Dummer in Langham in about 1949; thought to be Worcester Pearmain x Beauty of Bath; introduced in 1963; crimson with pale yellow russeted dots; crisp, juicy and fairly sweet; good in fruit salad* • **Doctor Harvey/Harvey** (c), *first recorded in Essex in seventeenth century; noted by most early commentators; 'A faire, greate, goodly apple and very well relished'; common winter apple in Norwich market in 1820s; variously claimed by Norfolk and Cambridgeshire* • **Edith Hopwood** (e), *Hornchurch* • **Eros** (e) • **Excelsior** (c), *Seabrook & Sons, Boreham* • **Flame** (e), *Seabrook & Sons, Boreham* • **Francis** (e), *Mr Thorrington, Hornchurch, 1925* • **Garnet** (e), *Seabrook & Sons, Boreham* • **George Cave** (e), *is perhaps the best early apple often ready before the end of July; thought to be a chance seedling nurtured by George Cave of Dovercourt about 1923; attractive yellowy-green flushed with crimson; crisp, juicy* and slightly acid • **Grey Pippin** (e), *found in 1980 by John Tann, may be same as late nineteenth-century variety* • **Maldon Wonder** (e), *Heybridge* • **Monarch** (c), *Seabrook & Sons, Boreham, grown in Essex for London markets in twentieth century, and popular during the Second World War as needs little sugar; good for grilling and cooks to a juicy fluff* • **Montfort** (e), *Woodford Green* • **Nolan Pippin** (e), *from Mrs Woodward of Colchester around 1920* • **Opal** (e), *Seabrook & Sons, Boreham* • **Pearl** (e), *Seabrook & Sons, Boreham* • **Queen** (c,) *a handsome exhibition variety raised by Mr Bull, a farmer of Billericay, in 1858, from pips of an apple bought at the local market; whitish-green flushed with flecks of red; distinctly acid, tender and very juicy; cooks to a yellow purée* • **Rosy Blenheim** (e), *Hornchurch* • **Ruby (Seabrook)** (e), *Seabrook & Sons, Boreham* • **Ruby (Thorrington)** (e), *Hornchurch* • **Seabrook's Red** (e), *Seabrook & Sons, Boreham* • **Stanway Seedling** (c), *first found in Essex, 1899* • **Sturmer Pippin** (e), *raised by nurseryman Ezekiel Dillstone in Sturmer, near Haverhill, around 1800 from Ribston Pippin x Nonpareil; his grandson Thomas took some scion wood with him to Australia; widely grown in Tasmania and imported to the UK – 800,000 bushels in 1934; susceptible in Britain to canker and needs a hot summer to produce its full flavour; high in* vitamin C; firm, fresh, juicy with a hint of gooseberry; excellent with cheese • **Sunburn** (e), *Hornchurch* • **Topaz** (e), *Seabrook & Sons, Boreham* • **Tun Apple** (e) • **West View Seedling** (e), *discovered by Mr Rainbird of Billericay in 1932* • **Woodford** (c), *origin unknown; pretty dark pink blossom.*

GLOUCESTERSHIRE

Ampney Red (e), *from Ampney Crucis* • **Ansell/Ancell** (ci) • **Arlingham School Boys** (d) • **Ashmead's Kernel** (e), *a long-standing favourite in the gardens of west Gloucestershire; raised by Dr Ashmead in the early 1700s; one of the finest aromatic apples with a sweet-sharp taste, reminiscent of fruit drops; yellowish-russeted flesh, firm, crisp, juicy, sugary* • **Ballast Apple** (ci) • **Barnett's Beauty** (e) • **Ben Lans** (d) • **Berkeley Pippin/Dafferton** (e) • **Blood Royal/Winter Quarrenden** (d) • **Box Kernel** (d), *thought to be from Box Farm, Awre* • **Bromsbury Crab** • **Brown French** (ci), *from May Hill* • **Bunch Apple** (ci) • **Bushy French** (c) • **Cambridge Quinning/Cambridge Queening** (d) • **Captain Kernel/Captain Nurse/Nurses Kernel/Chaceley Kernel/Chexley Kernel/Chatley's Kernel** (e), *may be the latter which is a Worcestershire variety; continuing research by Gloucestershire Orchards Group* • **Chaxhill Red** (c ci e), *may be same as*

Duni Red, raised 1873 by Mr Bennett of Chaxhill near Westbury-on-Severn • **Corse Hill/Corset Hill/Cosset Hills** (ci), *from Corse, near the border with Worcestershire* • **Councillor** (ci), *Berkeley area* • **Dent's Favourite** (d) • **Duke of Bedford** (c) last heard of in 1884 has been discovered recently in south Gloucestershire • **Dymock Red/Peggy's Apple** (ci) • **Eden** (e), *E.J. Ingleby, Forest and Orchard Nurseries, Falfield, 1948* • **Elmore Pippin** (e) • **Evans' Kernel** (d), *found in Ruardean* • **Fawke's Kernel** (d), *19th century at Dymock by the Fawke family; once common in Dymock* • **Fletcher** (ci), *may be from Shepperdine* • **Flower of the West** (e), *Minsterworth* • **Fon's Spring** (e) • **Foxwhelp** (ci), *old variety; old trees, large with upright limbs, can still be found in parts of Herefordshire and Gloucestershire; irregular shape, with markedly striped flush* • **Forest Styre** • **Gilliflower of Gloucester** (e), *Saul* • **Gloucestershire Costard** (d) • **Gloucester Royal** (e) • **Gloucestershire Underleaf** (d) • **Green Two Year Old** (d) • **Green Underleaf** (d) • **Gypsy Red** (ci), *Oldbury-on-Severn* • **Hagloe Crab** (ci), *may be from seventeenth century from Hagloe near Awre* • **Hard Knock** (d), *Oxenton* • **Hens' Turds** (ci), *Rodley* • **Holbrooke** (d), *Berkeley area* • **Hunt's Duke of Gloucester** (e) • **Jenny Lind** (e), *named after the Swedish opera singer, who died locally in 1887* • **Kenchy Pippin** (ci), *Hal-more, near Berkeley* • **Kernel Underleaf** (d) • **Kill-Boys** (ci), *Oldbury-on-Severn area* • **King Apple** (d), *Bollow, near Westbury-on-Severn* • **Lake's Kernel** (e) • **Leathercoat/Leatherjacket** (d) • **Lemon Pippin of Gloucestershire** (e) • **Lemon Roy** (d) • **Lodgemore Nonpareil/Clissold Seedling** (e), *Lodgemore, near Stroud* • **Longney Russet** (e) • **Longstalk** (ci) • **Maiden Blush** • **Martins Kernel** (e), *Arlingham* • **Molly Kernel** (d), *Oldbury-on-Severn* • **Morning Pippin** • **Newpools** (d) • **Nine of Diamonds** (ci) • **Nine Squares** (d) • **Norman Pippin** (d), *lower Berkeley Vale* • **Northland Pippin/Seedling** (e), *Tetbury* • **Old Tankard** (ci) • **Over Apple** (ci) • **Overleaf** (ci) • **Overton Red** (d) • **Parlour Door** (d), *found growing in the Apperley area and nearer Gloucester* • **Pear Box** (d), *Oldbury-on-Severn* • **Pedington Brandy** (ci), *found growing near Oldbury-on-Severn* • **Phelp's Favourite** (d) • **Port Wine Pippin/Port Wine Kernel** (d) • **Pretty Beds** (d), *Arlingham peninsula* • **Prince's/Princess Pippin** • **Puckrup Pippin** (e) • **Red Styre** (ci) • **Red Two Year Old** (d) • **Reynold's Kernel/Reynold's Crab** (d) • **Rhead's Reinette** (e) • **Rock Kernel** (ci) • **Rose of Ciren** (e) • **Royal Turk** (c), *Churchdown* • **Severn Bank/Lassington (c)** • **Sheep's Nose of Oldbury** (d) • **Shepperdine Silt/Black Tanker** (ci) • **Shilling** (e) • **Shopground Kernel** (d) • **Siddington Russet** (e) • **Spout Apple** • **Stanway**

Kernel (d) • **Sugar Pippin** (d) • **Taynton Codlin/ Cow Apple** (c ci), *Taynton* • **Tewkesbury Baron** (e) • **Tippetts** (d) • **Transparent Codlin** (d) • **Upright French** (ci) • **Vallis** • **Welsh Druid** (d), *southern Forest of Dean* • **White Flanders** • **White Styre/Wick White Styre** (ci) • **Yellow Styre** (ci).

HAMPSHIRE & ISLE OF WIGHT

Beauty of Hants (e), *raised at Bassett some time before 1850 from a Blenheim Orange; flesh creamy white, fine-textured, soft and juicy; taste similar to parent* • **Benenden Early** (e), *raised around 1945 by J.J. Gibbons of Southampton; introduced by Stuart Low Ltd of Benenden in Kent* • **Easter Orange** (e), *introduced by Hillier & Sons of Winchester,1897* • **Hambledon Deux Ans** (c), *an old garden variety, from Hambledon in the mid-eighteenth century; can keep for two years; 'A large noble apple, richly flavoured but rather deficient in juice'* • **Howgate Wonder** (c), *raised in 1916 by Mr Wratton, Howgate Lane, Bembridge, Isle of Wight; light green, flushed, striped with orange-brown; popular for exhibitions on account of its size; fruit a little flavourless in comparison with the Bramley, but holds some of its shape when cooked* • **Isle of Wight Pippin** • **James Saunders** • **Jersey Beauty** (e), *Newport, Isle of Wight* • **King George V** (e), *raised in Bembridge, Isle of Wight, in late nineteenth century* • **Lady Thorneycroft** • **Lord Kitchener** • **Sir John Thorneycroft** (e), *Isle of Wight* • **Steyne Seedling** (e), *Isle of Wight.*

BROWN SNOUT

HEREFORDSHIRE

Adam's Pearmain (e), *contested Norfolk/ Herefordshire, where it was once known as Hanging Pearmain* • **Ball's Bittersweet** • **Bringewood Pippin** • **Brown Snout** • **Byford Wonder** (c), *introduced by Cranston's Nurseries in 1894, named after the riverside village near Hereford* • **Cherry Pearmain** • **Collington Big Bitters** (c ci) • **Colwall Quoining** (e) • **Cowarne Red** • **Credenhill Pippin** • **Crimson Quoining/ Crimson Queening/Herefordshire Quoining/ Herefordshire Queening** (c ci e), *recorded 1831 thought to be much older* • **Doctor Hare's** (c) •

Downton Pippin (e) • Gennet Moyle (c ci), *grown in fifteenth century, Archenfield area* • Golden Harvey/Brandy Apple (e ci), *may be same as Round Russet of early 1600s* • Herefordshire Beefing (c), *'beefing' may come from 'beau fin'; dried in cooling bread ovens (as Norfolk Beefings) sold for gifts in London; dark red, dry apple* • Herefordshire Russet (c e), *see* Worcestershire • King's Acre Bountiful (c), *introduced in 1904 by Kings Acre Nursery in Hereford* • King's Acre Pippin (e), *King's Acre Nurseries, Hereford, 1899; Sturmer Pippin x Ribston Pippin; well worth growing despite its unattractive appearance; dull green, slightly flushed with brownish-red; a firm, juicy, coarse-textured fruit with a rich aromatic flavour, good in salads* • Lady's Finger of Hereford • Lord Hindlip (e) • New German (d) • Pig's Nose Pippin (e), *described by Hogg 1884* • Pomeroy of Herefordshire/Sugar Apple (e), *thought to be a very old variety* • Prince's Pippin/King of the Pippins/Golden Winter Pearmain/Shropshire Pippin (ci e), *origins debatable, synonyms or thought by some to be different varieties; common in farm orchards in Herefordshire where known as Prince's Pippin* • Redstreak (ci), *thought to have been raised at Holme Lacy by Lord Scudamore in the early 1600s; became well known, establishing the county's reputation for cider; the original variety was a*

pitcher – would grow its own roots from cuttings • Sam's Crab (c ci e) • Skyme's Kernel (ci), *old cider variety, promoted and distributed by the Woolhope Naturalist's Field Club in the late 1800s* • Stoke Edith Pippin (e), *recorded 1872, possibly from Foley estate in Stoke Edith* • Strawberry Norman • Ten Commandments (ci e), *exhibited 1883, named after the ten red spots around core; small dark red apples* • Tillington Court (c), *Burghill Fruit Farm* • Tyler's Kernel (c), *thought to be an old county variety, exhibited in 1883* • Wormsley Pippin.

HERTFORDSHIRE

Beauty of Waltham • Brownlees' Russet (e), *'a favourite russet for the private gardener', well known for its beautiful blossom, a rich cerise-pink; introduced by William Brownlees, nurseryman, Hemel Hempstead around 1848; green, russeted with brown-yellow ochre; pleasantly nutty taste, aromatic* • Bushey Grove (c) • Crimson New Wonder (c), *Holywell Fruit Farm* • Dawn (e) • Edwin Beckett • Fairie Queen (e) • Gavin (e), *raised by Gavin Brown at the John Innes Institute, Bayfordbury, 1956* • Golden Reinette (e), *'The farmer's greatest favourite'; widely grown around London in the 1850s and 'reputed to be at its perfection in Hertfordshire'; likes light, warm soil; 'An old, deservedly* esteemed table apple' • **Hitchin Pippin** (e), *from Hitchin area, 1896* • **Hormead Pearmain** (c) • **Lane's Prince Albert** (c), *'It is a lovely fruit which takes the highest polish of any variety'; named by nurseryman Henry Lane, who planted it out immediately after cheering the Queen and Prince Albert through Berkhamsted in 1841; the original tree was still in a high street garden in 1936; Russet Nonpareil x Dumelow's Seedling; bright green, slightly flushed with red stripes; juicy, brisk, acid; good for pies* • **Voyager** (e), *Barnet* • **Warners King** (c), *early known as King Apple; Mr Warner, a small nurseryman of Gosforth, Yorkshire, gave it to nurseryman Thomas Rivers of Sawbridgeworth, Hertfordshire, who renamed it; yellowish-green, crisp, juicy; cooks well to a sharp purée. See also* Kent, Yorkshire • **Winter Hawthornden** (c) • **Young's Pinello** (e), *raised by Miss Young, Letchworth, around 1930s. From River's Nursery, Sawbridgeworth:* **New Hawthornden** (c) • **Prince Edward** (e) • **Rivers' Early Peach** (e) • **Rivers' Nonsuch** (e) • **Rivers St Martins/St Martins** (e) • **Thomas Rivers** (c).

HUNTINGDONSHIRE

Hunter's Majestic (d), *raised before 1914 by Miss E. Balding of Upwell* • **Huntingdon Codlin** • **Murfitt's Seedling** (c), *dates from 1883, probably introduced by nurserymen Wood and Ingram of Huntingdon; once popular in Cottenham and Histon* • **Perfection** (e), *is grown around Heath Farm, Bluntisham; bred for the owners by Seabrook & Sons, Boreham, Essex in the 1960s.*

KENT

Bascombe's Mystery (e), *since mid-nineteenth century* • **Beauty of Kent** (c), *popular cooking apple in late Victorian period as very large, but considered 'too ugly for present-day commercial use'; greenish-yellow flushed, speckled and striped with red; tender flesh, very juicy and deliciously perfumed; cooks to pretty lemon-coloured slices* • **Bountiful** (c), *raised by Dr Alston at East Malling Research Station (EMRS) in 1964. EMRS was established as the fruit research station in 1921. Different rootstocks can limit the size of a tree – M when referring to a rootstock remembers Malling and MM Merton Malling where they were developed* • **Bow Hill Pippin** (c), *raised by A.S. White of Bow Hill, Maidstone; introduced by G. Bunyard & Co., a Maidstone nursery in 1893* • **Brenchley Pippin** (e) • **Castle Major** (c) • **Christmas Pearmain** (e), *introduced by G. Bunyard & Co., Maidstone* • **Cobham** (e) • **Colonel Vaughan/Kentish Pippin** (e), *thought to be from Kent in the late seventeenth century* • **Diamond Jubilee** (e), *Rainham* • **Falstaff** (e), *EMRS* • **Faversham Creek** (c), *found* by H. Ermen in the 1970s growing by Faversham Creek, copes with salt water • **Fiesta/Red Pippin** (e), *EMRS, 1972* • **Flower of Kent**, *see also Isaac Newton's Tree*, Lincolnshire • **Folkestone** (e), *from Chandler & Dunn in Ash, 1964* • **Foster's Seedling** (c), *introduced by G. Bunyard & Co., Maidstone* • **Fred Webb** (e) • **Gascoyne's Scarlet** (d), *raised by Mr Gascoyne of Sittingbourne; one of the best varieties for chalk; originally grown for decoration – owing to its attractive fruit – carmine red on milky green; sharp, subtle, perfumed flavour; breaks up, but not completely, when cooked* • **George Neal** (d), *raised by Mrs Reeves of Otford, in 1904; introduced by R. Neal & Sons of Wandsworth, 1923; greeny-yellow with small patches of russet; excellent flavour, crisp, juicy and acid, some claim it the best for apple sauce, slices remain intact on cooking* • **Gooseberry Apple** (c), *recorded in 1831, grown in Kent for London markets in nineteenth century* • **Granny Giffard** (d), *raised by Mr Swinherd, head gardener to John Swinford of Minster, near Margate* • **Great Expectations** (e), *raised by Mr A. Nobbs, a retired gardener, in about 1945; introduced by Hammond Stock Nursery of Bearsted* • Greensleeves (e) • **Grenadier** (c), *origin unknown; recorded in 1862; exhibited by nurseryman Charles Turner of Slough but promoted later by G. Bunyard & Co.,*

Maidstone • **Jester** (e) • **Jupiter** (e), *EMRS, 1966* • **Kent/Malling Kent** (e), *EMRS, 1949* • **Kentish Fillbasket** (c) • **Kentish Quarrenden** (e) • **Lady Sudeley** (e), *raised in about 1949 by Mr Jacobs, perhaps bailiff of Sharsted Farm, Chatham and named Jacob's Strawberry; he then took the apple to Petworth with him; renamed by G. Bunyard & Co., Maidstone* • **Lamb Abbey Pearmain** (e), *raised in 1804 by Mrs Mary Malcolm, Lamb Abbey, Dartford, from a pip* • **Mabbott's Pearmain** (e), *grown around Maidstone in nineteenth century* • **Maid of Kent** (c) • **Maidstone Favourite** (e), *G. Bunyard & Co., Maidstone* • **Michaelmas Red/Tydeman's Michaelmas Red** (e) • **Orange Goff** (c) • **Polly Prosser** (e) • **Red Devil** (e), *raised in 1875 by H.F. Ermen of Faversham* • **Robin Pippin** (e), *Brenchley* • **Rossie Pippin** (c), *G. Bunyard & Co., Maidstone* • **Smart's Prince Arthur** (c), *grown around Maidstone for London markets in nineteenth century* • **South Park** (e), *raised by W. Barkway, a gardener at South Park, Penshurst, 1940* • **St Alban's Pippin** (e) • **Sunset** (e), *raised 1918 by G.C. Addy of Ightham; sweet, yellowish flesh, tasty and juicy* • **Suntan** (e), *EMRS, 1956* • **Tydeman's Early/Tydeman's Early Worcester** (e), *raised by H.M. Tydeman, EMRS, 1929* • **Tydeman's Late Orange** (e), *EMRS, 1930; frost-resistant blossom* • **Wanstall Pippin** • **Warner's**

King/Killick's Apple (c), *contested: known in 1700s as King Apple; may have originated in an orchard in Weavering Street, Maidstone, where known as Killick's Apple. See also* Hertfordshire, Yorkshire.

LANCASHIRE

Duke of Devonshire (e), *'quite indispensable for late use'; raised in 1835 by Mr Wilson, gardener to the Duke of Devonshire at Holker Hall, Cark-in-Cartmel; rich, nutty flavour; firm, fairly juicy and slightly acid; at its best well after Christmas* • Florence Bennett (d), *raised by Mrs F. Bennett of Crosby Green, West Derby, Liverpool, in the 1950s, possibly from an apple core thrown on to the garden rubbish heap* • Gold Medal/Ryland Surprise (d), *raised in Preston around 1882 by nurseryman Mr Troughton* • Golden Spire/Tom Matthews (ci), *found in Lancashire in about 1850 and introduced by Richard Smith, a nurseryman in Worcester, also widely grown in Scotland* • Hargreaves Greensweet • Harvest Festival (c), *Lytham* • John Huggett (d), *Grange-over-Sands* • Hutton Square • Keswick Codlin (c), *a distinctly angular and rather ugly apple found growing behind a wall at Gleaston Castle near Ulverston some time before 1793. See* Cumberland • Lady's Delight (d), *1851; tree has drooping habit; juicy, sweet, brisk* • Lady's Finger of Lancaster • Lancashire Scotch Bridget, *exhibited from Preston in 1893, and reputed to be slightly later in maturing than Scotch Bridget (c); thought to have originated in Scotland but popular around Lancaster in nineteenth century and still found there; grows in difficult conditions* • Lange's Perfection (d), *Wigan, 1983* • Lord Clyde (c), *raised by nurseryman B.W. Witham of Reddish and appeared in catalogue in 1866* • Lord Suffield (c), *raised by Thomas Thorpe, a weaver from Middleton, near Manchester; first distributed in 1836; unsuitable for areas with high rainfall; the largest of the codlin-type cooking apples; once grown widely as an early cooker; crisp, juicy and acid; cooks well, breaking up completely; frothy baker* • Minshull Crab/Lancashire Crab (c), *from Minshull village, recorded in 1777; was grown for the cotton towns; hard apple, keeps shape when cooked, and makes stiff purée; very sharp taste* • Pott's Seedling (c), *raised by Samuel Potts of Ashton under Lyne; made popular by nurseryman John Nelson of Rotherham, who found it in a garden in Oldham in the 1850s* • Proctor's Seedling (d), *raised in the Longbridge area* • Sowman's Seedling (c), *raised in 1914 at the County Agricultural Station at Hutton by A.G. Sowman; cooks to a sharp froth, needing sugar* .

LEICESTERSHIRE

Annie Elizabeth (d), *named in memory of his daughter (who died aged thirteen months) by Samuel Greatorex; raised from a Blenheim Orange pip sown in a nearby allotment in Knighton in 1857; introduced by Harrison's Nurseries of Leicester in 1868; one of the best varieties for a small garden, being of 'upright growth, sturdy and compact in habit, making an excellent pyramid'; brilliant red and yellow when ripe, handsome ribbed fruit; an excellent late kitchen apple, but good for dessert if kept until spring; good for stewed apple since the slices remain intact* • **Barnack Orange** (e), *Belvoir Castle* • **Belvoir Seedling** (e), *Belvoir Castle* • **Betty Geeson** (c), *raised from a pip by Betty Geeson, near Belvoir; small; late keeper* • **Dumelow's Seedling/Wellington** (c), *known further north as May Day Apple; a Victorian favourite; accredited to Mr Dummeller, a farmer at Shakerstone; original tree was flourishing in 1800; thought to be a seedling from Northern Greening. 'The wood of the young shoots is of a dark brown colour thickly covered with large greyish white dots, which readily distinguish this from almost every other variety'; yellowish-green; useful in mincemeat for its sharp, acid flavour; keeps without shrivelling until March or later* • **Marriage Maker** (e) • **Prince Charles** (e), *Burbage* • **Queen Caroline** (c), *raised by Mr T. Brown, nurseryman, at Measham, Ashby-de-la-Zouch, in early nineteenth century.* • **St Ailred** (e).

LINCOLNSHIRE

Allington Pippin/South Lincoln Beauty (d), *raised by Thomas Laxton at Stamford 1884* • **Broadholme Beauty** (c), *raised in 1980 in Broadholme near Lincoln by plantsman Henry Lovely from a James Grieve pip; keeps well, needs no sugar* • **Brown's Seedling** (d), *raised at Brown's Nurseries at Stamford, 1874* • **Dewdney's Seedling/Baron Wolseley** (c), *raised by Mr Dewdney, Barrowby, 1850* • **Doctor Clifford** (c), *a seedling found by William Ingall, a nurseryman of Grimoldby near Louth, around 1898* • **Ellison's Orange** (e), *raised by the Rev. C. Ellison at Bracebridge, Lincoln, and by Mr Wipf, gardener at his brother-in-law's home at Hartsholme Hall in 1904, from a Cox's Orange Pippin x Calville Blanc; grows best in dry, well-drained soils; crisp and juicy; known for its lovely aniseed flavour when ripe; good in salads and apple dumplings; excellent cropper; Lawrence D. Hills points to its frost-resisting blossom* • **Grimoldby Golden** (c) • **Herring's Pippin** (e), *spicy and strongly perfumed* • **Holland Pippin/Kirton Pippin** (d) • **Hunthouse Pippin**, *raised by Rowson Bros Nursery, West Torrington Gardens, 1883; rediscovered*

2004. See also Yorkshire • **Ingall's Pippin** (e) • **Ingall's Red** (e) • **Isaac Newton's Tree** (c), *also known as the Gravity Tree; one of Britain's oldest varieties, descended from the tree that grew in Isaac Newton's garden at Woolsthorpe Manor near Colsterworth, in the 1660s and reputedly gave Newton his Great Idea; fruit 'distinctly ugly' – pale silvery-green, greenish-yellow flushed with red; flesh soft, coarse-textured and sub-acid; cooks to a purée; thought to be Flower of Kent first mentioned in 1629* • **Peasgood's Non-such** (d), *'one of the largest and most handsome of all apples'; planted by Mrs Peasgood as a child in the 1850s in Grantham from a Catshead Cod-lin pip; needs a warm, rich, well-drained soil to flourish; pale yellowish-green overlaid with orange and bright red stripes; 'A very handsome highly coloured apple, whose beauty gives it a place on the dessert table though its best virtues are culinary'; good for baking and dumplings* • **Philadelphia** (d), *Alford* • **School Master** (c), *thought to be from a seedling of a Canadian apple grown in the garden of Stamford Old Grammar School around 1855; but may be from Herefordshire* • **Sleeping Beauty** (c), *grown for Boston markets* • **Stamford Pippin** • **Uland** (c), *raised by William Ingall, 1922.*

MIDDLESEX and LONDON

Fearn's Pippin • **Grange's Pearmain** (d), *raised by James Grange, a market gardener of Kingsland* • **Hounslow Wonder** (c), *introduced by nurseryman Spooner from Hounslow, recorded 1910* • **London Pearmain** (e) • **Morris's Russet** (e), *raised by Morris, a market gardener in Brentford; described 1851* • **Royal Jubilee/ Jubilee/Graham** (c), *raised by John Graham of Hounslow; introduced in 1887, Queen Victoria's Golden Jubilee year; once recommended for frost pockets, and still popular in foothills of the Alps* • **Scarlet Pearmain** (e), *introduced in about 1800 by Bell, the land steward of the Duke of Northumberland, Syon House* • **Storey's Seedling** (e), *raised by R.O.C. Storey of Northolt Park, 1927.*

NORFOLK

Adam's Pearmain (d), *Norfolk or Herefordshire; a scion of wood from Norfolk sent to the Horti-cultural Society in London in about 1826* • **Admiral/Gloria** (e), *pip brought from Japan by Mr A.K. Watson in 1921, once known as Togo of Upton* • **Banns** (e), *Norwich, 1928* • **Baxter's Pearmain** (d), *introduced by George Lindley, nurseryman of Catton near Norwich, in 1821* • **Captain Palmer** (e), *a seedling found at Gissing, near Diss, 1900* • **Caroline** (e), *from Blickling Hall Gardens near Aylsham 1822; named after*

Lord Suffield's wife • **Doctor Harvey**, *perhaps originated Essex but claimed as one of Norfolk's long popular varieties; may be named after the master of Trinity Hall, Cambridge,during the 1830s* • **Dutch Mignonne** (d), *probably from Holland, introduced by Thomas Harvey of Catton Hall, near Norwich in 1771* • **Emneth Early/Early Victoria** (c), *See* Cambridgeshire • **Five Crowned Pippin/London Pippin** (c), *may be from 1500s; known in Somerset as London Pippin; sold in Norfolk in 1700s as a Norfolk variety* • **Golden Noble** (c), *discovered in old orchard in 1820 by Patrick Flannagan, gardener at Stowe Hall near Downham Market; one of the best cookers; acid, with a distinct fruity flavour; good for baking, and in apple pie; cooks to a golden froth.* • **Green Roland** (d), *probably from East Norfolk in 1800s; known as Norfolk Green Queen, and also as John Shreeve around Rollesby; planted during Second World War throughout East Anglia during sugar rationing as it needs little in cooking, forms a firm purée* • **Hanworth Codlin** (c), *a seedling found in gardens of Hanworth Rectory, near Aylsham, 1948* • **Happisburgh** (e) • **Harling Hero** (e), *raised or found by Frank Claxton, a local game dealer from East Harling, near Attleborough, before 1930s* • **Herbert Eastoe** (d), *New Costessey* • **Horsford Prolific/Queen Anne** (e), *found in the vicarage garden in Horsford in early 1900s by the* Rev. Mr Mountford • **Hubbard's Pearmain** (e), *dates from 1796; popular in Norfolk gardens in nineteenth century* • **Hunter's Majestic** (d), *raised before 1914 by Miss E. Balding of Upwell, near Wisbech; grown commercially in Fens in 1930s* • **Jordan's Weeping** (e), *found growing in a garden at Horning, in the Broads, before 1940* • **Leeder's Perfection** (d), *Postwick* • **London Pearmain** (e), *origin 1848; rediscovered growing at Attleborough Hall in 1948* • **Look East** (e), *raised by Ormonde Knight at Yaxham, 1971; named after the regional BBC television news programme* • **Lynn's Pippin** (e) • **Norfolk Beauty** (c), *raised by Mr Allan, head gardener at Lord Suffield's Gunton Hall, near North Walsham, 1901; acidic, breaks up in cooking* • **New Costessey Seedling** (e) • **Norfolk Beefing** (c), *earliest record thought to be 1698, Mannington Hall estate; may be from France or Holland; keeps well – ' its season is January to June' – purple flush; good for drying and baking; best eaten after Christmas; very popular in Norwich up to the 1950s, sold as Norfolk Biffins by bakers – after dinner sweetmeats (dried slowly in cooling bread ovens and then coated in melted sugar)* • **Norfolk Royal** (d), *found as a chance seedling at Wright's Nurseries, North Walsham, 1908; shiny crimson and yellow skin; crisp, juicy, sweet, and cooks well* • **Norfolk Royal Russet** (e), *found* growing in garden of the Rev. C. Wright at Burnham Overy Staithe and introduced in 1983 • **Park Farm Pippin** (e), *named after the farm on the Royal Sandringham Estate* • **Pine Apple Russet** (e), *known in East Anglia since early eighteenth century* • **Red Ellison** (e), *found in fenland orchards of Harold Selby at Walpole St Peter, 1948; a sport of Ellison's Orange* • **Red Falstaff** (e), *East of England Apples and Orchards Project suggests found growing at Woodlands Orchard, Ashill, near Swaffham, by Michael Rowe in 1989, while Joan Morgan believes it to be a sport of Falstaff from East Malling Research Station, Kent* • **Robert Blatchford** (c), *raised by F. Chilvers at Hunstanton, introduced 1914; named after the editor of the* Clarion *who taught at High House School, Heacham* • **Sandringham** (e), *raised by Mr Penny, head gardener at Sandringham, 1883* • **St Magdalen/Magdalene** (e), *found growing at Wiggenhall St Mary, near Downham Market, in the orchards of H. Bridge, 1890* • **Striped Beefing** (c), *found growing in garden of Crowe of Lakenham near Norwich, 1794, by George Lindley, nurseryman* • **Summer Broaden/Norfolk Summer Broadend** (c), *recorded in 1800s as popular in cottage gardens* • **Vicar of Beighton** (c) • **Winter Majetin** (c) • **Winter Broaden**.

NORTHAMPTONSHIRE

Attractive • **Barnack Beauty** (e), *very sweet, juicy yellow flesh* • **Eady's Magnum** (c), *raised around 1908 by Miss D.A. Eady of Wellingborough* • **Lord Burghley** (e), *found in waste ground at the gardens of Burghley Park, southeast of Stamford, in 1834; Bunyard considered it one of the best dessert apples; firm, yellow, juicy with a slight pine flavour* • **Thorpe's Peach** (e), *raised by Miss Goodwin at E. J. Thorpe's nursery in Brackley, in 1899.*

NORTHUMBERLAND

Mrs Lakeman's Seedling (d), *raised around 1900, Stocksfield.*

NOTTINGHAMSHIRE

Baron Ward (c) • **Beauty of Stoke** (c), *raised by Mr Doe, head gardener at Rufford Abbey; recorded in 1889* • **Bess Pool** (e), *found in a wood by the young Bess Pool; she brought some fruit home and they were admired so much that grafts were taken; first recorded in 1824; grown commercially by J.R. Pearson in Chilwell whose son reported 'before the duty on foreign apples was taken off it would fetch 5s a peck, now (1869) I am selling it at 1s the peck'; milky, mottled red and green; good to eat at Christmas with cheese* • **Bramley's Seedling** (c), *most* famous and popular culinary apple; planted as a pip by Mary Ann Brailsford between 1809 and 1813, in Church Street, Southwell, later owned by Mr Bramley; the original tree survives in the garden today; cuttings were taken by Henry Merryweather and sold commercially from 1876; the tree 'is very hardy, and its blossoms seem able to withstand the spring frosts so successfully that it is a constant and regular bearer'; bright green; rich in vitamin C; juicy, strong flavour; the premium English cooking apple – excellent for pies • **Domino** (c), *grown around Southwell in the nineteenth century* • **Mead's Broading** (c), *from Pearson's nursery, Chilwell, described 1884* • **Pickering's Seedling** (e), *nineteenth century* • **Radford Beauty** • **Winter Quarrenden** (e), *introduced by Pearson's nursery, Chilwell, recorded 1896.*

OXFORDSHIRE

Blenheim Orange (d), *r*aised around 1740 by a tailor, George Kempster, in his garden in Manor Road, Old Woodstock, 'within ten yards of walls of Blenheim Park'; the tree was a local landmark – coaches would pause in passing and 'thousands thronged from all parts to gaze on its ruddy ripening orange burden; then gardeners came in the springtime to collect the much coveted scions'; known as Kempster's Pippin

until 1811, 'a lasting monumental tribute and inscription to him who first planted the Kernel from whence it sprung'; slow to come into crop, sweet, nutty flavour; excellent for apple charlotte; Roy Genders calls it 'one of the great apples of England' • **Foulkes' Foremost** (e), *raised by F. Foulkes of Headington, Oxford, in 1938* • **Farmer's Glory** • **Hanwell Souring** (c) • **Old Fred** • **Pheasant's Eye** • **Sergeant Peggy** • **Eynsham Challenger** (c) • **Eynsham Dumpling** (c) • **Jennifer** (e) • **Jennifer Wastie** (e) • **Oxford Beauty** (e) **Oxford Conquest**, **Oxford Hoard** (e) • **Oxford Sunrise** (e) • **Oxford Yeoman** (c) • **Peggy's Pride** (e) • **Red Army** (e), *Raised by W.F. Wastie of Eynsham, 1920s–40s.*

RUTLAND

No varieties known specific to the county.

SHROPSHIRE

Bringewood Pippin • **Brookes's** (e), *recorded 1820* • **Lady's Fingers** • **Shropshire Pippin/ Prince's Pippin/King of the Pippins/Golden Winter Pearmai**n (e ci), *debate over origins, only DNA analysis will reveal if actually different varieties; common in farm orchards in the area, for eating and cider making* • **Moss's Seedling** (e), *raised around 1955 by Chetwynd End nurseries, in Newport* • **Onibury Pippin** (e), *raised* by Thomas Andrew Knight in early nineteenth century, Onibury being the location of one of his nurseries • **Springrove Codlin** • **Yellow Ingestrie** (e), *raised by the famous pomologist Thomas Andrew Knight of Downton Castle around 1800, and named after the seat of the Earl of Talbot (in Staffordshire); Cox's Orange Pippin x Golden Pippin; crisp, juicy, yellow flesh; 'A delightful little yellow apple for September'.*

SOMERSET

Ashton Bitter (ci), *raised by G.T. Spinks 1947 at Long Ashton Research Station (LARS), Bristol, which specialised in cider varieties* • **Ashton Brown Jersey** (ci), *tested at LARS, early 1900s* • **Backwell Red** (ci), *grown around Backwell in early 1900s* • **Bailbrook Seedling** (e) • **Bartletts Glory** (e) • **Bath Russet** • **Beauty of Bath** (e), *from Bailbrook; introduced by Mr Cooling of Bath in 1864; a good early eater, pale greenish-red, mottled; pleasantly sharp, sweet and juicy* • **Beauty of Wells** (e) • **Bell Apple/Sweet Sheeps Nose** (c ci), *Somerset/Devon border* • **Black Dabinett** (ci), *from Kingsbury Episcopi* • **Black Vallis/Redskins** (ci), *from North Somerset* • **Bridgwater Pippin** (c) • **Broadleaf Jersey** (ci) • **Brockhead** (e) • **Burrow Hill Early** (ci), *from Burrow Hill, Kingsbury Episcopi, 1980s; thought to be older variety, but name unknown* • **Cadbury/**

Pounset/Royal Wilding (ci) • **Camelot** (ci) • **Cap of Liberty** (ci) • **Cheddar Cross** (e), *raised at LARS by G.T. Spinks in 1916* • **Chisel Jersey** (ci), *from Martock, in the nineteenth century, popular locally for cider until 1970s* • **Churchill** (ci) • **Cider Lady's Finger** (ci) • **Coat Jersey** (ci), *from Coat, Martock; recorded 1950s* • **Congresbury Beauty** (ci), *almost lost but trees propagated from last survivor, now growing in Congresbury Millennium Orchard* • **Coopers Favourite** • **Court of Wick** (e ci), *arose at Court of Wick, Claverham, near Yatton, introduced 1790, although thought to be older; said to be a hardy variety, widely grown in nineteenth century, particularly in West Country* • **Dabinett** (ci), *from a hedge in Middle Lambrook found by William Dabinett in the early 1900s; still a popular cider apple* • **Dorset** • **Dove** (ci), *from Glastonbury; recorded 1899 but probably older* • **Dufflin** (ci), *from Taunton; grown in West Country; sweet cider* • **Dunkerton's Late** (ci), *raised near Glastonbury in 1940s* • **Dunnings Russet** • **Early Blenheim** (d) • **Early Red Jersey/Port Wine/Royal Jersey II** (ci) • **Even Pearmain** • **Exeter Cross** (e), *developed at LARS in 1924 by G.T. Spinks* • **Fair Maid of Taunton/Moonshines** (ci), *probably from Taunton, now found around Glastonbury* • **Fill Barrell** (ci), *from Woolston, near Sutton Montis, late nineteenth century* • **Gatcombe** (ci) •

Gin (ci) • **Glory of the West** (d) • **Golden Farmer** (e) • **Golden Knob** (e), *from late 1700s at Enmore Castle; popular with Kentish market gardeners supplying London markets in the nineteenth century* • **Golden Wonder** • **Green Pearmain** (c) • **Hagloe Pippin** (e) • **Hangdown/Horners/ Hangydown/Pocket Apple** (in Devon) (ci), *known in Somerset and north Devon* • **Harry Master's Jersey** (ci), *thought to have been raised by Harry Masters in Yarlington in the late nineteenth century* • **Hereford Cross** (e), *raised at LARS in 1913 by G.T. Spinks* • **Hoary Morning** (d), *thought to be from Somerset; first recorded in 1819; large and handsome but evocative name not matched by taste* • **Honeystring** (ci) • **Kingston Black** (ci), *probably from Kingston, near Taunton, in mid– late nineteenth century; now a favourite for cider– making* • **Lambrook Pippin** (ci) • **Lambrook Seedling** (e) • **Langworthy/Wyatt's Seedling** • **Le Bret** (ci) • **Long Tom** (d), *probably from north– west Somerset* • **Lorna Doone** (c ci), *Wellington* • **Mealy Late Blossom** (c) • **Melmouth** (e), *raised around the 1890s by Florence Melmoth in Yeovil* • **Merchant Apple/Merchant Apple of Ilminster** (e), *thought to be from Ilminster; described 1872 by Mr Scott, nurseryman* • **Morgan Sweet** (ci) • **Neverblight** (ci) • **Newport Cross** (e), *raised at LARS in 1920 by G.T. Spinks* • **Nine Square** (e) • **Norton Bitters** (ci) • **Pennard Bitter** (ci),

propagated by Mr Heal of Glastonbury in late nineteenth century; named after West Pennard • **Plymouth Cross** (e), *raised at LARS in 1916 by G.T. Spinks* • **Pomeroy of Somerset** (e) • **Porter's Perfection** (ci), *from orchard of Charles Porter, East Lambrook, in nineteenth century; now found around Martock* • **Pyleigh** • **Radcliffe Nonpariel** (e) • **Red Jersey** (ci • **Red Worthy** (ci) • **Rich's Favourite** • **Royal Jersey** (ci) • **Royal Somerset** (c ci), *described in 2001, but not same variety as that described 1884 by Hogg* • **St Ivel Pippin** • **Shoreditch White** (e ci), *known by Hogg 1884* • **Silver Cup** (ci) • **Somerset Lasting** (c), *Devon/Somerset border* • **Somerset Redstreak** (ci), *probably from Sutton Montis area* • **Stable Jersey** (ci), *probably from Shepton Mallet, thought to be an old variety* • **Stembridge Cluster** (ci), *from Mr Sam Duck of Stembridge, Kingsbury Episcopi* • **Stembridge Jersey** (ci), *probably from Stembridge* • **Stoke Red** (ci), *thought to be from Wedmore; also found at Rodney Stoke in 1920s* • **Stubbard** (d) • **Taunton Cross** (e), *raised at LARS in 1919 by G.T. Spinks* • **Taunton Golden Pippin** (e) • **Taunton Nonpariel** • **Taylor's Sweet/Taylor's** (ci). *probably from South Petherton; sold by Porter's nursery there in nineteenth century, thought to be older* • **Tommy Rodford** (ci), *from Kingsbury Episcopi* • **Tom Putt** (c ci), *stories differ: thought to have been raised* by Tom Putt, rector of Trent near Sherborne in the late 1700s, or perhaps by his uncle on the family estate in Gittisham, Devon; also thought to be same as Tom Potter and Devonshire Nine Square of Gittisham, near Honiton, in 1700s; much prized in the West Country and also West Midlands until early twentieth century • **Vallis Apple/Redskins** (ci) • **Wear and Tear** (e ci), *from around Glastonbury* • **White Close Pippin** (ci) • **White Jersey** (ci), *thought to be from near Cadbury Castle in the nineteenth century* • **Woodbine/ Runaway/Rice's Jersey** (e ci) • **Worcester Cross** • **Yarlington Mill** (ci), *from Yarlington near Cadbury; found growing in a wall by a water- wheel in early 1900s and replanted at Yarlington Mill* • **Yellow Redstreak** (ci), *used more for rootstock than cider* • **Yeovil Sour** (ci).

STAFFORDSHIRE

Betsy Baker, a *Cannock apple rediscovered some years ago* • **Roland Smith**, *Weston Park.*

SUFFOLK

Catherine (c), *from the garden of the pub now known as Live and Let Live at Combs, near Stowmarket, before 1900* • **Clopton Red** (e), *a seedling raised by Justin Brooke of Clopton Hall, Wickhambrook, in 1946* • **Honey Pippin** (e), *Clopton Hall, Wickhambrook* • **Lady Henniker**

(d), *from seedling found in cider must at Thornham Hall near Eye, in the 1840s; introduced by John Perkins, gardener in 1873; best in December/January when it has lost some acidity; lovely flavour, cooks well* • **Lord Stradbroke/ Fenn's Wonder/Fenn's Seedling** (c), *raised, or found, around 1900 by Mr Fenn, Lord Stradbroke's head gardener, at Henham Hall, near Wangford* • **Maclean's Favourite** (e), *raised by Dr Allan Maclean of Sudbury around 1820, although Joan Morgan suggests he was from Colchester, Essex* • **Maxton** (e), *Assington, 1939; a sport of Laxtons Superb* • **Red Miller's Seedling** (e), *sport of Miller's Seedling, from a garden in Sudbury in the first half of the twentieth century* • **St Edmund's Pippin/St Edmund's Russet** (e), *raised by Mr R. Harvey at Bury St Edmunds; first recorded in 1875; one of the best flavoured of all October apples; crisp, juicy, fresh; bruises easily* • **Suffolk Pink** (e), *found in orchards at Braiseworth, near Eye, around 1990.*

SURREY

Albury Park Nonsuch • **Barchard's Seedling** (e), *raised by Mr Higgs, head gardener to R. Barchard of Putney, recorded 1853; grown by market gardeners for London in 1880s* • **Braddick's Nonpareil** (e), *nineteenth century, Thames Ditton* • **Byfleet Seedling** (c), *raised by George Carpenter,* head gardener at West Hall, Byfleet, in 1915 • **Carswell's Honeydew** (e), *raised 1939 by J.W. Carswell of Ashtead* • **Carswell's Orange** (e), *from Ashtead* • **Cellini** (d), *raised by nurseryman Leonard Phillips, Vauxhall, 1828; popular with London's market gardeners in the late nineteenth century; recently undergoing revival as the Vauxhall Apple* • **Claygate Pearmain** (e), *found growing in a hedge near Claygate by John Braddick during the 1820s; who sent some to a RHS meeting in 1822; one of the finest of all dessert apples, firm, crisp, juicy, sweet and aromatic* • **Cleeve** (e), *raised at Cleeve, Weybridge, pre-1930 from a Canadian pip* • **Cockle Pippin** (e), *originated with Mr Cockle at Godstone, Redhill, in about 1800, and was extensively grown there and in surrounding counties; first-class rich flavour, sweet and aromatic; excellent with cheese* • **Colonel Yate** (c) • **Comrade** (e) • **Curl Tail** (d), *thought to be from Woking, recorded 1872; named for its curved stalk* • **Duchess's Favourite** (e), *raised in late eighteenth/early nineteenth century by nurseryman Cree of Addlestone; admired by the Duchess of York, who lived near the nursery, grown in gardens as well as market gardens* • **George Carpenter** (e), *raised by himself in 1902* • **Hannan Seedling** (d), *raised by Mrs I. Hannan of Walton-on-Thames in 1928 from an Australian pip* • **Harry Pring** (e) • **High View Pippin** (e) •

Joybells (e), *thought to have been raised by Robert Lloyd, head gardener of Brookwood Hospital, near Woking, in the early 1900s* • **June Crewdson** (e) • **King of the Pippins/Reine de Reinettes** (d), *and many more synonyms as it become popular across England and Europe; Joan Morgan writes that its upright growth, casting little shade, appealed to market gardeners, who planted strawberries and blackcurrants between rows; nutty with almond undertones* • **Lingfield Forge**, *recently grafted from last remaining tree into Lingfield Community Orchard* • **Lady Isabel** (d), *found on a compost heap by Mrs Reading of Guildford, 1939* • **May Beauty** (e) • **Mitchelson's Seedling** (c), *raised by Mitchelson, a market gardener, in Kingston-upon-Thames, during the nineteenth century* • **Nanny** (e), *either Sussex or Surrey; recorded 1842* • **Palmer's Rosey** (e) • **Pixie** (e), *raised at RHS Wisley, 1947* • **Scarlet Nonpareil** (e), *raised around 1773 in the garden of an inn at Esher* • **Shoesmith** (c), *raised by George Carpenter* • **Victory** (c), *raised by George Carpenter* • **Wadey's Seedling** (e) • *The following were all raised by M.B. Crane at the John Innes Horticultural Institute, Merton, during the early-mid twentieth century:* **Chad's Favourite** (e) • **Merton Beauty** (e) • **Merton Charm** (e) **Merton Delight** (e) • **Merton Joy** (e) **Merton Knave** (e) • **Merton Pearmain** (e) • **Merton Pippin** (e) •

Merton Prolific (e) • Merton Reinette (e) • Merton Russet (e) • Merton Worcester (e).

SUSSEX

Aldwick Beauty (e), *from Mrs D.M. Alford of Aldwick, Bognor Regis* • **Alfriston** (c), *raised at Uckfield, by Mr Shepherd, in the late eighteenth century. Originally called Shepherd's Seedling/ Pippin and renamed by Mr Brookes of Alfriston in 1819; very popular in Victorian period; deep bright green to greenish-yellow; large, sugary and brisk; cooks to a golden-brown with a delicious pear-like flavour* • **Ashdown Seedling** • **Brighton** • **Coronation** (e) • **Crawley Beauty** (d), *discovered by J. Cheal & Sons around 1870 in a cottage garden near their nursery, now under Gatwick airport* • **Crawley Reinette** (e), *J. Cheal & Sons* • **Doctor Hogg** (c), *raised by the head gardener at Leonardslee, Horsham; introduced about 1880; named after the Victorian pomologist* • **Duck's Bill** (e), *Petworth House, 1937; may be ancient variety of same name* • **Eastbourne Pippin** (e) • **Edmund Jupp** (d), *from Horsham, recorded 1862* • **Egremont Russet** (e), *most commercial of all the russets with frost-resistant blossom; thought to have been raised by Lord Egremont in the 1870s at Petworth; rich nutty flavour; crisp, firm and dry; holds its shape well when cooked* • **First and Last** • **Forge** (d), *a favourite cottager's apple from the former iron-working area around East Grinstead and Crawley; first described in 1851* • **Golden Bounty** (e), *Scutes Farm, Hastings, 1940* • **Golden Pippin** (e), *a seventeenth century variety from Parham Park near Arundel* • **Goodwood Pippin** • **Hawkridge** • **Knobby Russet** (e), *from Haslar Capron of Midhurst, 1820, knobbly, russeted with a strong flavour* • **Lady Hopetown** (e) • **Lady Sudeley** (e), *raised in Kent about 1949 by Mr Jacobs who took the apple to Petworth with him. Renamed by George Bunyard & Co nursery, Maidstone, Kent* • **Mannington's Pearmain** (e), *from about 1770; grew in cider pomace thrown over a garden hedge by Mr Turley, a blacksmith, in Uckfield; in 1847 his grandson, John Mannington, sent it to the RHS; rich, nutty* • **Old Middlemas** • **Petworth Nonpareil** • **Saltcote Pippin** (e), *raised by James Hoad of Rye; recorded 1818* • **Sussex Mother** (e), *grown around Heathfield in nineteenth century* • **Tinsley Quince** (e), *Crawley* • **Wadhurst Pippin** (e).

WARWICKSHIRE

Shakespeare • **Wyken Pippin** (e), *planted at Wyken near Coventry; believed to have come from the pip of an apple eaten by Lord Craven on his travels from France to the Netherlands in about 1715; greenish, dotted with russet; delicious* yellow flesh, juicy, sweet, tender; best between Christmas and Easter.

WESTMORLAND

Bradley's Beauty, *found growing on mosses of Witherslack around 1990* • **Falbarrow Favourite**, *rediscovered in an orchard in Crosthwaite in 2004; perhaps named after Falbarrow Park at Bowness-on-Windermere* • **Irish Reinette**, *rediscovered in Storth, 2004; said by Hogg to have been popular in Westmorland and Lancaster* • **Lemon Square**, *from Eden Valley (Cumberland and Westmorland)* • **Longstart** (d), *first recorded 1851; favoured cottage-garden apple around Westmorland and Lancaster in the nineteenth century* • **Rank Thorn** (e), *thought to be an old variety; may be from the farm of the same name at Cartmell Fell* • **Taylor's Favourite**, *Lyth Valley* • **Wheaten Loaves**, *Lyth Valley.*

WILTSHIRE

Bedwyn Beauty (d), *raised by Mr Stone of Great Bedwyn near Marlborough in 1890* • **Burn's Seedling** (e), *thought to be the variety raised by Henry Burn, head gardener at Tottenham Park near Marlborough in the nineteenth century* • **Celt** (e), *Melksham* • **Chorister Boy** (e), *found in a garden in Wiltshire, introduced by Keynes, Williams & Co. of Salisbury, 1890* • **Corsley**

Pippin (e), *thought to originate from trees planted at Corsley School in early twentieth century by the headmaster, Mr Latham; found in gardens in the village* • **Dredge's Fame**(e), *introduced by nurseryman William Dredge of Wishford, 1802* • **Mary Barnett** (d), *raised by Mrs Barnett, Steeple Ashton, from a pip, on her wedding day in 1920* • **Roundway Magnum Bonum** (e), *raised by Mr Joy, gardener at Roundway Park, near Devizes, 1864; delicious pear-like flavour, a valuable and distinctive fruit;according to Dr Hogg, 'Flesh yellowish white, tender, crisp, very juicy and with a fine aroma'.*

WORCESTERSHIRE

Betty Geeson (c), *introduced by Dr Davies of Pershore, 1854; see also Leicestershire* • **Chatley Kernel** (d) • **Dick's Favourite** (c), *raised at Rowe's Nurseries, Worcester, by the foreman, Mr Carless, in the late nineteenth century* • **Edward VII** (c), *introduced by Barbourne Nurseries, Worcester, around 1908; very late flowering, pretty pink blossom, escapes late frosts; cooks to purée* • **Gladstone** (e), *a chance seedling originating around 1780; first called Jackson's Seedling; introduced by Blakedown Nursery, Kidderminster; re-named after the prime minister* • **Green Purnell** (e) • **Herefordshire Russet** (d), *a new variety in 2005, from F.P. Matthews in Tenbury,*

Worcestershire, bred by Nick Dunn; 'russet nuttiness…crisp creamy flesh…mouth-tingling acidity…rich apple juice…classic golden russeted skin, with greeny yellow undercolour, is thin and crunchy' • **Hope Cottage Seedling** (e), raised from a pip by Mrs Oakley, Rochford, near Tenbury Wells, in 1900 • **King Charles' Pearmain** (e), sent to Dr Hogg in 1876 by John Smith, a nurseryman in Worcester • **King Coffee** (e), from Worcester • **Madresfield Court** (e), thought to have been raised by William Crump, head gardener at Madresfield Court; introduced 1915 • **May Queen** (e), raised by Mr Haywood of Worcester; recorded 1888 • **Newland Sack** (d), thought to be from late eighteenth century; found in discarded cider pomace at Newland Court near Great Malvern; keeps well, and becomes sweeter for eating after Christmas; propagated by the Marcher Apple Network from the last known surviving tree at Newland Court, near Great Malvern in 2002 • **Pitmaston Nonpareil/Pitmaston Russet Nonpareil** (e), raised at Pitmaston by John Williams, exhibited 1818 • **Pitmaston Pine Apple** (e), thought to have been raised at Witley by Mr White around 1785, marketed by John Williams of Pitmaston; variable in taste according to year, 'honey and musk' or 'pineapple'; 'its distinct and delicious flavour should give it a place in the gardens of connoisseurs', E.A. Bunyard •

Rushock Pearmain/King Charles Pearmain (e), raised 1820 by Charles Taylor, a blacksmith, at Rushock • **Sandlin Duchess** (e), raised by Mr Gabb of Sandlin, near Malvern, 1880, and introduced by William Crump, head gardener at Madresfield Court • **Whiting Pippin** • **William Crump** (e), raised either at Madresfield Court or by the Rowes' nurseries of Worcester • **Worcester Pearmain** (e), thought to have originated at Swan Pool, near Worcester, around 1870; raised by Mr Hale from a Devonshire Quarrenden pip; introduced by Messrs Smith of Worcester, in 1873; frost-resistant blossom; crisp, attractive fruit with a red skin; white flesh, with a hint of strawberry; good for sorbet.

YORKSHIRE

Acklam Russet (e), Acklam, 1768 • **Cockpit** (c), recorded in 1831; cooks to a purée • **Fillingham Pippin** (e), thought to have been raised by Mr Fillingham, a carter between Swanland and Hull; popular in the East Riding in the 1940s; a pitcher • **Flowery Town**, Backhouse nurseries of York, attractive pink flesh • **Green Balsam** • **Grandpa Buxton** (c), an early cooker raised from a pip in a garden at Copt Hewick, 1990s; grows well in the north • **Hunt House**, a long keeper; it is said that this apple went out with the long-distance whaling boats from Whitby, even with Captain Cook; see *also* Lincolnshire • **Improved Cockpit** • **Nancy Jackson** • **Northern Greening** • **Ribston Pippin** (e), *discovered in the gardens at Ribston Hall near Knaresborough, thought to have grown from a pip brought from Rouen and planted in about 1707; 'One of the most richly-flavoured apples, crisp, juicy and strongly aromatic', Scotts Nurseries; olive-green, flushed with orange-brown and striped with scarlet; boasts the highest vitamin C content of any apple* • **Sharleston Pippin** (e), *from Sharleston, near Wakefield* • **Sykehouse Russet/English Hospital Reinette**, *rediscovered by the RHS Northern Fruit Group in the Millennium Survey for the Whitby area, North Riding, 2000; a tree still stands in Sykehouse village* • **Warner's King**, *see* Hertfordshire • **Yorkshire Beauty/Hawthornden/Oxford Peach**, **Greenup's Pippin**; *see also* Cumberland and Midlothian • **Yorkshire Greening/Yorkshire Goosesauce** (c), *listed in 1769 by nurseryman William Perfect in Pontefract; cooks to a sharp purée.*

SCOTLAND

Craig Pillans' pioneering work on Scottish apples is acknowledged; his booklet *Historic Apples of Scotland* has been invaluable in exciting interest.

Origin unknown

Bloody Ploughman • **Clydeside** • **Early Julyan** (d), *known before 1800; thought to be Scottish variety; 'rather small, yellow skin, juicy and with a brisk, balsamic flavour'* • **Lady of the Lake** (e) • **Lady of Wemyss** • **Lord Rosebery** (e) • **Maggie Sinclair** • **Oslin** (d) *aniseed flavour* • **Scotch Bridget** (c), *recorded in 1851, probably from Scotland and popular around Lancaster in the late nineteenth century; large, juicy, sweetens enough to eat* • **Scoth Dumpling** • **Stoup Leadington**, *first recorded 1831* • **Tam**

Montgomery • **Thorle Pippin/Whorle Pippin/ Lady Derby** (e), *recorded 1831; very popular in Scotland around turn of the twentieth century; juicy, sweet, refreshing* • **White Paradise.**

ANGUS

Arbroath Pippin/Oslins (e), *possible introduction to Arbroath Abbey from France, seventeenth century or earlier; aromatic* • **Hood's Supreme** • **Seaton House/Niton House** (c), *raised before 1860 at Seaton House, Arbroath* • **Tower of Glamis** (c), *origin uncertain; known before 1800, widely planted in the Carse of Gowrie and Clydesdale; bright green, ripening to sulphur yellow; crisp, juicy, firm flesh and distinctive perfume.*

EAST LOTHIAN

East Lothian Pippin (c), *first recorded 1883* • **Leadington**, *original name of Lennoxlove House.*

FIFE

Lady of Wemyss (c), *first recorded in 1814, perhaps from the Wemyss family seat in East Lothian, or Wemyss in Fife.*

LANARKSHIRE

Cambusnethan Pippin (d), *thought to have been raised by the gardener of Cambusnethan House, near Wishaw, in Clydesdale around 1750, although* some say it is from the earlier monastery there • **White Paradise** (c), *thought to be from Clydesdale.*

MIDLOTHIAN

Cutler Grieve (e), *from Midlothian* • **Green Kilpandy Pippin** (c) • **Hawthornden**, *from southeast Edinburgh, first catalogued in 1780; once very popular throughout Britain. See other claims in Cumberland as Greenup's Pippin, Yorkshire as Yorkshire Beauty.* • **James Grieve** (d), *raised by James Grieve in Edinburgh around 1890 and commercially cultivated by Dickson's nurseries, his employers; is one of the best mid-season apples; prefers the north, eaten as dessert apple in England but stored or cooked in Scotland where it grows sharper; blossom notably scented; greasy skin, bright yellow-green, speckled and striped with orange-red; refreshing flavour, soft and very juicy; cooks well.*

MORAYSHIRE

Beauty of Moray (c), *documented since 1883.*

PEEBLESSHIRE

Stobo Castle (c), *introduced by Storrie of Glencarse, around 1900, but may originate from Stobo Castle.*

PERTHSHIRE

Bloody Ploughman (d), *first recorded 1883,*

associated with the Carse of Gowrie • **Lass O'Gowrie** (d), *from Carse of Gowrie* • **Lord Rosebery** • **Port Allen Russet** (e), *from Port Allen, Errol.*

ROSS-SHIRE

Coul Blush (e c), *raised in Coul in Easter Ross in 1820s; probably Britain's most northerly variety.*

ROXBURGHSHIRE

Pine Golden Pippin (e), *first recorded about 1860 by Dickson & Son of Hassendean Burn near Hawick; pineapple flavour* • **White Melrose/Melrose** (d), *may date from sixteenth century and the monks of Melrose Abbey; sweetish with a hint of melon.*

STIRLINGSHIRE

Stirling Castle (c), *raised by John Christie, nurseryman in Causewayhead, around 1830, tender, acid, juicy: bright yellowish green flushed with red; excellent cooker for September.*

WIGTOWNSHIRE

Galloway **Pippin** (c), *possibly dating from sixteenth century and the Wigtown monastery; a Christmas eater; flavours of white wine.*

WALES

The work of the Marcher Apple Network is acknowledged.

Origin unknown

Bakers Delicious (e), *one of the most delicious of early apples; found in Wales and introduced by Bakers of Codswell, Wolverhampton, in 1932; yellow flushed with bright red; firm, crisp, juicy* • **Cadwalader** (ci), *rediscovered growing in Herefordshire's Golden Valley, 2004, by the Marcher Apple Network.*

BRECKNOCKSHIRE

Monmouth Green/Landore (d), *'Landore' commoner in Herefordshire; grown around the Black Mountains since mid–late nineteenth century and thought to be much older; for cooking early; dessert after November; keeps until after Christmas.*

CAERNARFONSHIRE

Bardsey Apple, *rediscovered growing on Bardsey Island off the north-west coast.*

CARMARTHENSHIRE

Marged Nicolas/Morgan Nicolas (d), *found on farms in Dinefwr area; for cooking and eating; keeps well until early spring* • **Pig Yr Wydd** (c), *found on farms around Dinefwr.*

MONMOUTHSHIRE

Breakwell's Seedling (ci), *found 1890s at Perthyre Farm, near Monmouth, then propagated by George Breakwell; once grown in the Herefordshire/Gloucestershire area, and still used commercially* • **Broom** (ci), *named after Broom House, south of Raglan* • **Frederick** (ci), *found in the nineteenth century in the Forest of Dean, Monmouthshire; also grown in Gloucestershire and Herefordshire* • **Monmouthshire Beauty/Cissy** (e), *raised around 1800 by Mr Tampling of Malpas, near Newport* • **Perthyre** (ci), *from Perthyre Farm, near Monmouth* • **Porter's Sharp** (ci), *from an unknown tree at Berllanderi Farm, Raglan; named after a former owner of the farm* **St Cecilia** (e), *raised by John Basham & Sons of Bassaleg, Monmouthshire, around 1900; also popular in the west of England* • **Twyn-y-Sheriff** (ci), *from an unknown tree at Twyn-y-Sheriff Farm, near Raglan.*

PEMBROKESHIRE

Pen Caled (ci), *from St Dogmaels* • **Pig Aderyn** (ci), *from St Dogmaels.*

RADNORSHIRE

Cummy Norman (ci).

IRELAND

See www.irishseedsavers.ie online Apple Catalogue, with descriptions of eighty varieties and Joan Morgan and Alison Richards, *The New Book of Apples.*

PRACTICAL ACTION & SOURCES

SAVE OUR ORCHARDS: ACTION NOTES

A development proposal threatens the old orchard in the centre of your village, at the back of the row of 1930s semis in your suburb, or in the Victorian garden at the heart of your town. Or perhaps a traditional orchard is to be grubbed out because there is no current commercial return for the fruit. What can you do to save it? It is wise to be prepared – get to know your locality intimately and gather support long before any threat emerges.

First you need to make arguments about the value of an orchard, and yours in particular, to galvanise local people and the media. Form a group to share long-term responsibility for the orchard as a community asset.

Why conserve old orchards?

Orchards are important to local distinctiveness because they:
- vary from place to place
- are a rich source of poetic inspiration
- are a source of good food, from apple pie to cider
- are healthy places to be and to work
- offer valuable habitats for wild life: bees love fruit blossom and blossom needs bees, bats, birds and butterflies. Old orchards are increasingly recognised as being as rich in biodiversity like wood pasture
- are historically important and link us with cultures all the way to the Tien Shan mountains on the Kazakhstan/China border
- create beautiful landscapes
- provide local jobs and reduce transport costs, the carbon burden and pollution
- harbour old varieties of fruit and wild fruit trees, which are irreplaceable

sources of genetic diversity and may be or may parent the disease-resistant strains of tomorrow
- have a long tradition of multiple use
- are imbued with local cultural significance
- may become the focus of a community, the moot, the playground, the festival field, the open-air classroom, the place for sharing knowledge.

Surveying, mapping and recording

Are there any orchards in your neighbourhood or parish? Are there many fruit trees in local gardens? Where are they and who is responsible for them?

Make a local apple register, noting the different varieties that grow in gardens, orchards and hedgerows, their locations and the number of trees. Search for varieties that are particular to your area. Do street names and old maps give clues to where orchards once were? Mark them on a county or town apple map or parish orchard map, then pin it up in your village or town hall, a local shop or other prominent place and ask people to add to it.

Trace the origins of varieties, especially those with local associations – you might discover a long-lost one. Research their stories and their histories: there may be old books and papers to consult in your local library or archive. Talk to and tap into the knowledge of older people: tape and transcribe their stories, memories and working knowledge of orchards and cider-making. Make this available to the County Record Office. Create a book.

Take photographs around the day and the year. Hold competitions. Make displays for your library. Keep a note of the wild life visiting local orchards or organise bird, bat, butterfly, insect, plant or fungi surveys. Inform Natural England and your County Wildlife Trust of any old orchards that you think are important wild life habitats.

Value wild fruits. Make a map of wild crab apple, cherry, bullace, sloe and other fruit trees, ensure that they are cared for in hedgerow, garden, park and wood.

Campaigning

Orchards and fruit trees are frequently undervalued by householders, farmers, developers and planners.

Encourage developers to include new community orchards in their plans, and the planting of local fruit trees in gardens. At the start of the twentieth century Dame Henrietta Barnett had apple trees of many varieties planted in the new gardens of London's Hampstead Garden Suburb. Many are still there. On the south side of Northampton, housing developers were persuaded to save Wilson's Orchard in the 1990s; the local community cares for the old trees and is planting new ones, and Apple Cause extends advice across the county.

Talk to local farmers or growers. Find out if they have any old orchards that they are prepared to let or sell to the local community. Environmental stewardship grants may be available for the maintenance of a traditional orchard: contact the countryside management team at your county or district council, Defra, and the Country Wildlife Trust.

Tell Natural England, County Wildlife Trust, Defra and your MP that you value your local orchards, especially if they are under threat: your voice counts.

Encourage the retention, planting and care of wild and cultivated fruit trees in hedgerows, especially where they are a feature of local distinctiveness. Ask your district or county tree officer to place Tree Preservation Orders on significant fruit trees in streets, parks and gardens. Explore the possibility of orchards being included in the Local Plan as important features of the area and in the Local Biodiversity Action Plan as vital habitats.

Encourage shops to sell a wider range of local fruit and fruit products. Ask for cider made from local cider apples rather than imported apple concentrate: obtain a copy of *The Good Cider Guide* published by CAMRA (the Campaign for Real Ale).

Twin with small orchards in other counties and countries. For example, community and wild-life orchards are known in Germany: build international bonds to help care for your local orchard.

If you own an orchard in a town or village, consider bequeathing it to the parish or town council, or the local wild life or civic trust. Research this carefully and write in caveats: even the most reputable bodies sell the family silver.

Tell Common Ground of your activities and local initiatives. Good examples are *vital* in encouraging and advising others embarking on similar projects.

Practical Action

Rediscover or create recipes using local varieties of fruit. Make the most of the distinctive flavour and qualities of old varieties. Collect recipes from neighbours and put them together in a local cookery book.

Install bird and bat boxes in your garden or your orchard. Manage your land, however small a patch it may be, so that it will support some wild life.

Take grafts from unusual trees. Follow Gabriel's Community Orchard's example in Somerset and start your own rootstock nursery for propagating local varieties.

Strive to manage your orchard organically. Contact local organic growers, the Soil Association or Garden Organic (HDRA) for advice.

Find out if any local commercial orchards are open to the public. Some have annual open days (usually in September or October) when you can visit, pick and taste the fruit. Open your old orchard for school visits or local seasonal festivities: bringing people into an orchard, particularly at harvest time, will increase local interest and sales.

Visit the nearest 'Pick Your Own' orchard and find out which varieties are grown. Suggest that the owner adopts a 'rent-a tree' scheme to involve local families and schools. Encourage them to grow local varieties and organise fruit events.

Grow local varieties of fruit in your own garden. Consult the Gazetteer of Local Varieties (see pages 179–213), local growers and gardeners about varieties of fruit particular to your area. Seek advice on appropriate pollinators. Plant your trees between November and March (before Christmas is preferable).

Take grafts from your favourite old trees – it's not as difficult as it might seem – or plant following local planting patterns. Set up a Community Orchard, re-establish a city orchard for the street, office or hospital or create a school orchard.

Encourage your local council to plant fruit trees on public land, in a corner of the park, on new estates and at the edge of a village, town or city. Ask your city farm to plant an orchard, to celebrate Apple Day and to provide orchard-skills training.

Offer your orchard for camping, let the grazing for sheep – but remember to install tree guards.

Sell any fruitwood to craftspeople. Ask them to make things for local sale using the orchard's name.

Hold juicing and cider-making, pruning and grafting days, climbing and bee-keeping courses.

Feed the immediate economy: sell fruit through local shops or box schemes and pannier markets. Some of the National Federation of Women's Institutes organise special markets for Apple Day, selling only apple products, pies, cakes and preserves.

Revelry

Encourage broad involvement. Wassail your orchard on Twelfth Night. Rejoice in the blossom in spring. Organise public picnics and barbecues in the summer.

Play apple games in the orchard: see Common Ground's book *Apple Games and Customs* for seasonal ideas, such as apple bobbing, crabbing the parson, a-griggling or Gruacach's Treasure.

Commission artworks for your orchard, such as seating, apple stores, game boards or ladders. Add to its local distinctiveness.

Try open-air plays, storytelling, poetry, meetings.

Offer the orchard for weddings in spring.

IDEAS FOR CELEBRATING APPLE DAY

Celebrate Apple Day on 21 October and All Fruits Eve the night before. Devise your own activities or join others in their celebrations.

Varieties and Tasting Most Apple Day celebrations include a display of local and regional varieties that you may never have seen before, let alone tasted. The different shapes, sizes, colours and smells are amazing. Some events offer tastings – you may be so enchanted by a particular variety that you decide to buy a tree for your garden.

Look out for places in your area where you can buy local varieties – a greengrocer (if you are fortunate enough to have one), farm shop or farmers' market. Ask them to sell a greater range, and suggest to your off-licence and pub that they carry a good, local cider.

Identification Experts on apple identification are thin on the ground – remember, there are more than 2,700 different apples, culinary, dessert and cider, to distinguish between. Reliable experts are booked up well in advance, and it is well worth bringing your mystery garden apple to an expert: it is one of the most popular Apple Day attractions, and several 'lost' varieties have been rediscovered.

Produce This is your chance to experiment with or sample a huge range of products made with apples, from jelly, chutney, cakes, pies, ice-creams and sorbets to single-variety juices, cider, wine and dishes featuring particular varieties. Local recipes and cookery books are often available. You may be able to bring along surplus apples for pressing. Ask your local pubs and restaurants to put on special apple menus and guest ciders.

Fruit Trees Specialist fruit-tree nurseries regularly attend Apple Days to showcase local and unusual varieties that will enable you to enjoy a wider choice of fruit in the future. They may also demonstrate grafting and pruning, and advise on planting and after care.

Gifting It was once traditional to give apples as a sign of friendship – in the past decorated apples were taken from house to house as a symbol of good luck and health. Tie a ribbon round a single apple or fill a basket with a mixture or a single variety and make gifting on Apple Day second nature as it is with eggs at Easter and cards at Christmas.

Games Try your hand at apple bobbing, fork apple, apple shy, pin the maggot on the apple, griggling, a-scraggling, pothering and ponking. Take part in the longest-peel competition – peel an apple as thinly as possible in one piece and measure the result. Common Ground runs a national competition – there are prizes!

Arts and Crafts Make apple prints, apple creatures, carvings from apple wood. Write new music and poems, enjoy storytelling, mummers plays.

Wild Life Join a guided walk through an old orchard and you will appreciate what an important habitat it is for wild life, from flowers, insects and fungi to birds and mammals. Traditional orchards, with widely spaced tall trees, are beautiful at any time of the year. And age brings character.

APPLE IDENTIFICATION

The gnarled or fallen apple tree in your garden may be the last of a unique variety, perhaps one that is well adapted to your soil and climate. Previous owners and neighbours may know about it, including its name. Before you consider felling the tree discover the qualities of the fruit – if correctly stored it may be an October cooker and a May eater. The tree may be perfectly happy lying horizontally, giving you a free seat, a character and something to stand on to pick its fruit as it redirects itself upwards. If you are forced to remove it, don't forget that apple and other fruitwood is sought after by craftspeople: woodcuts and engravings rely upon fruitwood blocks; wooden bowls and cups, spoons and ladles, cheese moulds, whistles, recorders, chains, love tokens and mill-wheel teeth use apple, pear or cherry wood. You may like to take or offer grafts to perpetuate the variety.

Identification at Apple Day

Apple Day, 21 October, is an ideal time to discover more about the mystery apple tree at the bottom of your garden many of the hundreds of events around the country offer a popular apple identification service – be prepared to queue: experts are few.

Bring three samples of typical mature fruit with a twig and leaves. Don't take misshapen, damaged or poor specimens as they may make identification impossible. An expert may ask about the age of your tree and orchard. An orchard planted in the 1900s is likely to have a different assemblage of varieties than one planted in the 1950s.

If an apple has been grown from a pip it will be a completely new variety: roadsides and railway cuttings are lined with wildings. No expert can identify them – they have no name. If the fruit is good, simply enjoy its anonymity, or take a cutting, keep careful information on the whereabouts of the wilding, name the fruit yourself and ask a good nursery to find out whether or not it has a future. To perpetuate a variety twigs are cut from the tree and grafted onto a rootstock or, rarely, encouraged to grow their own roots, otherwise the variety dies out.

Each year Common Ground produces a list of Apple Day events being held around the country which is available with a SAE or online www.commonground.org.uk.

Lost and Found

Apparently lost apple varieties have been identified at Apple Day events, often brought in from a lone garden tree by its curious owner. The White Quarantine turned up at Probus Gardens in Cornwall in 1991, and the Profit at Kingston Maurward, Dorset in 2001. The Gypsy King apple, last recorded in the nineteenth century, was rediscovered on Apple Day 2004 at Church Stretton in Shropshire. Charles Martell, unique champion of his home county, has been searching for decades; he says: 'I think the total of Gloucestershire apples in existence is now 102. The Duke of Bedford, a culinary variety which seems not to have been heard of since 1884 has recently come to light in South Gloucestershire.' Grafts from rediscovered trees are taken for propagation so they can grow in the locality once more. The identification of fruit has often been the starting point for surveys or maps of fruit trees in an area. Each year Orchards Live in north Devon add new local varieties to their Devon Pomona as do many other local and regional orchard groups.

Postal Identification

The Royal Horticultural Society and the Brogdale Horticultural Trust offer a fruit identification service to members and others for a fee. To make use of these services:

- Send three samples of typical mature undamaged fruit, with a twig and leaves.
- Provide as much detail about the tree as possible: age and habit/shape of tree; any particular characteristics of blossom or growth; whether the fruit is dessert, culinary, or both; season of use of fruit; the locality of the tree if different from your address; soil type if possible.
- Make sure you number each sample gently on the skin with a ballpoint or marker pen – stick-on labels fall off in the post. Make a note for yourself of the tree and number because the fruit cannot be returned.
- To ensure the fruit arrives in good condition, wrap each piece in newspaper, bubble-wrap or polystyrene granules, and pack in a strong box. Do not use boxes that have previously contained strongly smelling products such as soap as this may mask the characteristic scent and flavour of the fruit.
- Enclose a stamped addressed envelope and the appropriate fee (in 2006 the cost ranged from £8 per variety for members to £19 for non-members):

The Director of Horticulture (Fruit Naming)
RHS Garden
Wisley
Woking
Surrey GU23 6QB
Tel: 0845 260 9000 or see www. rhs.org.uk
or
Fruit Identification
Brogdale Horticultural Trust
Brogdale Road
Faversham
Kent ME13 8XZ
Tel: 01795 535286 or see www. brogdale.org

Local knowledge

Local horticultural societies and colleges, fruit-growers, specialist nurseries, county or local orchard groups may be able to help with identification. The number of people with fruit-identification skills is rapidly diminishing, though, and as it takes many years of experience to accumulate such knowledge, we need to share it before it is lost. Why not enrol on a training course? Visit www. england-in-particular.info to find out what happens in your county from the Orchards Gazetteer. Contact local groups and regional experts to see if they can offer training.

Suggested Reading for DIY Identification The following books contain photographs, drawings and detailed descriptions of a number of varieties and may prove a useful starting point.

Bultitude, John, *Apples: a guide to identification of international varieties*, Macmillan Reference, 1983

Bunyard, Edward A., *A Handbook of Hardy Fruits More Commonly Grown in Great Britain*, (2 vols) Picton Publishing, 1994

Copas, Liz, *A Somerset Pomona*, Dovecote Press, 2001 (cider apples)

Hogg, Dr Robert, and Graves Bull, Dr Henry, *The Herefordshire Pomona*, Woolhope Naturalists Field Club, 1885; Wheeler, Richard (Ed.) CD ROM, The Marcher Apple Network, 2005

Morgan, Joan and Richards, Alison, *The New Book of Apples*, Ebury Press, 2002

Sanders, Roseanne, *The English Apple*, Phaidon Press, 1988

Wheeler, Richard (Ed.) *Vintage Fruit – Cider Apples and Perry Pears*, CD ROM, The Marcher Apple Network, 2007

The Applekey™ is a database to aid identification by the Northern Fruit Group: www.nat-orchard-forum.org.uk

Brogdale National Fruit Collection: many varieties are photographed and described at www.brogdale.org

BLOSSOM WALKS & FESTIVALS

With their coy pink buds and turning-white flowers among the bright, emerging leaves, apple trees in blossom can take the breath away. Fruit trees are among the most beautiful: an orchard in flower is a magnificent sight, and to be under the trees with the hum of insects or the petals falling is an unforgettable experience. Tall standard apple trees, and the huge cherry and perry pears, have so much more presence than today's bush varieties.

Flowering times vary according to the weather, and with climate change, most seem to be getting earlier. A rough rule of thumb suggests cherry, damson and plum in March, pear in April followed by apple until May/June. Joan Morgan notes that 'The main flowering period in southern England [for apples] is early to mid May, although in recent years mild winters have advanced the period to mid April. There are varieties which blossom at least two weeks before the majority of apples, and others that do not come into flower until June.' Vita Sackville West's 'The Land' is a tribute to the season's beauty:

> Sometimes in apple country you may see
> A ghostly orchard standing all in white,
> Aisles of white trees, white branches, in the green,
> On some still day when the year hangs between
> Winter and spring, and heaven is full of light.

It is surprising how much apple blossom colour and fragrance vary. James Grieve flowers are scented. Roy Genders finds the cerise-pink blossom of Brownlees Russet particularly striking, but the Arthur Turner is alone in having a RHS award for its blossom. Why have we not introduced a festival at which we can admire the blossom as the Japanese have with *hanami*? Their flower-viewing season starts with the cherry blossom in March. Armagh, the orchard county in the north of Ireland, puts on an apple-blossom festival at the end of April, almond blossom is celebrated in Italy, Morocco, Gran Canaria, Portugal and Australia while in the USA cherry and apple are welcomed in spring.

Once, Kent was loved for its springtime displays of fruit blossom, and local authorities promoted trips from London to see them. But since 1945 more than 90 per cent of the county's orchards have been grubbed up and at least one local authority no longer thinks it appropriate to designate blossom routes.

In *Burcombes, Queenies and Collogetts*, Virginia Spiers reminds us that, between Devon and Cornwall, 'in the nineteenth century, the orchards of the Tamar Valley were particularly prolific, the whole area famous for its extraordinary variety of fruit and the remarkable beauty of springtime blossom, which was much admired by trippers on the famous Tamar paddle-steamers'.

Blossom routes once common now seem confined to the Vale of Evesham, with walking or coach tours, bicycle rides and signed routes. 'The white plum and damson is the first to appear, followed by the pink apple and white pear around 10–14 days later', depending on the weather, between the end of March and early May.

Where to see Blossom

In Somerset and Devon cider apples predominate. You will find the white blossom of damsons in hedgerows and at field edges around Wenlock Edge in Shropshire and they march with the stone walls along the Lyth and Winster valleys of Westmorland. The low-lying froth of commercial orchards prevail in parts of Essex, and Cambridgeshire supports tall rambling Bramley trees near Wisbech.

The two main areas in Kent for fruit-growing are between Sittingbourne and Canterbury and in the Low Weald, roughly south of Maidstone from Sandhurst to Wye, though much of this is now covered with bush orchards.

The Vale of Evesham and the Teme Valley in Worcestershire are still known for their plums and apples. The Wychaven Blossom Trail is described in a leaflet with a map showing orchards and other places of interest around Evesham and Pershore, available from the District Council Tourism Department, tel: 01386 565373, or www.worcestershires-heritage-garden.org

The glorious old perry-pear and cider-apple orchards along the Marcle Ridge in Herefordshire are celebrated with walks, and wild cherries are scattered through broadleaf woodland in the Wye Valley between Gloucestershire and Monmouthshire. The Severn Vale is still home to apple, perry pear, plum and other orchard fruits, celebrated by Leonard Clark in 'Apple Trees':

…Massed, orchards of them,
Transmuting Severn's skies
To every shade of pink,
Taming the primroses at their feet,
And so full of song, the hill
Is one continuous fire of trembling sound.

The East of England Apples & Orchards Group and the Brogdale Horticultural Trust may organize blossom walks. Visit their websites for details.

Cross Lanes Fruit Farm, at Mapledurham in Berkshire hosts a Blossom Day one Sunday in May. You can picnic in the orchard, which contains sixty varieties of apples and pears. For further details, tel: 01189 723167. In the north, Norton Priory, at Runcorn in Cheshire, puts on a Blossom Day in the Walled Garden on or near to 1 May. For further details, contact the Cheshire Landscape Trust, tel: 01244 376333.

Each May, the Big Apple in Herefordshire runs a celebration of blossom with walks, cider tasting and tea. For further details, contact the Ledbury Tourist Centre, tel: 01531 636147.

In April, Damson Day in Westmorland's Lyth Valley may coincide with the damson's blossoming – delicate and white, contrasting with the tree's dark trunk and branches. The trees are scattered through the valley, along stone walls, in field corners, near schools, anywhere that the thin soils will allow them to grow. See the Westmorland Damson Association's website: www.lythdamsons.org.uk

Some National Trust properties (www.nationaltrust.org.uk) and RHS Wisley (www.rhs.org.uk) highlight their orchard trees at blossom time.

Cider and Apple Juice Routes

You can buy direct from the makers of juice and cider at any time of year, but the freshest juice will be available in the autumn, and cider needs at least six months to mature. The most exciting time to visit is during autumn when the apples are in vast heaps waiting for transformation. Look out for a roadside board with 'CIDER' scrawled across it. CAMRA's *Good Cider Guide* lists producers, pubs and other outlets. The tourism departments of Somerset, Herefordshire and Kent county councils produce informative leaflets with maps highlighting juice- and cider-makers selling from cider mills and farms. Cider cycling routes have been created for Ledbury and Pembridge in Herefordshire. The leaflets go in and out of print: keep asking, and browse the tourist information centers, and the tourism sections of council websites.

'Pyo' will appear on signs in some orchard areas. At West Bradley in Somerset you can pick at least eight varieties and look across to Glastonbury Tor beaming memories from the Isle of Avalon. A great way to gain access to the countryside is by tree adoption with, for example, Dragon Orchard's cropsharers scheme in Herefordshire; you can visit for picnics during the year as well as picking your own fruit in the autumn.

Some branches of CAMRA arrange cider-pub trails to celebrate National Cider Month in October. Tel: 01727 867201 or see www.camra.org.uk

Cumbria Leader+ (a European funded project) offers a fold-out leaflet, 'Apple Appeal', with a map showing apple orchards and local orchard producers. The Westmorland Damson Association and Cumbria Leader+ have created a Damson Walk through the Lyth Valley, and have produced a leaflet with map, directory and history. Tel: 01768 869533, or visit www.fellsanddales.org.uk

In Herefordshire, a twenty-mile cycling route circling Ledbury and a nineteen-mile Pembridge Route take in cider/apple-juice producers, orchards and pubs. A fold-out leaflet with a map is available from the Ledbury Tourist Information Centre, tel: 01531 636147, and at other tourist information centres around the county. See also www.ciderroute.co.uk

The Herefordshire Cider Route is a circular drive around cider producers and specialist retailers. A fold-out leaflet with a map is available from Herefordshire Tourism, tel: 01432 260621or visit www.ciderroute.co.uk

A Taste of Mid Kent have produced a fold-out leaflet with a map showing their Fruity Trail, a three-mile circular walk within the Kent Downs Area of Outstanding Natural Beauty, taking in old and new orchards. It includes a directory of cider/juice-makers and apple-growers. Tel: 01271 336020 or visit www.kenttourism.co.uk

The Kent National Trail along the North Downs Way takes in orchards, including No Man's Orchard (a Community Orchard and local nature reserve), at Chartham Hatch near Canterbury. See www.nationaltrail.co.uk

Somerset's fold-out leaflet with a map and list of local orchards, cider- and juice-makers, history and other useful information, researched and written by James Crowden, is now available on www.somerset.gov.uk/tourism

In Devon, the campaign website www.saveyalbertonvalley.org.uk includes an old newspaper article that features a lovely cider trail through Yalberton valley.

APPLE SEASONS

a rough guide

In Britain different varieties ripen from mid-July to the following May. This short guide, based on Scott's Nurseries catalogue, offers a start to seeking out and asking for apples during their season from greengrocers and markets. Every year is different and apples mature later in the north.

EATING APPLES	Early mid July - August	September Early October	Second Early October	Mid/Late Autumn	Late/Mid Winter	Late/New Year	Good Keepers
Beauty of Bath	●						
Discovery	●						
George Cave	●						
Devonshire Quarrenden	●						
Baker's Delicious		●					
Ellison's Orange		●					
James Grieve		●					
Laxton's Fortune		●					
Michaelmas Red		●					
Miller's Seedling		●					
Worcester Pearmain		●					
Charles Ross				●			
Egremont Russet				●			
Herring's Pippin				●			
King of the Pippins				●			
Lord Lambourne				●			
Spartan				●			
St Edmund's Pippin				●			
Sunset				●			

(Eating apples continued)	Early mid July - August	Second Early September October	Mid/Late Autumn	Late/Mid Winter	Late/New Year	Good Keepers
Tom Putt			●			
Blenheim Orange				●		
Chivers Delight				●		
Cox's Orange Pippin				●		
Gascoyne's Scarlet				●		
Kidd's Orange Red				●		
Norfolk Royal				●		
Pitmaston Pine Apple				●		
Ribston Pippin				●		
William Crump				●		
Ashmead's Kernel					●	
Cornish Aromatic					●	
King's Acre Pippin					●	
Laxton's Superb					●	
Orleans Reinette					●	
Rosemary Russet					●	
Winston					●	
Allen's Everlasting						●
Brownlees' Russet						●
Claygate Pearmain						●
Cornish Gilliflower						●
Court Pendu Plat						●
D'Arcy Spice						●
Roundway Magnum Bonum						●
Sturmer Pippin						●
Suntan						●
Tydeman's Late Orange						●

COOKING APPLES

	Summer & Autumn	Winter keepers
Arthur Turner	●	
Bountiful	●	
Collogget Pippin	●	
Emneth Early/Early Victoria	●	
George Neal	●	
Golden Noble	●	
Grenadier	●	
Hawthornden	●	
Keswick Codlin	●	
Lord Derby	●	
Peasgood's Nonsuch	●	
Queen	●	
Rev W. Wilks	●	
Stirling Castle	●	
Warner's King	●	
Alfriston		●
Annie Elizabeth		●
Barnack Beauty		●
Bess Pool		●
Bramley's Seedling		●
Catshead		●
Crawley Beauty		●
Doctor Harvey		●
Dumelow's Seedling/Wellington		●
Edward V11		●
Howgate Wonder		●
Isaac Newton's Tree / Flower of Kent		●
Lane's Prince Albert		●
Monarch		●
Newton Wonder		●
Norfolk Beauty		●
Tower of Glamis		●

STORING APPLES

Some apple varieties are at their best straight from the tree, others mellow with age, transmuting from cooker to eater. Some are inedible for months. In years of plenty, stewed apple and apple sauce can be frozen, but it is wonderful to have stored cooking and dessert apples to use or eat fresh.

Storing apples requires an equable, frost-proof space, dark and cool with circulating air. A cellar, insulated garage roof-space, north-facing loft, unused outside lavatory can all work well with wooden or chicken-wire shelves. The apples must be dry and laid out so that they do not touch. Once rot sets in it transmits quickly to neighbouring fruit. They can be wrapped in newspaper, but Roy Genders, professional gardener, offers dry straw or dried bracken, and Bob Flowerdew of the BBC's *Gardener's World* suggests dried nettles (see Bob Flowerdew's recipe p 137–8). The space must repel small visitors: mice and rats will be attracted by the lovely smell. Wooden apple racks are available to buy: check that they are made from Forestry Stewardship Council approved wood from not too far away. They must not smell or they will taint the apples: beech, chestnut and non-resinous pine all make good racks.

Commercial apple storage in huge warehouses, or shipping from the other side of the world requires manipulation of the atmosphere, cooling, lowering the oxygen while increasing the carbon dioxide in the container. Picked early and prevented from breathing, it is no wonder that so many travelled or far-too-late apples are disappointing. Better to buy locally and eat them in season or store in your own way.

SMALL-SCALE APPLE JUICE- & CIDER-MAKING

DIY apple juice

From the moment the first Discovery, Emneth's Early or Beauty of Bath is picked in July/August you can quench your thirst all the way through spring with juices of different hues and flavours as each apple comes into its season. Single-variety apple juices are wonderfully varied, or you can blend juices to satisfy different tastes, sharp or sweet.

We need around 66 mg of Vitamin C each day and a single Ribston Pippin will provide around 56mg. Apples also contain flavonoids, which guard against heart disease, and fruit fibre, some of which remains in the juice, making it cloudy, and helps to reduce the risk of bowel cancer.

Juicing is a simple, enjoyable process and can be a source of income. On Apple Day you may see an industrious presser servicing a long and expectant queue.

Every neighbourhood, even in the city, should boast a Community Orchard. While you are helping yours to grow, remember that a mature Bramley tree can produce more than two hundred pounds of apples. Those who can't pick their own fruit may let you take their harvest in exchange for a few bottles of juice or cider. Some growers offer juicing-grade fruit at low prices if the buyer collects from them.

Choose ripe fruit: it contains the highest sugar levels. Don't use rotten fruit: it may have started to ferment, which will taint the flavour of the juice and reduce its shelf life. Fruit with deep bruising, mould or rot may contain the naturally occurring toxin patulin, which can poison you. Please ask for advice or contact the Food Standards Agency. Collect and discard mouldy fruit, but slightly bruised fruit is welcomed by the birds and other winter visitors, such as badgers, foxes and squirrels.

Milling or Crushing To extract the most juice, the apples must be crushed or milled to a pulp – pomace – before pressing. The simplest method is to put them into a strong tub and pound them with a length of timber – a section of untreated three by three is ideal. The Ingenio mills invented in the sixteenth century and based on the design of a Cuban sugar-cane press – speeded up the process of tearing the apples into a pulp with intermeshing teeth. The old method, which survives in the West Country and Midlands, depended upon the apples being crushed by horse-drawn stone rollers in a trough ring. A variety of purpose-built mills are now available, starting with extension bars for household drills; a small hand-cranked mill costs around £150. The fruit pulp is acidic, so your containers should be made of stainless steel, wood, food-quality plastic containers or an old ceramic sink. Vigo Limited, based in Devon, offer everything for the cider- and juice-maker, amateur and professional.

Pressing For making larger amounts, the pomace, restrained in straw, horsehair or nylon matting is piled into a cheese on a wooden platform, with a heavy timber plate above. When the screw is turned, the plate presses down on the pomace, the juice runs out.

The small-scale juice- or cider-maker is best served by a basket press. This consists of a wooden or steel cylinder into which the pulp is poured, then compressed with a plate screwed into the cylinder. The juice escapes through gaps in the cylinder walls and collects in a channel at the base of the press. The fruit should not come into contact with bare metal to prevent tainting. Basket presses cost between £100 and £400 new, depending on size; some groups will lend or hire them. Members of the Hertfordshire Orchards Initiative bought a large second-hand press, which they will hire cheaply. The Shropshire Apple Trust and Greenwood Trust in Coalbrookdale, near Telford, sell ten-litre basket presses of local oak for £250. They have also constructed a traditional-style wooden cider press for community use.

Spent pomace or must was often fed to pigs to flavour the pork. Sans pigs, add it to your compost heap or scatter it in a corner of the garden or orchard to see what new varieties arise from the pips.

Storage Apple juice will taste best, and its vitamin C content will be higher, if drunk straight from the press. If it is not for immediate consumption, take steps to avoid fermentation. When bottling, siphon the juice from below the froth that is produced during pressing to reduce the amount of fruit debris. Fresh raw

juice will keep in the fridge for about a week. To freeze it, pour the juice into freezer bags supported in empty juice or milk cartons.

For longer-term storage the juice can be pasteurised. The simplest method is to fill clean screw-top glass bottles with juice and stand them carefully up to their necks in hot water. When the juice reaches 72°C, keep the temperature constant for twenty minutes. Then cap the bottles and lay them on their sides. This ensures that the hot juice comes into contact with the cap and that a partial vacuum is formed as the juice cools. Pasteurised bottled juice will keep at least until the next crop is ready. However, the process diminishes the flavour, so avoid treating juice with a delicate taste, such as Worcester Pearmain in this way.

Ragman's Lane Farm, in Gloucestershire, runs courses on juice- and cider-making. They make juice as follows:

> We pick the fruit by hand, shaking it from the trees and collecting it in sacks. The fruit is then washed and milled and pressed on a small Vigo Press. Thirty apples to the bucket, five buckets to the bag, forty bags to the tonne. Thirty bags fill a pickup. A tonne makes 650 bottles of juice. The juice is left to settle overnight before being heated to 72°C in the bottle to pasteurise – this kills any harmful bacteria and increases the shelf life. No sugar is added. We try to source the fruit locally. By paying for apples from remnant orchards we hope to preserve old fruit trees within the landscape. These orchards are largely unmanaged and have had no sprays. We sell our juice locally through farmers' markets and local retailers cutting food miles and packaging.

Juice brings in seasonal income to a Community Orchard management fund – but health and trading standards must be met. For advice contact the Food Standards Agency or see www.food.gov.uk

DIY Cider

Cider is a very ancient drink and the knowledge of its making is as much about culture as it is about chemistry. Making cider on a small scale is a simple and satisfying occupation, the more so when it is done with others.

There are two traditions of cider-making in England and Wales, which divide on a notional line between the Wash and the Solent. To the east, ciders are made from the blended juices of locally grown culinary or dessert apples; to the west, cider apples are cultivated to produce sharpness, bitterness or sweetness, the juices blended to the desired flavour. The sugars in a cider apple will determine the alcohol content of the drink, while its acidity will add sharpness; tannin adds body and bitterness.

Small-scale cider-making involves five stages: picking, crushing and pressing as with juice-making (see p 245), followed by fermentation and ageing.

Cider apples are collected from the ground after they have fallen from the tree. In cider production, a degree of recent bruising won't matter. The fruit must be ripe so that the sugar content is high, and some cider-makers claim that apples which are just beginning to rot help fermentation. But the patulin toxin (see p 245) won't be destroyed during fermentation so err on the side of caution: leave rotting fruit for the birds and wash your fruit before you press it.

Fermentation Yeast drives fermentation; first, it converts the apple sugars into alcohol, then turns the malic acid in the apple juice into lactic acid and carbon dioxide. It occurs naturally on the skin of the apples, and each variety harbours its own strain. The traditional cider-maker need do no more than allow the yeast to get on with its job. A wooden cider press will pick up yeast from the juice, so each farmhouse press will produce a distinct cider.

Pour the pressed juice into a scrupulously clean demijohn or a large bucket with a lid and leave it to stand in a warm place at 15° – 20°C. A brown scum on top of the liquid will tell you that it has begun to ferment. If you are using a bucket, skim off the scum occasionally with a spoon, or if using a demijohn, by replacing bungs of sterile cotton wool. The juice should bubble as it ferments vigorously for about three days. If the cider does not ferment well, perhaps because the temperature is too cool or the concentration of natural yeast is too low, you could add a little dried wine yeast.

When the initial vigorous fermentation has subsided, fit an airlock to the container and leave it for 3–6 months. Then transfer it into new demijohns fitted with an airlock (to allow carbon dioxide out but no air in), taking care not to stir up the dead yeast cells and fruit pulp at the bottom of the fermentation vessel. The cider should be reasonably clear by now and ready for bottling or storing in an oak barrel. At the bottling stage, some people like to add a little honey for colour and extra flavour. Others add a little sugar to sweeten, which encourages a second fermentation in the bottle, resulting in sparkling cider. In this case, use bottles and corks that are capable of withstanding pressure, such as champagne bottles. Store them in a cooler place at 10–15°C for 6–8 weeks for secondary fermentation.

Ageing Your cider will be ready to drink about six months after bottling when its acidity will have diminished, but it will probably be at its best after two years. Old wooden barrels impart flavour, and some, such as ex-rum barrels, even clear it.

A visit to the Cider Museum in Hereford, or the Rural Life Museum in Glastonbury, Somerset, will give you a good idea of the farm methods of the past.

Orchardless Cider-makers A passion for good cider drove two Berkshire families to invest in a small press and make their own. The New Road Cyderists collected apples from friendly neighbours and, late in 1994, produced their first vintage: their Cyder Nouveau was highly commended at Caversham Court Apple Day, even though it was a bit gum puckering. They went on to win a European environmental award and produce a small book – *Apples, Berkshire, Cider*.

ORCHARD HONEY

Which came first: the blossom or the bee? Domesticated and wild bees (more than 250 species) thrive in orchards and perform an invaluable job in pollinating the blossom ensuring a good crop. Without insects, especially bees, apple trees and most other fruit trees would not set fruit.

Intensive farming, with its monocultures, herbicides and pesticides, has denied wild bees a place to live and work, yet we need them, wasps and flies to help with pollination – the more so since our domestic honeybee population is under threat. Wild honeybees became extinct in Britain after 1992 when the parasitic varroa mite, now endemic here, arrived, and now a new species of bee-destroying hornet is likely to migrate from continental Europe.

Today fruit-growers have special pollination contracts with beekeepers: bees are shunted around the country on trucks to work as specific crops come into flower. As the Department for Environment, Food and Rural Affairs (Defra) in a restrained tone points out: 'Pollinating animals provide almost incalculable economic and ecological value to humans, flowering plants and wildlife.' But in 2007 in an attempt to put a figure on the specific work of bees they suggested that 'The economic value of crops grown commercially in the UK that benefit from bee pollination is estimated at around £120m–£200m p.a. By contrast, the value of honey production in the UK fluctuates between £10m and £30m p.a.' If unexplained 'colony collapse disorder' spreads in the UK, as it has in the USA, so honey is likely to become increasingly expensive. The cost to orchard owners and other growers will be disastrous.

The extent of our reliance on bees and other insects really is *incalculable*: their role is fundamental to our wellbeing. Without them, *we* shall have to flit between blossoms to set the fruit.

A few decades ago beehives were commonly kept in a corner of a farm or commercial orchard: the blossom of fruit trees and other crops offered colonies an important source of pollen, which enabled them to build up their population and, in good years, produce surplus honey. Now British beekeepers contribute just 10 per cent of the honey we eat, so there is much work to be done in encouraging the spread of beekeeping.

Crapes Fruit Farm, Aldham, near Colchester in Essex, hosts sixty hives, some owned by retired head teacher Derek Webber who instructs on beekeeping two evenings a week throughout the summer and holds the exams in the orchard. The produce is sold as Essex honey in Crapes apple mail-order boxes. In Herefordshire David Tindall sees the economic sense in making orchard honey: with five colonies in the Top Orchard he will 'segregate the ensuing honey in order that it can be specially labelled as Tidnor Wood Orchard Honey'. Since 2005, the National Trust's Killerton Estate in Devon has been working with Vivian's Honey Farm who provide bees to pollinate the blossom in the estate's five cider orchards. Using traditional methods they produce Killerton Orchard honey, which is used in the restaurant at Killerton House and is sold in the gift shop. Visitors love to buy local products such as honey as a souvenir of their visit. James Hamill, of the Hive Honey Shop in London, approached things differently. He planted a four-acre orchard, near Kingswood, Surrey with seventy-six apple varieties in which to put his thirty beehives. The British Beekeepers Association offers all kinds of advice as do Bees and Trees in the West Midlands. Somerset Orchard Link offer subsidised vocational training for orchard owners who wish to keep bees. London beekeepers do it on their roofs and you too could be making your own golden nectar. William Lawson (1618) advised:

> *you must have an house made along a sure dry wall*
> *in your Garden, neere, or in your Orchard*
> *for Bees love flowers and wood with their hearts.*

MISTLETOE

Ancient reverence for 'the golden bough', alive in winter when all else seems dead, has bestowed on mistletoe magical powers and mystery, and the kissing bough was once known as an aphrodisiac. This semi-parasite drinks from its host trees but photosynthesises for itself. Visible against the winter sky as clumps among the branches, mistletoe grows especially well in the lichen-encrusted orchards of Herefordshire, Worcestershire, Gloucestershire and Somerset and helps to give them their distinctive character. Female plants carry the berries that feed the mistle-thrush and blackcap among other birds, and can bring a modest source of income. Gathered sensitively, and not from the same tree every year, mistletoe supports the seasonal market and occasional pruning will prevent it damaging its host.

The Tenbury Wells Mistletoe Enterprise has done much to revive the threatened traditional mistletoe auction/market in late November and early December and now sells mistletoe by mail order for Christmas and ripe mistletoe berries for growing in February. Their website tells much about this strange plant: www.mistletoe.org.uk

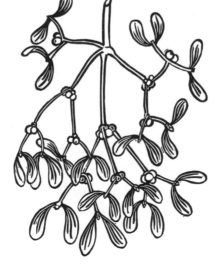

GROWING YOUR OWN

The best time to plant is in early winter when the soil is still warm and the tree is dormant – this is vital for bare-root trees. Ensure that the place you have selected for planting is well drained, sheltered from prevailing weather and frost free (or choose a late flowering variety). Dig the hole just before you plant, and never plant on a day when the ground is waterlogged or frozen. Choose fruit trees that are known to grow best in your locality and ask about disease resistance.

Buy from a reputable nursery. Trees become available in November, although climate change is altering the start of the tree-planting season because the warming weather is delaying dormancy. Make your order well in advance: less common varieties may take a year to prepare.

When buying a young tree, think about how tall and how spreading you want it to be. Everything depends on the rootstock, which imparts or represses vigour. Out of the range of rootstocks M25 supports a tall standard tree, best for wild life, shade and landscape, if you have room; M26 indicates a bush or trainable tree, and M27 a miniature that you can grow in a pot on your balcony. Discuss how far apart trees should be spaced: the convention may vary in different areas but as a rough guide, a standard should be positioned 30 feet from its neighbours, half-standard 20 feet, a bush 15 feet.

Apple trees that are self-fertile do not need a pollinator; others need pollen from a tree that blossoms at the same time (these are diploids) and a few, such as Bramley's Seedling, Blenheim Orange and Ribston Pippin (triploids), need two pollinators. Good nurseries will help you work out the best neighbours. Bees do their work better when they do not have to journey far.

Rabbits, sheep, deer and other herbivores like apple bark and twigs in winter; competitive grasses may slow a tree's growth in its first few summers. Guarding and mulching may be sensible. Water during the first growing season or two.

Fruit trees need a lot or a little looking after, depending on your personality and your demands of them. Take advice on planting, spacing, pruning and disease, but remember that trees know very well how to grow and fruit, given a fair chance and if you are not seeking a commercial crop.

SPECIALIST NURSERIES/ SUPPLIERS

The listed nurseries or projects stock a range of apple varieties and many also stock other orchard fruit trees. If a nursery in your area cannot supply the variety or size of tree you are looking for others may offer a mail-order service. Any good nursery will be able to offer advice.

East of England Apples and Orchards Project
Contact: treesales@applesandorchards.org.uk
(01328 838403); www.applesandorchards.org.uk
Sells around 180 varieties of apples and pears associated with the east of England.

BUCKINGHAMSHIRE

Bernwode Plants, Kingswood Lane, Ludgershall,
HP18 9RB (01844 237415);
www.bernwodeplants.co.uk
Approximately three hundred varieties of apple, around forty varieties of pear, plus plums, gages, damsons, cherries, quinces, medlars and mulberries. Mail-order service.

Buckingham Nurseries & Garden Centre,
Tingewick Rd, Buckingham MK18 4AE
(01280 822133); www.buckingham-nurseries.co.uk
Around fifty varieties of apples, pears, plums, damsons and gages. Mail-order service.

CAMBRIDGESHIRE

See *Bedfordshire*, East of England Apples and Orchards Project.

CORNWALL

Bodmin Plant & Herb Nursery, Laveddon Mill,
Laninval Hill, Bodmin PL30 5JU (01208 72837);
www.bodminnursery.co.uk
Range of apple varieties, including about ten Cornish varieties, plus Cornish plums and other fruit trees.

Cornish Apple Trees, Perranwell, Truro (01872 864409)
Over 50 Cornish apple varieties plus Cornish plum varieties.

Duchy of Cornwall Nurseries, Penlyne, Cott Rd, Lostwithiel, PL22 0HW (01208 872668); www.duchyofcornwallnursery.co.uk
Around fifty apple varieties including fifteen Cornish varieties. Mail-order service.

James MacFarlane, Trevothen Common, Coverack, Helston, TR12 6SD (01326 280594)
Specialises in Cornish varieties of apples.

Trelowarren Estate Nursery, Trelowarren, Mawgan, Helston (01326 221224)
More than a dozen Cornish apple varieties.

DEVON
Adam's Apples, Egremont Barn, Payhembury, Honiton EX14 3LA (01404 841166); www.talatonplants.co.uk
More than a hundred varieties of apple, plus pears, cherries, plums and gages. Also offers grafting service, local orchard planning and renovation. By appointment only.

Caroline and Richard Vulliamy, Tamar Valley Orchard Volunteers (01579 370411); email: carolinevulliamy@hotmail.com
New young stock grafted from local trees, which makes them ideal for local conditions, plus advice to orchard owners and workshops.

Thornhayes Nursery, St Andrews Wood, Dulford, Cullompton EX15 2DF (01884 266746); www.thornhayes-nursery.co.uk
Kevin Croucher has more than two hundred apple varieties, including seventy cider varieties and many from the south-west, thirty plum, thirty pear, including perry, Devon specials including mazzards (particular cherries) and Tamar Valley cherries. Also, design and advisory service, and mail order.

ESSEX
See *Bedfordshire* for East of England apples and Orchards Project.

Ken Muir Ltd, Honeypot Farm, Rectory Road, Weeley Heath, Clacton-on-Sea CO16 9BJ (01255 830181); www.kenmuir.co.uk
Around seventy varieties of apple, plus pear, plum, gage, damson, cherry, quince, medlar and nuts. Mail-order service.

GLOUCESTERSHIRE
Dave Kaspar, Day's Cottage Cider, Brookthorpe (01452 813602)
Gloucestershire apple varieties, and juice from their own orchards.

Lodge Farm Trees, Lodge Farm, Rockhampton, Berkeley GL13 9DY (01454 260310); www.lodgefarmtrees.co.uk
Around seventy varieties of apple, plus pears, cherries, plums, medlar and quince.

Sarah Juniper, 109 Woodmancote,
Dursley GL11 4AH (01453 545675);
www.sarahjuniper.co.uk
An identifier, who supplies Gloucestershire
varieties, offers workshops and displays of apple
varieties for Apple Day events.

HAMPSHIRE

Blackmoor Plant Centre, Blackmoor, Liss
(01420 488822); www.blackmoorplants.co.uk
Sells around a hundred apple varieties.

Family Trees, Sandy Lane, Shedfield
SO32 2HQ (01329 834812)
Around 150 varieties of apple, pear, cherry,
plum, damson, gage, quince, medlar and nuts.
Mail-order service.

HEREFORDSHIRE

H.P. Bulmer Ltd, The Cider Mills, Plough Lane,
Hereford HR4 0LE (01432 294302)
Thirty varieties of cider apple, plus perry pears.

Paul Jasper, The Lighthouse, Bridge Street,
Leominster HR6 8DU (Fax: 01568 616499);
www.jaspertrees.co.uk
More than a hundred apple varieties plus pears,
plums, grapes, cherries and damsons, all bare root.

HERTFORDSHIRE

Aylett Nurseries Ltd, London Colney, St Albans
(01727 822255); www.aylettnurseries.co.uk

Around thirty apple varieties, plus plums,
damson, gages, pears and cherries.

See *Bedfordshire* for East of England Apples and
Orchards Project.

ISLE OF WIGHT

Deacon's Nursery, Godshill PO38 3HW
(01983 840750); www.deaconsnurseryfruits.co.uk
More than two hundred apple varieties,
including several Scottish ones, plus some ciders,
pears, plums, cherries; grafting stock available.
Mail-order service.

KENT

Brogdale Orchards Ltd, Brogdale Rd,
Faversham ME13 8XZ (01795 535286);
www.brogdale.org
This is the old national fruit-trials establishment:
they have the national collections of around two
thousand varieties of apple, plus pear, cherry and
plum. Also, graft while-you-wait (March) and
bud while-you-wait (August) events from stock
grown at farm; will bud or graft from your own
trees and identify varieties.

Keepers Nursery, Gallants Court, East Farleigh,
Maidstone ME15 0LE (01622 726465);
www.keepers-nursery.co.uk
Three hundred apple varieties, plus many pears,
plums, cherries other fruits and nuts. Also
grafting, budding and mail-order service.

LINCOLNSHIRE

See *Bedfordshire* for East of England Apples and Orchards Project.

NORFOLK

See *Bedfordshire* for East of England Apples and Orchards Project.

Chris Bowers & Sons, Whispering Trees Nurseries, Wimbotsham PE34 8QB (01366 388752); www.chrisbowers.co.uk
170 apple varieties, plus pears, plums, gages, damsons and cherries.

NOTTINGHAMSHIRE

Cool Temperate, 45 Stamford Street, Awsworth, Notts NG16 2QL (0115 916 2673); www.cooltemperate.co.uk
Around forty apple varieties, plus pears, plums, gages, damsons, quinces, medlars, mulberries and nuts. Profits fund research into growing trees on their own roots. Visit by appointment only.

SOMERSET

Cider Apple Trees, 'Kerian', Corkscrew Lane, Woolston, Nr North Cadbury, Somerset BA22 7BP (01963 441101); www.ciderappletrees.co.uk
Stocks thirty cider-apple varieties, and sixty eating and culinary varieties.

Scotts Nurseries (Merriott) Ltd, Merriott TA16 5PL (01460 72306); www.scottsnurseries.co.uk
More than two hundred apple varieties, including cider apples, plus perry pears, pears, plums, cherries, quinces and medlars. Mail-order service.

SUFFOLK

See *Bedfordshire* for East of England Apples and Orchards Project.

Botanica, Campsea Ashe, Wickham Market (01728 747113); www.botanica.org.uk
Offers a wide range of fruit trees, including apple varieties of East Anglian origin. Botanica follow the Flora Locale code of conduct for the supply of native and wild plants.

Perryhill Nurseries, Hartfield (01892 770377);
www.perryhillnurseries.co.uk
Around fifteen apple varieties, plus medlar,
mulberry, pear, plum, quince and others.

Barters Plant Centre, Chapmanslade,
Westbury BA13 4AL (01373 832294);
www.barters.co.uk
Around twenty apply varieties, plus cherries,
walnuts, cobnuts, plums, damsons, gages, quinces
and mulberries, advice on rootstocks and
pollination groups. Barters grafted the Corsley
Pippin, named after the school where the original
tree was found.

Landford Trees, Landford, Salisbury
SP5 2EH (01794 390808);
www.landfordtrees.co.uk
Around thirty apple varieties, plus cherry,
medlar, mulberry, pear, plum and quince.
Trees can be collected or mail-ordered.

Trees For Life (formerly Frank P Matthews),
Berrington Court, Tenbury Wells WR15 8TH
(01584 810214); www.trees-for-life.com
Hundreds of varieties of apple, plus extensive
range of graft wood available; also pears,
cherries, hazelnuts, gages, medlars, damsons,
plums, quinces, walnuts, and mulberries.
Minimum order of £50.

Walcot Organic Nursery, Lower Walcot Farm,
Walcot Lane, Drakes Broughton, Pershore,
WR10 2AL (01905 841587); www.walcotnursery.co.uk
Certified organic fruit, around twenty-five apple
varieties, plus pears, plums, cherries and quinces.
Mail-order service.

R.V. Roger Ltd, The Nurseries, Pickering
YO18 7JW (01751 472226); www.rvroger.co.uk
At least eighty apple varieties, plus pears, plums,
damsons, cherries, medlars, mulberries, quinces
and nuts, also rootstock, grafting scions and
budding eyes. Mail-order service.

Butterworth's Organic Nursery, Garden Cottage,
Auchinleck Estate, Cumnock, Ayrshire
KA18 2LR (01290 551088);
www.butterworthsorganicnursery.co.uk
Fifty-plus apple varieties, many originating in
Scotland, plus plums, pears, and a book about
growing apples in Scotland. Mail-order service.
Visitors by appointment only.

J. Tweedie Fruit Trees, Maryfield Road Nursery, Maryfield, Nr Terregles, Dumfries DG2 9TH (01387 720880)
Around a hundred apple varieties, plus pears, plums, cherries and other fruit.
Mail-order servicce.

WALES

Dolau-Hirion Fruit Tree Nursery, Dolauhirion, Capel Isaac, Llandeilo SA19 7TG (01558 668744)
Welsh varieties, disease resistant in the Welsh climate; traditional varieties (pre-1850) for Wales, England and Scotland; grafting service, accessories.

Gwynfor Nurseries, Pontgarreg, Llandysul SA44 6AU (01239 654151); www.gwynfor.co.uk
Can supply and advise on Welsh apple varieties, and varieties that will grow well in the Welsh climate.

IRELAND

Irish Seed Saver Association (ISSA), Capparoe, Scariff, Co. Clare (00 353 61 92186); www.irishseedsavers.ie
Many Irish apple varieties available, ISSA having worked with the Armagh Orchards Trust to track down old and lost Irish varieties and help to set up the national collection at University College Dublin and at Caparroe. So far, they have gathered 140 varieties. Grafted trees are sold for planting in domestic gardens; an orchard restoration and creation service is

offered. Online apple catalogue lists more than eighty varieties with descriptions. ISSA says: 'Native apples are more intense in flavour than those now grown commercially. Varieties grown before the advent of pesticides are more resistant to scab, mildew and canker because the trees are acclimatised to the warm and damp Irish weather conditions.'

SPECIALIST
SUPPLIERS
OF FRUIT

The following list gives details of some fruit farms, growers and suppliers who sell an interesting selection of fruit. Some produce mail-order boxes and may make up Apple Day gift packs. Please remember that those offering a postal service need notice of your requirements, so place your order a few months in advance,

especially if you are ordering for Apple Day or Christmas. Remember, also, that the varieties you request may not always be available, due to seasonal vagaries, but most growers will replace them with something equally interesting.

BERKSHIRE

Cross Lanes Fruit Farm, Mapledurham, Reading RG4 7UW (01189 723167); www.crosslanesfruitfarm.co.uk
Around fifty apple varieties, plus damsons, four plum varieties and nine pear varieties grown and sold from the farm shop. Mail-order service.

BUCKINGHAMSHIRE

Home Cottage Farm, Bangors Road South, Iver SL0 0BB (01753 653064); www.homecottagefarm.co.uk
Thirteen apple varieties, plus pears, plums and soft fruit, sold through farm shop and pick-your-own.

Peterley Manor Farm Shop and PYO, Peterley Lane, Prestwood, Great Missenden HP16 0HH (01494 863566); email: info@peterley.co.uk, and www.peterleymanorfarm.co.uk
Apples include Cox's, Bramley's, Katy, Discovery, and juice. Also five cherry varieties, seven plums and damsons, plus cobnuts and walnuts.

CAMBRIDGESHIRE

Cambridge Organic Food Company (01223 873300); email: info@cofco.co.uk
Runs a box scheme for organic fruit and

vegetables, eggs, flour and other produce. Their apples, Bramley's, Spartan and Lord Lambourne, are grown in their own organic orchard at Aston Organic Orchard, Risby, Bury St Edmunds, converted to organic status in 1988. They also buy in apples from Farmer Kit's Organics, Little Bowsers Farm, Little Walden, Saffron Walden.

CHESHIRE

Haworth's of Eddisbury Fruit Farm, Yeld Lane, Kelsall (01829 759157) www.eddisbury.co.uk

Around twenty-six apple varieties, plus pears, plums, damsons, apple juice, cider and fruit wine. Available from farm shop or as PYO.

Willington Fruit Farm, Hillside Farm, Chapel Lane, Willington, Tarporley CW6 0PH (01829 751216)

Fifteen apple varieties, from September to January, plus home-pressed juice.

DEVON

Barnstaple Pannier Market (01271 379084)

Francis Hancock sells apples on Fridays at the market from August to spring. He grows forty varieties (mostly dessert and culinary).

West Lake Farm, Chilla, Beaworthy EX21 5XF (01409 221991); www.west-lake.co.uk

Hires out a portable press, and offers pressing at the farm. They press their own organic apples for juice, cider and cider vinegar.

DORSET

Elwell Fruit Farm, Waytown, Bridport DT6 5LF (01308 488283)

Thirty apple varieties, and pears grown in their own orchards, plus apple juice; PYO in September only. Telephone orders only for collection at the farm gate.

ESSEX

Crapes Fruit Farm, Rectory Rd, Aldham, Colchester CO6 3RR (01206 212375)

More than 150 apple varieties; available in mixed seasonal 7lb, 8lb, 13lb or 20lb boxes by mail order or from the farm shop. Some plums, cherries, pears and quinces, also honey from orchard bees. Their popular Apple Day demonstration selections should be ordered well in advance.

Lathcoats Farm, Beehive Lane, Galleywood, Chelmsford CM2 8LX (01245 353021); www.eapples.co.uk

Forty apple varieties, plus twelve single-variety juices available from farm shop. PYO and 'rent-a-tree'.

Park Fruit Farm, Pork Lane, Great Holland, Frinton-on-Sea (01255 674621); www.parkfruitfarm.co.uk

Forty apple varieties, four pear varieties, ten varieties of plums and damsons. PYO or sold from the farm shop and at local farmers' markets. Also fresh-pressed apple juice, mixed and single varieties, cider and cider vinegar.

Spencer's Farm Shop, Wickham Fruit Farm, Wickham St Pauls, Halstead (01787 269476); www.spencersfarmshop.co.uk
Twenty apple varieties over the season from their own orchards, plus cherries. Also PYO.

GLOUCESTERSHIRE
Hayles Fruit Farm, Winchcombe, Cheltenham (01242 602123); www.hayles-fruit-farm.co.uk
Around fifteen apple varieties, plus pears, plums from their own orchards, cobnuts, apple and pear juice, and cider.

Lea Court Farm, Upper Framilode, Gloucester (01452 740304/741013)
Unsprayed fruit, with around sixteen apple varieties, plus pears and seventeen plum varieties for sale in farm shop.

Longborough Fruit Farm, Manor Farm, Longborough, Moreton-in-Marsh (01451 830469); www.longboroughfarmshop.com
Around forty apple varieties, plus several pear and plum varieties grown in their orchards a mile from the farm shop. Plums available as PYO.

HAMPSHIRE
Blackmoor Estate, Blackmoor (01420 473782); www.blackmoorestate.co.uk
Apples, pears, plums, apricots and quinces, from their own orchards, sold at the farm shop and at farmers' markets. Gift boxes and a jute gift bag of apples available.

Durleigh Marsh Farm and Farm Shop, Rogate Road, Petersfield GU31 6AX (01730 821626)
Grows and sells twelve plum varieties (PYO available), plus apples from Blackmoor Estate, local ciders and apple juices.

Fruitwise, 96 Winchester Street, Botley, Southampton (01489 796790); www.fruitwise.net
Around forty apple varieties, including cider varieties, and plums grown in their own orchards. They also produce their own cider. Available at farmers' markets in Winchester, Fareham and Southampton, and Fruitopias greengrocer's in Southampton. Boxes of apples can be collected from the farm by prior arrangement.

HEREFORDSHIRE
Dragon Orchard Cropsharers, Dragon Orchard, Putley, Ledbury HR8 2RG (01531 670071); email: info@dragonorchard.co.uk, and www.dragonorchard.co.uk
A twenty-two-acre traditional fruit farm run by Norman and Ann Stanier, the fruit is picked by subscribers to the crop-sharing scheme, who may attend four open weekends each year, enjoy seasonal celebrations, guided walks and a newsletter, as well as apples and orchard produce, including juice and cider.

KENT
Brogdale Horticultural Trust, Brogdale Farm, Brogdale Road, Faversham ME13 8XZ (01795 535286); www.brogdale.org
The National Collection of Apples.

**Chegworth Valley Fruit Farm, Chegworth,
Maidstone ME17 1DE (01622 859272);
www.chegworthvalley.com**

Around forty varieties of apples and pears across
the season, plus apple and pear juice, including
single varieties. Chegworth sell their fruit and
juice at eleven farmers' markets across London.

**Perry Court Farm, Bilting, Ashford TN25 4ES
(01233 812408); www.perrycourt.com**

More than a hundred apple varieties and ten
pears grown in their own orchards, available
from farm shop and at local farmers' markets.

**Pippins Farm, Stonecourt Lane, Pembury,
Tunbridge Wells TN2 4AB (01892 824544)**

Thirty apple varieties grown in their own
orchards, available from the farm shop; also
plums, apple juice and cider.

LONDON

**Hive Honey Shop, 93 Northcote Road,
SW11 6PL (020 7924 6233);
www.thehivehoneyshop.co.uk**

Stocks apples in season from their own orchard
in Kingswood, Surrey, where they grow seventy-
six varieties, of which around twenty-five on sale
in the shop at any one time in season.

**Neal's Yard Dairy, 17 Shorts Gardens,
Covent Garden, WC2H 9UP (020 7240 5700),
and 6 Park Street, Borough Market,
SE1 9AB (020 7645 3554); www.nealsyarddairy.co.uk**

Stocks a range of British apple varieties over the
month around Apple Day to enjoy with their
range of cheeses.

**Fresh & Wild, 69–75 Brewer Street,
W1F 9US (020 7434 3179)**

Stocks a range of British apples in season,
plus apple juice.

NORFOLK

**The Apple and Pear People, Tunstead Road,
Hoveton, Wroxham NR12 8QN (01603 783850)**

Up to sixty varieties of apples and pears from
orchards across Norfolk, plus single-variety
juices.

New Creation Farm Shop, Furnace Lane, Nether Heyford, Northampton NN7 3LB (01327 344511)

Grows more than twenty apple varieties across the season, plus pears and plums. Also, apple juice, and honey from hives in the orchard.

Millets Farm Centre, Kingston Road, Frilford, Abingdon (01865 391555); www.milletsfarmcentre.com

Nine apple varieties grown in traditional 'big tree' orchard: Discovery, Katy, Lord Lambourne, Greensleeves, Howgate Wonder, Bramley's, Spartan, Cox's, and Egremont Russet; plus plums and pears, for PYO and for sale in farm shop. Also fruit juices pressed on the day of picking.

Waterperry Gardens, Waterperry, Nr Wheatley (01844 339254); www.waterperrygardens.co.uk

Around sixty varieties of apples, pears and plums, grown in own orchard, plus single-variety juice and apple trees.

Honeysuckle Wholefoods, 53 Church Street, Oswestry (01691 653125); email: info@honeysuckle-wholefoods.co.uk

Sells between fifteen and twenty apple varieties across the season, plus plums, pears and quinces, all organic.

Charlton Orchards, Charlton Road, Creech St Michael, Taunton TA3 5PF (01823 412959); www.charltonorchards.com

Grows around thirty apple varieties and makes fourteen single-variety apple juices; available from farm shop, local farmers' markets and by mail order.

North Perrott Fruit Farm, Townsend Farmhouse, North Perrott, Crewkerne TAI8 75R (01460 73451); wwwparettbrand.co.uk

Grows twenty-four apple varieties, including cider, four plum and ten pear varieties. Most sold wholesale through the Wye Fruit Co-op, but some also sold at the North Perrott Garden Centre in Crewkerne. Farm-produced Perrott single-variety apple juice also available by mail order.

Quiet Corner Farm, Henstridge BA8 0RA (01963 363045); email: quietcornerfarm@aol.com

Grows apples including Bramley's, Cornish Aromatic, Russets, King of the Pippins and Warrior, a Dorset variety for cooking and eating; Conference pears, all hand-picked and unsprayed; available at farmers' markets in Somerset and Dorset; apple juice for sale in season.

**West Bradley Fruit Farm, Glastonbury
BA6 8LT (01458 850227)**
Around twenty varieties of dessert apples and
pears grown, around ten available in middle
three weekends of September for PYO. Ten
cider-apple varieties sold to local cider-makers.
No farm shop.

SUFFOLK

**Ashill Fruit Farm, Swaffham Road, Watton
IP25 7DB (01760 440050)**
Around forty varieties of apples, plus pears,
plums, apple juice, honey and preserves available
at the farm shop.

**High House Fruit Farm, Sudbourne,
Woodbridge 1P12 2BL (01394 450263);
www.high-house.co.uk**
Apples, including Discovery, Worcester
Pearmain, James Grieve, Egremont Russet,
Cox's. Bramley's; pears, plums, cherries.

**Dan Neuteboom, The Orchards,
Oaktree House, Braiseworth, near Eye
IP23 7DS;
www.realenglishfruit.co.uk**
Around thirty varieties of organic apples and
pears, also trees. Consultancy service.

**Rookery Farm Shop, Tattingstone,
Ipswich IP9 2LU (01473 327220);
www.rookeryfarm.co.uk**
Sells a range of apples.

**Stoke Farm Orchards, Battisford,
Stowmarket
IP14 2NA, (01449 774944);
email: rebeccaupson@btinternet.com**
Ten apple varieties and four pear, plus
single-variety apple juice and pure pear juice.
Available direct from the farm.

**Suffolk Heritage Orchards, The Hall,
Church Hill, Monks Eleigh, Ipswich
IP7 7JQ (01449 740478);
email: gh.orchards@ukonline.co.uk**
George Hodgkinson grows old and rare local
varieties of apples, greengages and plums,
including St Edmunds Pippin and Sturmer
Pippin, plus the Suffolk plum, Coe's Golden
Drop. Telephone or email to order.

SUSSEX

**Laurel Tree Fruit Farms, Boar's Head,
Crowborough TN6 3HD (01892 661637)**
Range of varieties grown; available from
September to March.

**Middle Farm, Firle, Lewes
(01323 811411);
www.middlefarm.com**
Range of apple varieties on sale in farm
shop in season; occasional presentation packs
of apples. Home to the national collection of
cider and perry, with bottled and draught cider
and perry on sale, including their own
Pookhill Cider.

Perryhill Orchards, Edenbridge Road, Hartfield TN7 4JJ (01892 770595)
Around ten apple varieties grown and sold in the farm shop, also PYO; juice and cider.

Ringden Fruit Farm, Hurst Green, Etchingham TNI9 7QY (01580 879385); www.ringdenfarm.co.uk
Wide variety of apples sold, plus around thirty single-variety juices.

Tullens Fruit Farm, Tullens Pickhurst Lane, Pulborough RH20 1DA (01798 873800); email: sales@tullens.co.uk, and www.tullens.co.uk
Established in the 1950s, in 2002 its new owners planted additional old apple varieties. Varieties available: Cox's, Worcester Pearmain, Bramley, Egremont Russet, Red Pippin, Lord Lambourne, James Grieve, Discovery, Blenheim Orange, Laxtons Superb, plus Comice and Conference pears. Also single-variety apple juices.

E.H. Wilson & Sons, Oakwood Farm, Poppinghole Lane, Robertsbridge TN32 5BL (01580 830893)
Around forty apple varieties, plus perry pears in their organic orchards. Apples sold at Lewes farmers' market, local shops and at the farm gate by appointment. Their organic perry and apple juice sold at Middle Farm Shop, Firle (see p269), and at the farm gate by appointment.

Feldon Forest Farm, Frankton, Rugby CV23 9PD (01926 632246); www.feldon-forest-farm.co.uk
A young orchard of thirty apple varieties, plus pears, plums, greengages, quinces and cherries; available at the local country market and from the farm by appointment.

Snitterfield Fruit Farm, Kings Lane, Snitterfield, Stratford-upon-Avon CV37 0QA (01789 731711)
Twenty-five apple varieties, plus a range of other fruit, juice, preserves.

Broomfields Farm Shop, School Plantation, Holt Heath, Worcester WR6 6NF (01905 620233); www.broomfieldsfarmshop.co.uk
Fifteen apple varieties from their own orchards. Mail-order service.

Clive's Fruit Farm, Upper Hook Road, Upton upon Severn (01684 592664); www.clivesfruitfarm.co.uk
Around twenty apple varieties, six pear, six plums, plus damsons. Ready-picked or PYO. Also apple juice, cider and perry.

Mill Orchards, Stourport Road, Great Witley (01299 896222); www.millorchards.co.uk
Around fifteen apple varieties, plus pear, plum and single-variety apple juices. Apples are sold at Knightwick farmers' market and juice at Great Witley post office.

Walsgrove Farm, Egdon, Spetchley WR7 4QL (01905 345371); http://welcome.to/walsgrove
More than sixty apple varieties across the season, plus seventeen plum varieties, available from farm shop, PYO, and as presentation boxes. Eight acres of orchard with hook-ups for five caravans.

YORKSHIRE

Yorkshire Orchards, White House Farm, Bolton Lane, Wilberfoss YO41 5NX (01759 380375); www.yorkshireorchards.co.uk
More than a hundred apple varieties grown in own orchards, including cider and crab apples; apples sold through their website, visits to the orchards by appointment only, plus open days throughout the year.

WALES

Berryhill Farm, Coedkernew, Newport, Gwent NP10 8UD (01633 680938); www.berryhillfruitfarm.co.uk
Twelve apple varieties, plus plums and pears, grown and sold through farm shop and PYO. Apple juice also available.

SCOTLAND

Pillars of Hercules Farm, Falkland, Cupar, Fife KY15 7AD (01337 857749); www.pillars.co.uk
Organic farm with small orchard, growing about ten apple varieties sold in the farm shop.

IRELAND

Irish Seed Savers Association, Caparroe, Scariff, Co. Clare (00 353 61 921866); www.irishseedsavers.ie

See also Common Ground's website **www.england-in-particular.info** and **www.commonground.org.uk**

COLLECTIONS OF FRUIT TREES

These gardens or orchards, mostly open to the public, are living collections of different varieties and types of fruit tree. Some counties are developing mother orchards with all of the varieties they can gather.

Be prepared. Not all these collections are of tall trees. Some are rows of small or trained bushes, storing the genetic stock but without the flamboyance of an orchard. The list below is not comprehensive but is offered as a starting point. Talk to landholders, growers, gardeners in your own locality and find out what varieties they grow.

For collections of damsons, pears, perry pears, quinces and walnuts, see www.england-in-particular.info

BEDFORDSHIRE
**Park Wood Community Orchard
and Local Nature Reserve,
Brick Hill Drive, Bedford.**
Around two hundred varieties, including many developed by Laxton Bros of Bedford. Apples, pears, figs, damsons, plums, medlars, quinces and walnuts were planted in 1999 by local residents and Bedford Borough Council.

BUCKINGHAMSHIRE
**Hughenden Manor (National Trust),
High Wycombe HP14 4LA
(01494 755573)**
A Victorian walled garden, containing apple, pear, Morello and sweet cherry trees trained against the walls, plus an orchard planted in the 1980s. Fifty-six apple varieties.

CHESHIRE
**Quarry Bank Mill (National Trust),
Styal, near Wilmslow SK9 4LA
(01625 527468)**
Local apples, pears, plums, damsons, grown in the eighteenth and nineteenth centuries.

CORNWALL
**Cotehele House & Gardens (National Trust),
St Dominick, near Saltash PLI2 6TA
(01579 351346)**
A mother orchard of around a hundred varieties, many from the Tamar Valley, mainly apples, with cherries, pears, walnuts, plums and medlars.

Trelissick Garden (National Trust), Feock, Nr Truro TR3 6QL (01872 862090)
Large orchard stocked with nearly a hundred Cornish apple varieties, plus quinces and medlars, under planted with Cornish daffodils.

Tresillian House Garden, near Newquay, (01637 877447)
Orchards and a restored walled garden with cordons of historic varieties of apples, peaches, cherries and pears, and espaliers of young and very old apples and pears. Twelve plum varieties, of which six are Cornish, including the Kea Plum, plus a collection of more than seventy Cornish apple varieties, grafted on original rootstock pre-1800, medlars and quinces were planted in the 1990s. Visits by appointment only.

CUMBERLAND
Acorn Bank (National Trust), Temple Sowerby, Nr Penrith CA10 1SP (01768 361893)
Collection includes a 1930s orchard and a new orchard of apple varieties from the north-west, begun in 2000, plus espalier pears, cherries, plums, damsons and a mulberry.

Brantwood, Coniston LA21 8AD (01539 441396); www.brantwood.org.uk
Orchard planted in memory of John Ruskin and his love of apple blossom; trained apple trees of local and northern varieties in the walled garden.

DERBYSHIRE
Calke Abbey (National Trust), Ticknall DE73 7LE (01332 863822)
An orchard in the eighteenth-century walled garden includes thirteen apple varieties from the East Midlands.

DEVON
Cockington Court (Torbay Coast and Countryside Trust), Cockington, Torquay TQ2 6XA (01803 606035)
Large orchard containing many Devon varieties.

Killerton House (National Trust), near Broadclyst, Exeter EX5 3LE (01392 881345)
A large collection of apple trees with varieties from the West Country: an orchard of thirty to forty varieties is open to the public while further varieties may be seen by appointment.

Royal Horticultural Society Garden Rosemoor, near Great Torrington, North Devon (01805 624067)
West Country varieties, cider-apple trees and others suitable for growing in Devon, in the orchard and trained in the fruit and vegetable garden.

ESSEX
Broadfields Farm Orchard, The Forest Centre, Broadfields Farm, Pike Lane, Cranham, Upminster RM14 3NS (01708 641880)
Part of Thames Chase Community Forest, planted in 1995 with around 150 standard trees of local apple and pear varieties.

Crapes Fruit Farm, near Colchester.
See Apple Suppliers p 265.

See Apple Suppliers p 265.

GLOUCESTERSHIRE

Gloucestershire County Collection,
Alan Watson, Arboriculture Officer,
Gloucestershire County Council,
The Malthouse, Standish GL10 3DL
(01453 794920)
Mother orchard of Gloucestershire varieties
from which new trees can be propagated.

Westbury Court Garden (National Trust),
Westbury-on-Severn (01452 760461)
Espalier apples, pears and plums
known before 1700.

HAMPSHIRE

The Vyne (National Trust), Sherborne St John,
Basingstoke RG24 9HL (01256 883858)
A half-acre orchard with local and Hampshire
varieties in the grounds and fruit trees in the
walled garden.

HEREFORDSHIRE

Berrington Hall (National Trust), Leominster
HR6 0DW (01568 615721)
Collection of sixty apple varieties, all
pre-1900, collected from old orchards in
the area. Varieties hail from Gloucestershire,
Herefordshire, Worcestershire and the
West Midlands.

Tidnor Wood Orchard Trust, Tidnor
(01369 840360); www.tidnorwood.org.uk
A collection of cider-apple trees intended as a
museum, gene bank and habitat for indigenous
wild life; includes old and new orchards with
more than 360 varieties so far. Visitors on
open days only.

HERTFORDSHIRE

Stanley Lord Orchard,
The Bothy, Shenley Park, Radlett Lane, Shenley
WD7 9DW (01923 852629); www.shenleypark.co.uk
More than 120 apple varieties, young and
old trees in an orchard that was part of the
grounds of Shenley Park Hospital; includes
Hertfordshire varieties.

KENT

Brogdale Horticultural Trust,
Brogdale Farm, Brogdale Road,
Faversham MEl3 8XZ
(01795 535286); www.brogdale.org
Home of the National Fruit Collections;
the largest collection in the world of varieties
of fruit trees and plants; apples and cider
apples included; smallish trees.

Museum of Kent Life, Lock Lane, Sandling,
Maidstone ME14 3AU (01622 763936);
www.museum-kentlife.co.uk
Sixty Kentish apple varieties, plus plums, pears
and cherries.

LANCASHIRE

Leighton Hall, Carnforth LA5 9ST (01524 734474); www.leightonhall.co.uk

A collection of northern apples is being assembled as cordons in the walled garden, with help from the RHS Northern Fruit Group; first trees planted in 2006. Open May–September.

NORFOLK

Felbrigg (National Trust), Felbrigg, Norwich NR11 8PR (01263 837444)

Eighteenth- and nineteenth-century apples, many of Norfolk and East Anglian origin.

Roots of Norfolk, Norfolk Rural Life Museum, Beech House, Gressenhall, East Dereham NR20 4DR (01362 860563)

An orchard of Norfolk varieties.

NORTHAMPTONSHIRE

Lyveden New Bield (National Trust), near Oundle, Peterborough PE8 5AT (01832 205358)

A sixteenth-century orchard is being re-created with more than three hundred trees, twenty-five apple varieties, plus pear, cherry, damson and walnut trees.

NOTTINGHAMSHIRE

Clumber Park (National Trust), Worksop S80 3AZ (01909 476592)

Around fifty apple varieties, plus pears and cherries; peaches and nectarines in the glass-house.

SOMERSET

Somerset Rural Life Museum, Abbey Farm, Chilkwell Street, Glastonbury BA6 8DB (01458 831197)

An orchard with old varieties of Somerset cider-apple trees.

STAFFORDSHIRE

Wolseley Centre, (Staffordshire Wildlife Trust), Wolseley Bridge, Stafford ST17 0WT (01889 880100)

A county collection of around thirty-five local and traditional apple varieties, planted in 2004.

SURREY

Polesden Lacey (National Trust), Great Bookham, near Dorking RH5 6BD (01372 452048)

Re-creation of the old orchard of fifty-two Surrey varieties, planted 2003. Not open to public until 2010.

Royal Horticultural Society Garden Wisley, Wisley, Ripley (0845 260 9000)

700 apple varieties, plus other orchard fruits, in the Fruit Field, Fruit Nursery and Demonstration Fruit Garden.

SUSSEX

West Dean Gardens, West Dean, Chichester PO18 0QZ (01243 818210); www.westdean.org.uk

A restored walled kitchen garden with a large collection of fruit trees, including 100 apple varieties, forty-five pear, and twenty-five plum.

**Castle Bromwich Hall & Gardens Trust,
Chester Road, Castle Bromwich,
Birmingham B36 9BT (0121 749 4100);
www.cbhgt.org.uk**
Restoration of this ten-acre walled garden
with an orchard of apple varieties known
before 1750, espalier and fan-trained
peaches, nectarines, pears and plums.

**Woodgate Valley Urban Farm,
Woodgate Valley Country Park,
Bartley Green, Birmingham
(0121 426 1871); http://wvurbanfarm.org.uk**
Collection of fourteenth century varieties.

**Sizergh Castle (National Trust), Nr Kendal LA8 8AE
(01539 560951); www.nationaltrust.org.uk**
An apple and fruit orchard, including
damsons, at the rear of the kitchen garden;
first plantings from the 1970s. The orchard is
being supplemented with northern varieties,
with help from the RHS Northern Fruit
Group. Other orchards on the property are
being restored.

**Ampleforth Abbey and College, Helmsley
(01439 766899); www.ampleforth.org.uk**
Around sixty-five varieties, many of them old
and regional, like Ribston Pippin. Orchards
open to visitors at certain times.

**Beningbrough Hall & Gardens (National Trust),
Beningbrough YO30 1DD (01904 470666)**
A collection of apples, pears, cherries and plums
within the walled garden.

**Harewood House, Nr Leeds LS17 9LG (0113 218
1010); www.harewood.org**
Collection of northern apple and pear varieties
being assembled by the Northern Fruit Group,
twenty-five so far.

**Helmsley Walled Garden, Cleveland Way, Helmsley
YO62 5AH (01439 771427);
www.helmsleywalledgarden.org.uk**
More than fifty apple varieties planted in the
millennium vegetable garden as espaliers,
cordons and stepovers.

**Yorkshire Apple Collection, Great Yorkshire
Showground, Harrogate (01423 541000)**
Sixteen Yorkshire varieties planted by members
of the Northern Fruit Group in 2001.

**Nunnington Hall (National Trust), Nunnington YO62
5UY (01439 748283)**
Apples grown in Rydale during eighteenth
century, and local pears.

**Parcevall Hall, Skyreholme, Appletreewick, Skipton
BD23 6DG (01756 720311);
www.parcevallhallgardens.co.uk**
Local apples in an orchard dating from the
1930s; new collection planted in the 1980s.

SCOTLAND

House of Dun (National Trust for Scotland), Montrose, Angus DD10 9LQ (01674 810264); www.nts.org.uk

Collection of trained Scottish varieties of apple and pear.

Kellie Castle & Garden (National Trust for Scotland), Pittenweem, Fife KY10 2RF (01333 720271)

An orchard with a number of old Scottish varieties, plus a collection of apples and pears as cordons.

Priorwood Garden (National Trust for Scotland), Melrose, Roxburghshire TD6 9PX (01896 822493)

Apples of all eras, from Roman times to the present day, plus regional varieties, in a two-acre walled garden.

WALES

Erddig (National Trust), Wrexham, Clwyd LL13 0YT (01978 355314)

More than a hundred varieties of seventeenth- and eighteenth-century apples, pears and plums.

Llanerchaeron (National Trust), Ciliau Aeron, Nr Aberaeron, Ceredigion SA48 8DG (01545 570200)

Around fifty apple varieties trained in the walled garden, including 150-year-old espaliers.

IRELAND

Armagh Orchard Trust, Drumilly Estate, Loughall (028 38 892312)

Began in 1995 to preserve apples once common in Ireland; has more than a hundred in the historic walled garden.

The Native Irish Apple Collection, University College Dublin, being replicated at the Irish Seed Savers Association, Caparroe, Scariff, Co. Clare (00 353 61 921866); www.irishseedsavers.ie

140 varieties found so far.

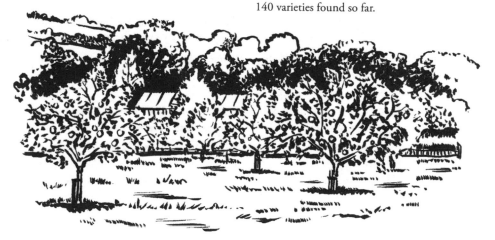

CONTACTS

See Common Ground's websites; www.england-in-particular.info gives information on the Save Our Orchards campaign, Community Orchards, food, calendar customs, a gazetteer and county particulars, as well as groups concerned with other fruit, such as cobnuts, damsons, pears and plums. Apple Day events are to be found in the autumn on www.commonground.org.uk

The Bat Conservation Trust, Unit 2, 15 Cloisters House, 8 Battersea Park Road, London SW8 4BG (020 7627 2629); www.bats.org.uk

British Beekeepers Association, The National Beekeeping Centre, National Agricultural Centre, Stoneleigh Park, Warwickshire CV8 2LG (02476 696679); www.bbka.org.uk

British Independent Fruit Growers Association, c/o Chittenden Orchards, Staplehurst, Tonbridge, Kent TN12 0EX (01580 891756)

British Trust for Conservation Volunteers, Sedum House, Mallard Way, Potteric Carr, Doncaster DN4 8DB (01302 388 888); www.btcv.org.uk
Co-ordinates environmental conservation volunteering throughout the UK and around the world. Supports many local conservation groups through its Community Network; helpful with insurance, courses, etc.

British Trust for Ornithology, The Nunnery, Thetford, Norfolk IP24 2PU, (01842 750050); www.bto.org
Promotes bird conservation through volunteer-based surveys.

Brogdale Horticultural Trust, Brogdale Farm, Brogdale Road, Faversham ME13 8XZ (01795 535286); www.brogdale.org
Largest collection of fruit-tree and plant varieties in the world, more than 2,300 different

apple varieties, 550 pear, 350 plum, 220 cherry, 320 bush fruits, as well as smaller collections of nuts and vines in 150 acres of orchard; apples, apple juice and trees for sale; also available courses, education and identification services.

Buglife, 170a Park Road, Peterborough, Cambridgeshire PE1 2UF (01733 201210); www.buglife.org.uk

Bumblebee Conservation Trust, School of Biological and Environmental Sciences, University of Stirling, Stirling FK9 4LA; www.bumblebeeconservationtrust.co.uk

Campaign to Protect Rural England, 128 Southwark Street, London SE1 0SW (020 7981 2800); www.cpre.org.uk
Promotes the beauty, tranquillity and diversity of rural England by encouraging the sustainable use of land and other natural resources. Campaigns and advises on planning issues.

Campaign for Real Ale (CAMRA), 230 Hatfield Road, St Albans AL1 4LW (01727 867201); www.camra.org.uk
As well as beer, CAMRA promotes real cider and perry, Cider Month in October, the National Champion Cider and Perry Competition, the Cider and Perry Pub of the Year Competition.

Common Ground, Gold Hill House, 21 High Street, Shaftesbury, Dorset SP7 8JE (01747 850820); www.commonground.org.uk and www.england-in-particular.info
Among other work, has campaigned since 1988 for traditional orchards, initiated and championed community orchards and Apple Day (21 October). Publications include *The Common Ground Book of Orchards* and *England in Particular*.

Department for Communities and Local Government, Eland House, Bressenden Place, London SW1E 5DU (020 7944 4400); www.communities.gov.uk
Information on the planning system.

Department for Environment, Food and Rural Affairs (Defra), Customer Contact Unit, Eastbury House, 30 – 34 Albert Embankment, London SE1 7TL (Helpline 08459 335577); www.defra.gov.uk
Information on orchards, the Common Agricultural Policy and the Environmental Stewardship Scheme, which provides grants for the restoration of traditional orchards.

Federation of City Farms and Community Gardens, The Greenhouse, Hereford Street, Bedminster, Bristol BS3 4NA (0117 923 1800); www.farmgarden.org.uk
Membership organisation offering support, advice and training.

Farming and Wildlife Advisory Group,
Stoneleigh Park, Kenilworth, Warwickshire
CV8 2RX (02476 696699);
www.fwag.org.uk

Food Standards Agency – carries out a range of work
to make sure food is safe to eat.
Food hygiene standards helpline 020 7276 8829;
www.food.gov.uk

Garden History Society, 70 Cowcross Street,
London EC1M 6EJ (020 7608 2409);
www.gardenhistorysociety.org
Promotes the study and protection of historic
parks, gardens and designed landscapes.

Garden Organic (the Henry Doubleday Research
Association), Ryton Organic Gardens,
Ryton on Dunsmore,
Coventry CV8 3LG (01247 6303517);
www.gardenorganic.org.uk
Advice on organic gardening, including
fruit growing.

Grasslands Trust, Wessex House,
Upper Market Street, Eastleigh,
Hampshire SO50 9FD
(02380 650093); www.grasslands-trust.org
Working to protect our wildflower-rich
grasslands.

Learning Through Landscapes, 3rd Floor, Southside
Offices, The Law Courts, Winchester, Hampshire
SO23 9DL (01962 846258); www.ltl.org.uk
Published the *School Orchards Pack* with
Common Ground, and offers resources for
making more use of school grounds.

The Mammal Society, 2B, Inworth Street,
London SW11 3EP (020 7350 2200);
www.abdn.ac.uk/mammal
Advises on and works to protect British mammals
and halt the decline of threatened species.

The National Council for the Conservation of Plants
and Gardens, The Stable Courtyard, Wisley Garden,
Wisley, Woking, Surrey GU23 6QP
(01483 211465); www.nccpg.com
Champions garden plants and runs national
plant-collections scheme.

National Orchards Forum:
www.nat-orchard-forum.org.uk
Established in 2002 to pool information and
expertise and provide a medium for discussion,
newsletter and information online.

National Trust, Heelis, Kemble Drive,
Swindon SN2 2NA (0870 242 6620);
www.nationaltrust.org.uk
Many properties maintain old orchards or local
fruit collections within their grounds and
organise Apple Day celebrations in England,
Wales and Northern Ireland.

Open Spaces Society, 25a Bell Street,
Henley-on-Thames, Oxfordshire RG9 2BA
(01491 573535); www.oss.org.uk
Protects commons, village greens and public
rights of way.

People's Trust for Endangered Species,
15 Cloisters House, 8 Battersea Park Road, London
SW8 4BG (020 7498 4533); www.ptes.org
Works to ensure a future for endangered
species of the world, and is surveying
traditional orchards in eight British counties:
Herefordshire, Gloucestershire, Worcestershire,
Cambridgeshire, Cumbria, Devon, Essex and
Kent, with specific interest in the endangered
Noble Chafer beetle; one reserve at Rough Hill
Orchard, Worcestershire.

Plantlife, 14 Rollestone Street,
Salisbury SP1 1DX (01722 342730);
www.plantlife.org.uk
Works to protect Britain's wild flowers and
plants, fungi and lichens, the habitats in which
they are found.

Royal Horticultural Society,
Fruit Officer, Wisley Gardens,
Woking, Surrey GU23 6QB (01483 211113);
www.rhs.org.uk
For horticultural advice, fruit identification,
training, etc; visit their model fruit garden, fruit
field and fruit nursery containing 700 apple
varieties, plus other orchard fruit.

Royal Horticultural Society Fruit Group,
RHS Garden Wisley, Ripley,
Surrey GU23 6QB;
contact the Curator's Office (01483 212342)

Royal Society for the Protection of Birds,
UK Headquarters, The Lodge, Sandy,
Bedfordshire SG19 2DL; www.rspb.org.uk
Working to secure a healthy environment for
birds and other wildlife.

Small Woods Association, Green Wood Centre,
Station Road, Coalbrookdale, Telford TF8 7DR
(01952 432769); www.smallwoods.org.uk
Supports and promotes the work done by the
owners of and carers for small woodlands.

Soil Association, South Plaza,
Marlborough Street,
Bristol BS1 3NX (0117 314 5000);
www.soilassociation.org.uk
Advice on organic growing, local food
links, organic certification.

SUSTAIN, 94 White Lion Street,
London N1 9PF (020 7837 1228);
Advocates food and agriculture policies
and practices that enhance the health and
welfare of people and animals, improve the
working and living environment; 2006/7
orchard project – good-practice guide.

Walled Kitchen Gardens Network, 70 Cowcross Street, London EC1M 6EJ; www.walledgardens.net
An informal group of national organisations and individual experts who offer an advisory service and news by email to subscribers; list of walled kitchen gardens to visit throughout the UK in progress.

The Wildlife Trusts, The Kiln, Waterside, Mather Road, Newark, Nottinghamshire NG24 1WT (0870 036 7711); www.wildlifetrusts.org
Headquarters of the network of county Wildlife Trusts, some of which manage orchard nature reserves for wild life.

The Woodland Trust, Autumn Park, Dysart Road, Grantham, Lincolnshire NG31 6LL (01476 581111); www.woodland-trust.org.uk
Dedicated to the care and protection of native woodlands; owns woodlands and other land, including some orchards, as well as restoring lost woodland and creating new.

ENGLAND

Arnside & Silverdale Area of Outstanding Natural Beauty Office, Countryside Management Service, The Old Station Buildings, Arnside, Lancaster LA5 0HG (01524 761034); www.arnsidesilverdaleaonb.org.uk
Research, surveys into local orchards, advice.

Bee Books—New and Old, John Kinross (01432 840529) mail order.

Bees & Trees, Whitton Cottage, Whitton, Leintwardine, Craven Arms, Shropshire LD7 1RE (01547 540374)
Training, restoration, advice; promotes orchards and old varieties of apples and other fruit; conserves native honey bees and the use of traditional straw skep hives; offers talks on bees, fruit trees, education days for schools etc.

Butterfly Conservation England, Manor Yard, East Lulworth, Wareham, Dorset BH20 5QP (0870 7744309); www.butterfly-conservation.org

Cheshire Orchard Project, Cheshire Landscape Trust, Fountains Buildings, Upper Northgate Street, Chester CH1 4EF (01244 376333)
Encourages community groups, schools and individuals to plant Cheshire varieties of apple and damson, and promotes the importance of orchards and fruit-growing.

Cornwall Orchards Project: Natural Environment Officer, Cornwall County Council, County Hall, Truro TR1 3AY (01872 222000); www.cornwall.gov.uk/trees
Advice, information packs about Cornish orchards and varieties.

Cornwall/Devon: Tamar Orchard Group, Tamar Valley Area of Natural Beauty, Kilworthy Park, Tavistock, Devon PL19 0BZ; AONB Project Officer (01579 351083); www.tamarvalley.org.uk
Events, pruning and grafting.

Cornwall/Devon: The Tamar Valley Orchard Volunteers (01579 370411)
Advice, pruning, grafting, practical tasks, workshops, orchard management; they grow new trees grafted from local varieties.

Cumbria: East Cumbria Countryside Project, Warwick Mill, Warwick Bridge, Carlisle CA4 8RR (01228 561601)
Woodlands officer; advice, including environmental stewardship.

Cumbria: Orchard Link Cumbria
A network of orchard owners and interested people, able to give advice on orchard management and planting – for example, Community Apple Press Association in Broughton in Furness, who have a mobile apple press for hire.

Devon: East Devon Coast and Countryside Service, Council Offices, Knowle, Sidmouth EX10 8HL (01395 516551)
Advice.

Devon: North Devon Coast and Countryside Service, Old Bideford Station, Railway Terrace, Bideford EX39 4BB (01237 423655)
Advice and volunteer days on orchard restoration.

Devon: Orchard Link, PO Box 109, Totnes, TQ9 5XR (07792 664710 or 01803 732212); www.orchardlink.org.uk

Training, newsletter, events and advice; will sell your surplus apples at farmers' markets and hire out its two mobile cider presses and mill; pressing days in October. Devon: Orchards Services - offers consultancy and practical work.

Devon: Orchards Live; www.orchardslive.org.uk
Based in North Devon; events including grafting days (February), pruning days (December to February), and budding days (July); started a Devon Pomona; Bootiful Apple Sale at South Molton Pannier Market in late October.

Dorset: Symondsbury Apple Project, c/o Treewise Co-op, The Office, The Old Post Office, Symondsbury, Bridport DT6 6EZ (01308 427449); www.appleproject.org.uk
Community orchard, advice, pruning, grafting and identification courses.

East of England Apples & Orchards Project; www.applesandorchards.org.uk
Researching varieties of the eastern counties, identification at Apple Day events; they also propagate and sell eastern varieties of apple trees, training workshops on creating and restoring orchards; increasing amount of information on Norfolk, Suffolk, Essex, Cambridgeshire, Bedfordshire, Hertfordshire and Lincolnshire.

Gloucestershire County Council, Arboriculture Officer, The Malthouse, Standish GL10 3DL (01453 794920)
Offers advice for planting and restoring orchards. mother orchard of Gloucestershire varieties.

Gloucestershire Orchards Group (01452 855677); www.orchard-group.org.uk/glos
Conserves, promotes and celebrates traditional orchards in Gloucestershire. website offers information on creating or restoring traditional orchards, Gloucestershire fruit varieties, events, etc; membership organisation offering training, advice and newsletter.

Gloucestershire: Ragmans Lane Farm, Lower Lydbrook GL17 9PA (01594 860244); www.ragmans.co.uk
Courses in cider- and juice-making, permaculture, etc.

Hampshire: Sparsholt College, Winchester SO21 2NF (01962 797277); email: cbird@sparsholt.ac.uk
Helped to establish a collection of Hampshire varieties at Sparsholt College, now propagating them; identification, pruning.

Herefordshire County Council, Countryside Service, Queenswood Country Park, Dinmore Hill, Leominster NR6 0PY (01432 260848)
Principal Countryside Officer advises on the restoration of old orchards and offers subsidised fruit tree kits for gardens with Herefordshire varieties as well as grants for traditional orchards in Herefordshire, the Malvern Hills AONB and the English side of the Wye Valley AONB.

Herefordshire: Dragon Orchard Cropsharers, Dragon House, Putley, Ledbury HR8 2RG (01531 670071); www.dragonorchard.co.uk

Herefordshire: Three Counties Cider and Perry Association, The Secretary, Gregg's Pit, Much Marcle, Ledbury, HR8 2NL; www.thethreecountiesciderand perryassociation.co.uk
Gloucestershire, Herefordshire and Worcestershire, technical expertise, regular meetings, supports members in trading legalities, health and safety matters, and on forthcoming legislation; tastings and social events.

Hertfordshire Orchards Initiative; (01727 847242)
Surveying, researching and conserving Hertfordshire's orchards and varieties; free leaflet available, advice.

Kentish Stour Countryside Project, Sidelands Farm, Wye, Ashford TN25 5DQ (01233 813307); www.kentishstour.org.uk
Helps to maintain No Man's Orchard, a local nature reserve and community orchard.

Lancashire Apples Project, in association with the Northern Fruit Group, Lancaster Seedsavers, Middlewood Trust and Lancashire County Council

Historic local varieties grafted, some for sale; a survey of orchards, some now being restored; a collection of northern apples planted in the walled garden of Leighton Hall.

London: East London Organic Gardeners; www.elog.org.uk

Juicing days; will lend a press.

Marcher Apple Network; www.marcherapple.net

Reviving interest in local apple varieties in the English and Welsh Marches; researching local varieties and establishing four museum orchards; events, training and identification.

National Forest Company, Community Liaison Officer, Enterprise Glade, Bath Lane, Moira, Swadlincote, Derbyshire DE12 6BD (01283 551211); www.nationalforest.org

Orchards included in National Forest Strategy; helping to establish community orchards.

Natural England, Northminster House, Peterborough PE1 1UA (01733 455252); www.naturalengland.org.uk

Land, nature and health; English Nature, now part of Natural England, has been researching traditional orchards as habitats, and in 2007 will add a Habitat Action Plan for orchards to the UK Biodiversity Action Plan.

Northamptonshire: Apple Cause, c/o South Court Environmental, 34 Bostock Avenue, Northampton NN1 4LW (01604 630719); www.scenorthampton.org.uk

Responsible with the local community for saving Wilson's Orchard in Northampton from development in the 1990s, caring for the trees and planting new ones; researching orchards in the county and can offer advice on saving and rejuvenating them.

Northern Fruit Group, Secretary, Harlow Carr Botanical Gardens, Crag Lane, Harrogate, North Yorkshire HG3 1QB

Courses and advice on varieties, propagating, planting and growing; surveying old orchards in parts of Yorkshire, annual fruit show, working on heritage collections.

Reaseheath College, Nantwich, Cheshire CW5 6DF (01270 613242); www.reaseheath.ac.uk

Horticultural training including fruit tree pruning and grafting.

Shropshire Apple Trust; www.shropshireapple.co.uk

Helped to create the Coalbrookdale community orchard; built a traditional twin-screw cider press, using green oak and salvaged metalwork; sells smaller oak table-top presses for £250; hires out tabletop and twin-screw presses or will bring them to events; juicing and cider-making weekend.

Somerset: Dobunni Fruit Farm, Brean Road, Lympsham, Somerset BS24 0HA
Traditional cider-making, orchard management; business assistance with Somerset Orchard Link.

Somerset Orchards, Environment Department, Somerset County Council, County Hall, Taunton, Somerset TA1 4DY (01823 355617)
Advice, grants for new standard orchards and replacement trees; encourages school orchards; traces and preserves local varieties.

Somerset Orchard Link, Sustainable Foodlinks, 10–11 Bridge Barns, Long Sutton, Langport TA10 9PZ (01458 241401); www.foodlinks.org.uk
Represents small-scale orchard owners who are seeking ways to market, add value to crop, etc.

Somerset Rural Life Museum, Glastonbury (01458 831197)
Orchard with old varieties of cider-apple trees, traditional cider-making exhibits.

Staffordshire Wildlife Trust, The Wolseley Centre, Wolseley Bridge, Stafford ST17 0WT (01889 880100)
Advice on local varieties and orchards, county collection at the Wolseley Centre.

Sussex: Chichester District Council, Environment Officer, East Pallant, Chichester PO19 1TY (01243 785166); www.chichester.gov.uk
Offers advice, funding. A *Guide to Setting Up Community Orchards* is available.

Vigo Vineyard Supplies, Dunkerswell, Honiton, Devon EX14 4LF (01404 890262); www.vigopresses.co.uk
Apple presses and everything for the amateur cider and juice maker.

Wittenham Hill Cider Portal; www.cider.org.uk

Worcestershire Orchard Workers, Countryside Officer, Worcestershire County Council (01905 766493)
Conservation and enhancement of traditional orchards, advice, training, restoration, pruning and grafting.

Worcestershire: Cider Academy, Mitchell F&D Ltd, 74 Holloway, Pershore WR10 1HP (01386 552324); www.cider-academy.co.uk

Worcestershire: Pershore College of Horticulture, Avonbank, Pershore WR10 3JP (01386 551126); www.pershore.ac.uk
Fruit-tree pruning courses, identification.

Worcestershire Wildlife Trust, Lower Smite Farm, Smite Hill, Hindip, Worcester WR3 8SZ (01905 754919); www.worcswildlifetrust.co.uk
Projects to save old orchards as habitats for wild life.

Wyre Forest Study Group, Willow Bank, Bliss Gate Road, Bewdley, Worcestershire DY14 9XT; email: studygroup@wyreforest.net
Leading biological survey work on old orchards.

SCOTLAND

Ayrshire Apple Network, John Butterworth, c/o Garden Cottage, Auchinlech Estate, Cumnock, Ayrshire KA18 2LR (01290 551088)

Butterfly Conservation Scotland, Balallan House, Allan Park, Stirling, FK8 2QG (0870 7706151); www.butterfly-conservation.org

Central Core Network, Greenbank House, West End, Abernethy PH2 9JL (01738 850566)
Orchard survey, advice, conservation and rejuvenation of orchards, community orchards, information pack, newsletter.

Galloway Orchards Project, New Milns Farm, Wigtown, Newton Stewart DG8 9DH (01988 403267)
Courses on pruning, budding, identification; promotes Galloway orchards and varieties.

The National Trust for Scotland, Wemyss House, 28 Charlotte Square, Edinburgh EH2 4ET (0131 243 9300); www.nts.org.uk

Scottish Natural Heritage, Great Glen House, Leachkin Road, Inverness IV3 8NW (01463 725000); www.snh.org.uk
Aims to secure the conservation and enhancement of the unique and precious natural heritage, the wild life, the habitats and landscapes that have evolved in Scotland through the long partnership between people and nature.

WALES

Butterfly Conservation Wales, 10 Calvert Terrace, Swansea, SA1 6AR (0870 7706153); www.butterfly-conservation.org

Countryside Council for Wales, Land Use Policy Officer, Plas Penrhos, Ffordd Penrhos, Bangor, Gwynedd LL57 2LQ (08451 306229)
Information on orchard conservation.

Welsh Assembly Government (0845 010 5500); www.wales.gov.uk
Administers Tir Gofal, the agri-environment grants scheme that includes traditional orchards.

Marcher Apple Network; www.marcherapple.net
Reviving interest in local apple varieties in the English and Welsh Marches; researching local varieties, established four museum orchards, events, training, identification.

Monmouthshire County Council, Biodiversity Officer, County Hall, Cwmbran NP44 2XH (01633 644843)
Advice on grants and managing orchards for wild life.

North East Wales Orchard Initiative;
www.welshorchardfruits.co.uk
Looking for lost varieties in north-east Wales to
create mother orchards; interested in unidentified
fruit trees in your garden or orchard; advice.

Perllanau Powys Project, Glasu, Antur Gwy, Park
Road, Builth Wells, Powys LD2 3BA (01982 552224);
www.glasu.org.uk
Promotes orchards in Powys and works
to make use of surplus windfalls. Advice,
contacts, forum.

The Tree Fruit Society of Wales
Talks, workshops, pruning and grafting.
At Scolton Manor, Pembrokeshire, they plan
an orchard of Welsh varieties and others that
grow well in Wales.

Welsh Perry & Cider Society, Fruit Officer (01291
673804); www.welshcider.co.uk
Festival in May; advice, training,
information exchange.

IRELAND
Armagh Orchard Trust (028 38 892312)
Began in 1995 to preserve apples once
common in Ireland, has more than a hundred
in the historic walled garden at Drumilly
Estate in Loughgall.

Butterfly Conservation N. Ireland,
Slemish Complex, Knockbracken Healthcare Park,

Saintfield Road, Belfast BT8 8BH
(028 90 796979);
www.butterfly-conservation.org

Irish Seed Savers Association,
Caparroe, Scariff, Co. Clare (00 353 61 921866);
www.irishseedsavers.ie
Leading Irish fruit organisation, searching
for the last surviving traditional Irish apple
varieties; more than 140 found and grown
at Caparroe. Grafted trees available, orchard
restoration and creation service; Apple
Catalogue online lists more than eighty
Irish varieties with descriptions.

REFERENCES
& FURTHER
READING

If you buy one book, this is the one:
Morgan, Joan, and Richards, Alison,
*The New Book of Apples, the Definitive Guide
to Apples including over 2000 varieties*,
Ebury Press, 2002

Baker, Harry, *The Fruit Garden Displayed*,
    Royal Horticultural Society,
    Ward Lock, 1998
Blackburne-Maze, Peter, *The Apple Book*,
    Collingridge, 1996
Bultitude, John, *Apples: a guide to the
    identification of international varieties*,
    Macmillan Reference, 1983

Bunyard, Edward A.,
    *A Handbook of Hardy Fruits more commonly
    grown in Great Britain*, 2 vols, Picton
    Publishing, 1994
Bush, Raymond,
    Tree Fruit Growing – 1. Apples,
    Penguin, 1943
CAMRA, *The Good Cider Guide*, CAMRA, 2005
Clark, Michael, *Apples, A Field Guide*,
    Whittet, 2003
Copas, Liz, *A Somerset Pomona: The Cider Apples
    of Somerset*, Dovecote Press, 2001
Crowden, James, *Cider: The Forgotten Miracle*,
    Cyder Press 2, 1999
Crowden, James, *Ciderland*, Birlinn, 2008
Ellis, Hattie, *Sweetness and Light: the mysterious
    history of the honey bee*, Sceptre, 2004
Flowerdew, Bob, *Bob Flowerdew's Complete
    Fruit Book, A Definitive Sourcebook to
    Growing, Harvesting and Cooking Fruit*,
    Kyle Cathie, 2000
French, R.K., *The History and Virtues of Cider*,
    Robert Hale, 1982
Garner, R.J., *The Grafter's Handbook*,
    Cassell/RHS, 1988
Grigson, Jane, *Jane Grigson's Fruit Book*,
    Penguin, 1982
Greenoak, Francesca, *Forgotten Fruits: the English
    Orchard and Fruit Garden*,
    Andre Deutsch, 1983
Hartley, Dorothy, *Food in England*, Futura, 1985
Hills, Lawrence D., *The Good Fruit Guide*,
    HDRA, 1984

Hogg, Robert, *British Pomology*, 1851

Hogg, Dr Robert, and Graves Bull, Dr Henry,
The Herefordshire Pomona,
Woolhope Naturalists Field Club, 1885;
CD, Marcher Apple Network, 2005

Hole, Christina, *British Folk Customs*,
Hutchinson, 1976

Juniper, Barrie E., and Mabberley, David J.,
The Story of the Apple, Timber Press, 2006

Kightly, Charles, *The Customs and Ceremonies
of Britain*, Thames & Hudson, 1986

Latimer, Jonathan, *Orchards Through the Eyes of
an Artist*, Langford Press, 2005

Lawson, William, *A New Orchard and Garden
with The Country Housewife's Garden (1618)*,
Prospect Books, 2003

Legg, Philippa, and Binding, Hilary,
Somerset Cider: The Complete Story,
Somerset Books, 1998

Mabey, Richard, *Flora Britannica*,
Chatto & Windus, 1996

MAFF, *Index of the Apple Collection at the
National Fruit Trials*, MAFF, 1985

Morgan, Joan, and Richards, Alison,
*A Paradise out of a Common Field: the
Pleasures and Plenty of the Victorian Garden*,
Century 1990

Pooley, Michael, and Lomax, John,
Real Cidermaking on a Small Scale, Nexus
Special Interests, from Shropshire Apple
Trust, n.d.

Roach, F A., *Cultivated Fruits of Britain*,
Basil Blackwell, 1985

Rowe, Alan, *Success with Apples and Pears to Eat
and Drink*, Groundnut Publishing, 2002

Sanders, Rosanne, *The English Apple*,
Phaidon Press, 1988

Smith, Muriel W.G., *The National Apple Register
of the United Kingdom*, MAFF, 1971

Taylor, H.V., *The Apples of England*,
Crosby Lockwood, 1936

Twiss, Sally, *Apples: A Social History*,
The National Trust, 1999

Ward, Ruth, *A Harvest of Apples*,
Penguin/Sage Press, 1997

Wheeler, Richard (Ed.), *The Herefordshire
Pomona – facsimile*
CD ROM, The Marcher Apple Network, 2005

Wheeler, Richard (Ed.), *Vintage Fruit:
Cider Apples and Perry Pears – facsimile*
CD ROM, The Marcher Apple Network, 2007

Williams, R.R., *Cider and Juice Apples*,
University of Bristol, 1988

Williams-Davies, John, *Cider Making in Wales*,
Welsh Folk Museum, 1984

Wilson, Bee, *The Hive*, John Murray, 2004

COMMON GROUND PUBLICATIONS

Orchards, 1989

The Apple Broadcast, 1994

Apple Games and Customs, 2005

Apple Map of Britain
A1 full colour poster and gazetteer, 1993

The Common Ground Book of Orchards: community, conservation and culture, 2000

Orchards and Wild Life – Report from Joint Common Ground–English Nature Conference, 1999

Community Orchard Manual, 2007

Pamphlets: *Save our Orchards*; *Community Orchards*; *Apple Day*; *Advice Notes*.

Ideas for saving old orchards and planting new ones for the enjoyment of the community, as a reservoir for local varieties and a refuge for wild life.

Some Country and Regional Books and Booklets

Butterworth, John, *Apples in Scotland, a practical guide to choosing and growing our favourite fruit*, Langford Press, 2001

Cheshire Federation of Women's Institutes, *Orchards of Cheshire*, CFWI, 1995

Cornwall County Council, Information packs about Cornish orchards and varieties

East of England Apple and Orchards Project, county varieties lists

Marcher Apple Network, *Apples of the Welsh Marches*, booklet

Mac, Fiona, *Ciderlore: Cider in the Three Counties*, Logaston Press, 2003

Mackay, Duncan, Hall, Pip, and Hay, Peter, *Apple Berkshire Cider*, Two Rivers Press, 1996

Merryweather, Roger, *The Bramley: a world famous cooking apple*, Newark and Sherwood District Council, 1992

Northern Fruit Group, *Fruit Varieties Recommended for the North of England*, n.d.

Pillans, Craig, *Lincolnshire to the Core*, Lincolnshire County Council, 1992

Pillans, Craig, *Historic Apples of Scotland*, 1987

Small, June, *Somerset Cider & Apple Juice Map, a list of Somerset apple varieties, orchard grants, etc.*

Somerset County Council, *Somerset's Orchards*, DVD

Spiers, Virginia, and Martin, Mary, *Burcombes, Queenies and Colloggetts – The Makings of a Cornish Orchard*, West Brendon, 1996

Squirrel, Kim and David, *Dorset Orchards*, Symondsbury Apple Project, 2005

Trewin, Carol, *Gourmet Cornwall*, Alison Hodge, 2005

ACKNOWLEDGEMENTS

Common Ground is small charity dependent on grants and donations. We offer our grateful thanks to our current funders: Defra Environmental Action Fund, Cobb Charity, John Ellerman Foundation, Garfield Weston Foundation, Headley Trust, Raphael Trust, Tedworth Trust and over a longer time frame, Countryside Commission and Agency, English Nature, Lyndhurst Settlement, Manifold Trust, J. Sheridan, Stanley Smith Horticultural Trust, Zephyr Charitable Trust, London Boroughs Grant Scheme and a London based trust.

The long list of acknowledgements below demonstrates the extent of participation and joint effort that has developed since Common Ground started working on orchard conservation in 1987. We are bound to miss out important people because of this – thank you to anyone who has raised a finger, a pruning saw or a spoon for orchards anywhere. Any mistakes are ours.

Special thanks to:

Common Ground's initial workers for their hard work and dedication at different stages: Dan Keech, Jane Kendall, Beatrice Mayfield, Neil Sinden and Stephen Turner; current workers Darren Giddings and especially Kate O'Farrell, who have helped us to continue campaigning and promoting Apple Day. We have never been able to raise enough funds to have a permanent orchards officer.

Our Director/Trustees who continue to give us great support, Barbara Bender, Robin Grove-White, Richard Mabey, Rupert Nabarro. We miss the enthusiasm and generosity of Roger Deakin our fellow founder director who died in 2006 whose book *Wildwood* was published this year. David Holmes, Common Ground's honorary art director who, since 1990 has designed and overseen posters and pamphlets, books and postcards as well as the Apple Map which helped us excite others with the quest to find out where apples originated. The late James Ravilious is constantly remembered; his outstanding black and white photographs of orchards of the West Country that we commissioned in the 1980s did so much to raise awareness about what is being lost. Some of the illustrations in this book echo his work. James Crowden, for his knowledge and passion for orchards and cider. Vivien Green at Shiel Land, who is always responsive and creative irrespective of our mood.

Philippa Davenport – without her this book would not have been possible. She was a generous and early champion of our work and we finally met when Common Ground won a special Glenfiddich Award in 1995. When we wrote asking for renewed permission to use her recipe from the first edition of this book, she recklessly offered to help us. Not only did she track down very busy people and persuade them to contribute recipes, but she discussed at length the use of appropriate apple varieties. Her introduction gives just a glimpse of her passion and care. We have learned much, and are proud to have worked with her.

Those who contributed essays – all special to us in different ways – Joan Morgan for 'An Apple for all Seasons'; Carol Trewin for 'Ten Green Apples'; Gail Vines on 'Attracting Wild Life to Orchards' and Dan Keech for work on 'Small-Scale Cider- & Apple Juice- Making'.

Those who have given time to hone recipes despite their hectic lives, we thank for their generosity and care: Darina Allen; Lindsey Bareham; Frances Bissell; Raymond Blanc; Joanna Blythman; Lynda Brown; Sally Clarke; Shona Crawford Poole; Tamasin Day-Lewis; Philippa Davenport; Elizabeth David; Charles Dowding; Gail Duff; Rose Elliot; Hattie Ellis; Hugh Fearnley-Whittingstall; Bob Flowerdew; Matthew Fort; Henrietta Green; Francesca Greenoak; Sophie Grigson; Skye Gyngell; Barny Haughton; Patricia Hegarty; Fergus Henderson; Shaun Hill; Mark Hix; Simon Hopkinson; Clarissa Hyman; Juliet Kindersley; Sue Lawrence; Jeremy Lee; Richard Mabey; Claire Macdonald; Laura Mason; Patricia Michelson; Joan Morgan; George and Barbara Morris; Grace Mulligan; Jill Norman; Tom Parker-Bowles; Sara Paston-Williams; Anna Pavord; Craig and Christine Pillans; Rose Prince; Simone Sekers; Nigel Slater; Delia Smith; Caroline Waldegrave; Andrew Whitley; Margaret Wilson; Alice Wooledge Salmon.

To the wonderful illustrators: Ivan Allen; Richard Allen; Matt Clervaux; Glyn Goodwin; Brian Grimwood; Clifford Harper; Lucinda Rogers; Stephen Turner; Will Webb; Dan Williams. And especially to Will Webb as art director and designer. The literary executor of Leonard Clark: 'Apple Trees', from *Selected Poems 1940–57*, Hutchinson, 1958. To Juliet Nicolson for permission to quote from Vita Sackville West's 'The Land'. To Jill Norman for permission to re-use the recipes that Elizabeth David had given us for the first edition. Thank you to Wendy Fogarty, Melanie Grocott, Leanda Pearman, Dominic Prince, Lucy Timmins, Kate Trusson, Jess Upton. To the great team at Hodder & Stoughton: especially to Rupert Lancaster, our commissioning editor, for seizing the moment and bringing enthusiasm and care to the process of creating new from old, and Hugo Wilkinson, his assistant; Lisa Highton, deputy managing director; Karen Geary, publicity director; Elizabeth Hallett, production director; Hazel Orme who edited the text.

Our thanks and tributes to the following who have made and are making orchards live again in so many places and ways:

Brenda Allen et al, Reeth Community Orchard, Yorkshire; Tim Allen (ex-Countryside Commission); Sue Anderson, National Forest, Derbyshire/Leicestershire; Peter Andrews, Bath Organic Group; Jim Arbury, Fruit Officer, Royal Horticultural Society; Steve Ashley; Harry Baker, ex-Fruit Officer, Royal Horticultural Society; Sue Bell; Rupert Best, Chief Steward, Orchards section, Royal Bath & West Show; James Bisset, Herefordshire County Council; David Bouch, Head Gardener, National Trust Cotehele, Cornwall; Jonathan Briggs, Botanical Society of the British Isles and Mistletoe Matters; Pauline Buttery; Sheila Camplin, Tamar Valley Orchard Volunteers; Ted Bruning, Mike Bennan, David Kitton, Mick Lewis, Gillian Williams at CAMRA; Peter Cartmell, Westmorland Damson Association; Barry Champion, National Trust, Trelissick Garden; Edward Chorlton, Environment Director, Devon County Council; Michael Clark, Tewin Orchard, Hertfordshire; Simon Clark and Hilary Wilson, Northern Fruit Group; Barbara Collier, Taunton Deane BC, Somerset; Derek Cooper, BBC Radio 4, The Food Programme; Liz Copas, Somerset; Phil Corbett, Own Root Fruit Trees Project; CPRE; Cumbrian Fells and Dales (Leader+); Mike Deegan, Graham Peake, Staffordshire Wildlife Trust and Orchards Initiative; Jackie Denman, The Big Apple, Herefordshire; Sheila Dillon, BBC Radio 4, The Food Programme; Ivor and Susie Dunkerton, Herefordshire; Matt Dunwell, Ragman's Lane Farm, Gloucestershire; John Edgeley, Pershore College, Worcestershire; John Ely, Shenley Park Trust and Hertfordshire Orchards Initiative; Hugh Ermen; Chris Fairs, HP Bulmer; Richard Farrington; Richard Fawcett, ex-Gloucestershire County Council; Lynn Fomison; Andrew Fraser, Worcestershire Wildlife Trust; Laurie Fricker; Meg Game, Kentish Cobnuts Association; Michael Gee, Orchards Live, north Devon; Margaret Gibson, Frieze Hill Community Orchard, Somerset; John Gittins, Cheshire Landscape Trust and Cheshire Orchards Trust; Harry Green, Worcestershire; Gill Goddard, ex-London Borough of Lewisham; Dennis Gould, Stroud, Gloucestershire; Paul Hand, Bees and Trees, Shropshire; Graham Harvey; Colin Hawke, Cornwall County Council and Orchards Project; Anita Hayes, Irish Seedsaver Association; Martin Hicks, Hertfordshire; Pat and Peter Hinde, Home Cottage Farm; Alex Hill, Vigo Ltd; Vicki Hird, Friends of the Earth; Randolph Hodgson, Neal's Yard Dairy; the late Nancy Holt, Carhampton Community Orchard; Ian and Gill Horsley formerly of the Brandy Wharf Cider Centre; Maureen Jeffrey, Sulgrave Manor; Dr Barrie Juniper, Oxford University; Roger Key, (English Nature) Natural England; Joe King, Gabriel's Community Orchard; Keith Goverd; Barry Lane; Tim Lang, Professor of Food Policy, City University; Sheila Leitch, Marcher Apple Network; Charles Martell; Philip McMillan Browse; Duncan Mackay, New Road Cyderists; James Marsden, (English Nature) Natural England; Margaret Miller, Gartmore School, near Stirling, Scotland; George Morris; Wade Muggleton, Worcestershire County Council; Peter Nalder, South Court Environmental; NFWI Cheshire; National Trust; Nancy O'Brien, ex-La Sainte Union School, Kentish Town; Claire Peasnall, ex-Cross O' Cliff Community Orchard; Dave Perkins, Roots & Shoots; Ben Pike, Orchard Link, Devonshire; Craig Pillans, Lincolnshire; Ian Pitcairn; Lucy Pitman, ex-Pythouse Walled Garden, Wiltshire; Michael Pooley, Shropshire Apple Trust; Phil Rainford, Lancashire Apples Project; Ben Ravilious; Robin Ravilious; Sonia Ritter, Lion's Part Theatre Company; Bob Roberts, (Countryside Agency) Natural England; Heather Robertson, Natural England; RV Roger Nurseries, Yorkshire; John Shelton, Kentish Stour Countryside Project; Martin Skipper, Claire Stimpson, Bob Lever, East of England Apples and Orchards Project; June and Robin Small, Charlton Orchards, Somerset; Ann Smith, Gloucestershire Orchards Group and National Orchard Forum; Christina Smith; Grant Sonnex BBC Radio 4, Natural History Unit; Virginia Spiers, Mary Martin and James Evans in the Tamar valley; Kim and David Squirrell, Symondsbury Apple Project, Dorset; Ann and Norman Stanier, Dragon Orchard; Phil Stone, Landscape Officer, Somerset County Council; SUSTAIN; Andrew and Anne Tann, Crapes Fruit Farm; Julian Temperley, Burrow Hill Cider/Somerset Cider Brandy Co; Trudy Turrell, Orchard Link, Devonshire; Patricia Tutt, ex-Bath & North East Somerset Council; Eddie Upton, Folk South West; Caroline and Richard Vulliamy, Tamar Valley Orchard Volunteers; Ruth Ward; Alan Watson ex-Somerset County Council; Brett Westwood BBC Radio 4, Natural History Unit; Rob Williams (English Nature) Natural England; Rosemary Winnall, Wyre Forest Study Group; Reverend Mervyn Wilson.

PICTURE CREDITS

Ivan Allen: 8, 25, 35, 36, 103, 185, 187, 190, 193, 257, 261, 263, 288, 292. Richard Allen: title page, 210. Matt Clervaux: 50. Glyn Goodwin: 13, 41, 43, 52, 239, 271, 277, 289, 290. Brian Grimwood: 6. Clifford Harper: 14, 19. Lucinda Rogers: 10, 21, 30, 40, 48, 54, 57, 65, 79, 155, 224, 226, 234, 258, 272. Stephen Turner: 42. Will Webb: 39, 47, 58, 125, 176-177, 178, 214, 220, 237, 243, 247, 252, 255, 262, 264, 267, 278. Dan Williams: 5, 11, 32, 44, 51, 216, 223, 229, 232, 235, 244, 251.

INDEX

A

acidity 21, 22, 69
Allen, Darina 88, 164
apple balsamic vinegar 83-4
apple brandy 39, 150
Apple Charoset 75
Apple Day 12, 53-4, 150, 158, 166, 170, 222-8, 278
Apple and Stilton Toasts 71-2
apple varieties
(see also Gazetteer of Local Varieties pages 179-213)
  Alfriston 139
  American Mother 89
  Annie Elizabeth 20, 23, 92, 157
  Antonovsky 140
  Arthur Turner 89, 98, 159, 165, 183, 233
  Ashmead's Kernel 24, 53, 77, 85, 94, 109, 116, 121, 124
  Backhouse('s) Flowery Town 33, 101
  Baker's Delicious 149
  Barnack Beauty 17
  Barnack Orange 17
  Beauty of Bath 16, 71, 88, 174
  Beauty of Kent 128
  Belle de Boskoop 82
  Ben's Red 106
  Blenheim Orange 13, 16, 20, 23, 64, 66-7, 77, 84, 86, 92, 94, 109, 128, 147, 157, 161, 175, 256
  Bloody Ploughman 74
  Bountiful 66, 69, 73, 114
  Braeburn 26, 27, 28, 128, 147
  Bramley 17, 23, 61, 69, 98, 128, 139, 151, 168
  Bramley's Seedling 20, 23, 88, 126, 149, 256

Breakwell's Seedling 104
Bridgwater Pippin 16
Brownlees Russet 101, 233
Burr Knot 33, 101
Carlisle Codlin 53
Catshead 33, 81, 101
Caville Blanc d'Hiver 86
Charles Ross 53, 94, 142, 153
Cissy 81, 157
Claygate Pearmain 157
Cobham 56
Cockpit 100
Cornish Gillyflower 18, 64, 72, 92, 94
Cornish Aromatic 131
Coul Blush 73, 74
Court Pendu Plat 28, 94, 109, 118, 157
Court of Wick 118
Cox 23, 26, 27, 28, 61, 63, 85, 111, 124
Cox's Orange Pippin 17, 24, 46, 53, 80, 88, 92, 113, 115, 134, 143
Crawley Beauty 53
Crimson Costard 153
Dabinett 104
D'Arcy Spice 16, 64, 66, 92, 94, 131, 157
Devonshire Quarrenden 16, 53, 72, 153
Discovery 24, 27, 70, 71, 111, 129
Dog's Snout 33, 101
Duchess of Oldenberg 70
Duke of Bedford 228
Dumelow's Seedling 20, 23, 99, 100, 121, 149
Early Victoria 19-20, 66, 139, 140, 165
Ecklinville Seedling 20
Egremont Russet 27, 82, 89, 90, 92, 115, 166
Ellison's Orange 24, 82, 92, 124

Emneth Early 16, 126, 139
Emperor Alexander 70
Encore 138, 149
Fair Maid of Devon 16
Flower of Kent 151
Forge 23
Foxwhelp 20, 37, 104
Fred Webb 56
Fuji 27
Gala 26, 27, 28
Galloway Pippin 13, 74, 108
George Cave 118
George Neal 72, 73, 129, 149
Gladstone 16
Glass Apple 114, 157
Gloria Mundi 157
Golden Delicious 17, 26, 27, 68, 88, 131
Golden Noble 20, 126
Gooseberry 100
Granny Smith 16, 26, 68, 131
Gravenstein 33, 100
Gravity Tree 17
Green Balsam 33, 100, 131
Grenadier 88, 111, 140, 165
Gypsy King 228
Hambledon Deux Ans 16
Hawthornden 20, 73, 74, 101, 139
Hoary Morning 118
Hockings Green 133
Holstein 24
Howgate Wonder 67, 98-9, 138, 159, 161
Idared 16
Improved Cockpit 96
Irish Peach 89
Isaac Newton's Tree 17
James Grieve 22, 72, 73, 88, 94, 115, 233
Jersey Beauty 157
Jonagold 27, 111
Kempster's Pippin 16

Common Ground
Save our Orchards